REVELATION AS TESTIMONY

REVELATION AS TESTIMONY

A Philosophical-Theological Study

Mats Wahlberg

William B. Eerdmans Publishing Company
Grand Rapids, Michigan / Cambridge, U.K.

© 2014 Mats Wahlberg
All rights reserved

Published 2014 by
Wm. B. Eerdmans Publishing Co.
2140 Oak Industrial Drive N.E., Grand Rapids, Michigan 49505 /
P.O. Box 163, Cambridge CB3 9PU U.K.
www.eerdmans.com

Printed in the United States of America

19 18 17 16 15 14   7 6 5 4 3 2 1

Library of Congress Cataloging-in-Publication Data

Walberg, Mats.
 Revelation as testimony: a philosophical-theological study /
 Mats Walberg.
       pages   cm
 Includes bibliographical references and index.
 ISBN 978-0-8028-6988-3 (pbk.: alk. paper)
 1. Revelation — Christianity.   2. Witness bearing (Christianity)
 3. Knowledge, Theory of (Religion)   I. Title.

BT127.3.W35   2014
231.7'4 — dc23

                                2014012166

Excerpts from Joe Houston, *Reported Miracles: A Critique of Hume,* 1994, Copyright Cambridge University Press, are reproduced with permission.

For my mother, Lena

Contents

ACKNOWLEDGMENTS ... ix

1. Introduction ... 1
2. Revelation and Knowledge of God ... 20
   - 2.1. Revelation, Propositions, and Personal Relations ... 25
     - 2.1.1. Propositional and Manifestational Revelation ... 28
     - 2.1.2. Misconceptions about Propositional Revelation ... 33
     - 2.1.3. Conclusion ... 41
   - 2.2. The Problem of Knowledge of God ... 42
     - 2.2.1. Kaufman's Challenge ... 43
     - 2.2.2. A Response to Kaufman's Challenge ... 47
3. Theories of Revelation ... 52
   - 3.1. Revelation as History ... 52
   - 3.2. Revelation as Inner Experience: Nonconceptual Experience ... 59
     - 3.2.1. Friedrich Schleiermacher ... 59
     - 3.2.2. Karl Rahner ... 64
   - 3.3. Revelation as Inner Experience: Conceptual Experience ... 71
   - 3.4. Revelation as Dialectical Presence ... 80
     - 3.4.1. Emil Brunner ... 81
     - 3.4.2. Karl Barth ... 84

3.5. Revelation as New Awareness	89
3.6. "Postliberal" Views of Revelation	91
3.6.1. Ronald Thiemann	92
3.6.2. John Milbank	97
3.7. Conclusion	101
4. Divine Speech	107
4.1. Locutionary and Illocutionary Acts	109
4.2. Double-Agency Discourse	110
4.3. Possible Ways for God to Speak	113
4.4. Biblical Interpretation	115
4.5. Where Does It All Start?	120
5. Knowledge by Hearsay	124
5.1. Reductionism and Anti-Reductionism	124
5.2. John McDowell's Anti-Reductionism	132
6. Entrance into God's Own Knowledge	144
6.1. The Prophet P	145
6.2. Doxastic Responsibility	150
6.3. Jesus	152
6.4. The Epistemic Function of Miracles	158
6.5. The Task Ahead	165
7. Responsible Belief	172
7.1. Trusting the Gospels	172
7.2. Believing Reports about Miracles	182
7.3. Believing in the Resurrection	200
8. Faithful Knowledge	213
8.1. Objections and Clarifications	214
8.2. What about *Faith*?	223
BIBLIOGRAPHY	234
INDEX	244

Acknowledgments

I would first like to thank Arne Rasmusson for his invaluable help and inspiring presence while I was writing this book. I am also very thankful to John Haldane, who read the manuscript at an early stage and chaired a seminar where it was discussed. Many others deserve special thanks, such as Carl-Magnus Carlstein, Leif Svensson, Ulf Zackariasson, and the participants of the theology seminar at Umeå University.

I had the privilege to discuss some chapters of the book at the higher seminar for theology and philosophy at the Newman Institute in Uppsala. I am indebted to all the participants in that seminar, and especially to Ulf Jonsson, Gösta Hallonsten, and Philip Geister. Nicholas Wolterstorff, who was happy to disclose his identity as a reviewer for Eerdmans, gave me important encouragement toward the end of the process.

A version of this book was defended as a doctoral dissertation (for my second doctorate) at the Faculty of Theology, Stellenbosch University, South Africa. I am grateful for the hospitality of all the people at the Faculty of Theology, not least its dean, Nico Koopman. Both during my stay in Stellenbosch and at home in Umeå, I have greatly enjoyed working and dialoguing with my advisors Gerrit Brand and Dirkie Smit. Sadly, Gerrit passed away before this book was completed. I am very grateful for having had the privilege of knowing him.

Finally, I want to thank my mother Lena and all my sisters and brothers — Maria, Margareta, Åke Jr., and Jan — and my friend Marta for their support. I dedicated my first dissertation, which was about natural theology, to the memory of my father, Åke. It feels very appropriate to dedicate

ACKNOWLEDGMENTS

the present book, which is about revelation, to my mother, Lena, who has led me to the fullness of the Christian faith.

M. W.

CHAPTER 1

Introduction

Testimonial knowledge is knowledge gained from the spoken or written words of other people. If Peter believes that it is raining because he believes his mother's assertion to this effect, and if his mother speaks sincerely and knows what she is talking about, then Peter has testimonial knowledge of the fact that it is raining.[1]

Most of our knowledge is testimonial. I have never seen a brain, but I know that there are brains in people's heads because people have told me so. I have never seen a woman give birth, but I know that children come from women because people have told me so. I know that Barack Obama is the president of the United States, that there once was a man named Winston Churchill, and that I was born on New Year's Eve, because people have told me all these things — orally or in writing.

Our knowledge of God, according to the historical Christian tradition, is mainly testimonial. We know certain important truths about God and divine things because God himself has told them to us. Saint Thomas Aquinas writes:

> In order that men might have knowledge of God, free of doubt and uncertainty, it was necessary for Divine matters to be delivered to them by way of faith, being told to them, as it were, by God Himself Who cannot lie.[2]

---

1. A further condition is that Peter does not have reason to think that his mother is misinformed or is lying.

2. *The Summa Theologica* (hereafter cited as *ST*), trans. L. Shapcote and D. J. Sullivan, 2nd ed. (Chicago: Encyclopedia Britannica, 1990), II-II, q. 2, a. 4.

Saint Clement of Alexandria: "We give to our adversaries this irrefutable argument; it is God who speaks and who, for each one of the points into which I am inquiring, offers answers in the Scriptures."[3]

Martin Luther: "The Scriptures are God's testimony of himself."[4]

John Calvin: "The first step in true knowledge is taken when we reverently embrace the testimony which God has been pleased [in the Scriptures] to give of himself."[5]

The First Vatican Council, in *Dei Filius*, declares:

> We believe that what he has revealed is true, not because the intrinsic truth of things is recognized by the natural light of reason, but because of the authority of God himself who reveals them, who can neither err nor deceive.[6]

In this book I will argue, on the basis of insights from contemporary philosophy of testimony, for the viability of the traditional understanding of revelation as divine testimony. God reveals by speaking, and we acquire knowledge of God and divine things by believing what God says.[7] That God *speaks* is not to be understood as a metaphor in this context. The premodern tradition took the claim that God speaks literally, and it regarded the Bible as composed of divine speech-acts (assertions, commands, promises, etc.).[8] This view, which an understanding of revelation as divine testimony presupposes, does not, as I will argue, commit one to holding some naïve and untenable doctrine of biblical inerrancy.

---

3. Clement of Alexandria, *Stromate V* (Paris: Éditions du Cerf, 1981); quoted in John Lamont, *Divine Faith* (Aldershot, UK: Ashgate, 2004), p. 32.

4. *Luther's Works,* vol. 34, ed. Lewis W. Spitz (Philadelphia: Fortress, 1960), p. 227.

5. John Calvin, *Institutes of the Christian Religion* (Grand Rapids: Eerdmans, 1989), p. 66.

6. Heinrich Denzinger, *Compendium of Creeds, Definitions, and Declarations on Matters of Faith and Morals,* 43rd ed., ed. Peter Hünermann (San Francisco: Ignatius Press, 2012), §3008.

7. The Christian tradition, of course, has never portrayed revelation as *exclusively* a matter of divine testimony. The tradition also conceives of the events of biblical history — interpreted as divine acts — as part of revelation, as is the self-manifestation of God in Jesus Christ (more about this below).

8. A *literal* understanding of the claim that God speaks can, needless to say, be *analogical*. Analogy is a form of literal speech (for a different opinion, see Richard Swinburne, *Revelation: From Metaphor to Analogy,* 2nd ed. [Oxford: Oxford University Press, 2007], chap. 3).

Introduction

The dominant tendency in modernity has been to either dismiss the idea of revelation altogether or to construe revelation as exclusively manifestational. God does *not* reveal by performing speech-acts but only by manifesting himself in diverse ways, for example, through historical events or in transcendental experience. The latter forms of revelation are generally perceived to be more acceptable than the idea of divine testimony. Believing things merely on (what one takes to be) divine say-so is seen as irrational and reflective of an authoritarian mindset.

Wolfhart Pannenberg, representing this attitude, writes:

> Until the Enlightenment, Christian theology was doubtless a theology of revelation in this sense, appealing to revelation as a supernatural authority. The authoritative revelation was found in the "Word of God," i.e., in the inspired word of the Bible. . . . But for men who live in the sphere in which Enlightenment has become effective, authoritarian claims are no longer acceptable.[9]

Austin Farrer has the divine testimony model of revelation in mind when he says:

> There is nothing superficially less attractive to a philosophical mind than the notion of a revealed truth. For philosophy is reasonable examination, and must resist the claim of any doctrine to exempt itself from criticism. And revealed truth is commonly said to be accepted on the mere authority of its revealer; not on any empirical evidence for it, nor on any logical self-evidence contained in it.[10]

The idea that beliefs "accepted on the mere authority" of God (mediated through the Bible or ecclesiastical authorities) cannot enjoy the status of being rationally justified is so firmly anchored in the contemporary theological mind that even a thinker like John Milbank, who is otherwise very sensitive to modern prejudice, seems to take it for granted.

> For the more science and politics were confined to immanent and autonomous secular realms, the more faith appealed to an *arational*

---

9. Wolfhart Pannenberg, "Response to the Discussion," in John Cobb Jr. and James Robinson, eds., *New Frontiers in Theology*, vol. 3 (New York: Harper and Row, 1967), p. 226; quoted in Lamont, *Divine Faith*, p. 20.

10. Austin Farrer, "Revelation," in Basil Mitchell, ed., *Faith and Logic* (London: George Allen and Unwin, 1957), p. 84.

positivity of authority invested with a right to rule, and sometimes to overrule, science and secular politics.[11]

One important purpose I have in this book is to show that the standard contemporary attitude, though understandable in light of historical misuses of appeals to divine authority, is based on inadequate conceptions of the nature of testimonial knowledge.[12] Farrer, for example, seems unaware of the circumstance that most of the everyday truths we take

---

11. John Milbank, "Intensities," *Modern Theology* 15, no. 4 (1999): 445-97 (italics added).

12. Is Karl Barth a counterexample to the negative contemporary attitude toward the conception of revelation as divine testimony? This is a difficult question. On the one hand, Barth says that "we have no reason not to take the concept of God's Word primarily in its literal sense. God's Word means that God speaks. Speaking is not a 'symbol' " (Karl Barth, *Church Dogmatics*, vol. I.1: *The Doctrine of the Word of God* [Edinburgh: T & T Clark, 1975], p. 132). Here it seems that Barth advocates a literal understanding of the traditional claim that God reveals by speaking, and hence a conception of revelation as divine testimony. This impression is strengthened when we read that "God reveals himself in statements, through the medium of speech, and indeed human speech. His word is always this or that word spoken by the prophets and apostles and proclaimed in the Church" (Barth, *Church Dogmatics*, vol. I.1, pp. 137-38). Barth does not, on the other hand, want to identify revelation (God's word) with the concrete statements of the Bible or of human preachers ("we distinguish the Bible as such from revelation" [Barth, *Church Dogmatics*, vol. I.2: *The Doctrine of the Word of God* (Edinburgh: T & T Clark, 1956), p. 463]).

God's speech, for Barth, always seems to be "beyond" the human words, sentences, utterances and speech-acts that mediate it. "As readers of Scripture and hearers of proclamation we can and must, of course, work with certain general conceptual materials, apparently repeating . . . what God has said to this or that man. . . . But in doing so we have always to bear in mind that these materials are our own work and are not to be confused with the concrete fullness of the Word of God itself which we recall and for which we wait, but only point to it. What God said and what God will say is always quite different from what we can and must say to ourselves and others about its content. Not only the word of preaching . . . but even the word of Scripture through which God speaks to us becomes in fact quite different when it passes from God's lips to our ears and our lips" (Barth, *Church Dogmatics*, vol. I.1, pp. 140-41). The rather loose relationship that Barth sees between concrete statements in human language and God's Word makes it unclear whether Barth really can be said to have a literal understanding of the claim that God speaks. Nicholas Wolterstorff has argued that "there's less in Barth on God speaking than first appears" (Wolterstorff, *Divine Discourse: Philosophical Reflections on the Claim That God Speaks* [Cambridge: Cambridge University Press, 1995], p. 72). This, however, is not the place to try to nail down Barth's exact position on the literal status of divine speech. Even if we were to understand Barth's doctrine of revelation as a version of the traditional testimonial model, we would still have to admit that the epistemological category of testimony plays a very marginal role in Barth's explication of the doctrine.

ourselves to know are truths that we have "accepted on the mere authority of [their] revealer[s]."[13] I do not have a cogent argument from my own personal experience to the truth that Karl Barth was born in 1886. I have just accepted the latter proposition (which I take myself to know) as true on the authority of some author who I know only by name and whose reliability I have no adequate evidence for. I could, of course, check with other sources, thereby acquiring premises for an argument-to-the-best-explanation, for example, along the following lines: three independent sources state that Karl Barth was born in 1886. The best explanation of this fact is that Barth really was born that year. The point, however, is that I have not done this. I have just consulted one book (which is also the case when it comes to innumerable other beliefs that I have). And even if I were to consult a number of books and find them in agreement, I would still not have a very solid argument for the truth of the proposition that Barth was born in 1886. There is always the rather likely possibility that all the books depend, directly or indirectly, on a common misleading source. In order to exclude this possibility, I may have to do quite extensive research.

But maybe — the critical reader will object — I can be said to possess a justification for my belief about Barth's birth in the form of the following argument: peer-reviewed books are usually trustworthy about the birth years of famous people; a peer-reviewed book states that Barth was born in 1886; therefore, Barth was probably born in 1886. An argument of this type would maybe suffice to give my belief about Barth's year of birth and similar beliefs the status of knowledge, thereby eliminating the need for me to simply trust an author. But how do I know the minor premise of the argument, that the book about Barth's birth that I am relying on is peer-reviewed? Because the publishing company's Web site says that it is? Then I would be relying "on the mere authority" of the publishing company's Web site (unless I have independent evidence for its reliability, which I probably do not). And what about the major premise — that peer-reviewed books are usually trustworthy? This is something that I cannot confirm on the basis of my own personal experience. I have acquired thousands of beliefs from peer-reviewed books. I have, however, only checked the truth of a very limited number of those beliefs for myself. So I do not know, on the basis of my own firsthand experience, that peer-reviewed books are *usually* trustworthy.

---

13. This is, in any case, what many contemporary philosophers of testimony claim. I will defend the claim in chap. 5 below.

Does all this mean that I do not really know that Barth was born in 1886? To draw this conclusion from the considerations above would be disastrous. It would force me to concede that I do not really know most of the things that I think I know. My evidence for most of the matter-of-fact propositions that I have come to believe in the course of my theological education is no better than my evidence for the year of Barth's birth. The only alternative to radical skepticism, therefore, seems to be to admit that it cannot in general be irrational — or nonrational, or arational — to accept something as true "on the mere authority of its revealer." This, at least, is what many philosophers of testimony argue today. To believe things merely on the say-so of others is as rational and indispensable as believing things on the basis of one's own firsthand experiences. Testimony, according to this view, must be conceived as a sui generis source of epistemic justification, like perception, memory, and inference. This means that "when we inquire into the basis of some claim by asking: 'Why do you believe that?' or 'How do you know that?' the answer 'Jones told me' can be just as appropriate as 'I saw it' or 'I remember it,' 'It follows from this.'"[14]

"Jones told me" can, in other words, constitute my *justification* for believing something, in the same sense as a perceptual experience or an inferential argument can. If Jones, as a matter of objective fact, is a reliable source of information about the relevant topic, then my justification for believing the proposition that I have heard from him is satisfactory. This means that what I have heard can count as knowledge. The testimony of Jones, moreover, can justify one of my beliefs even if I lack any evidence whatsoever for Jones's trustworthiness in the relevant respect. The only thing that matters, according to this view, is that I do not have positive evidence *against* Jones's trustworthiness. If you think that this sounds strange, ask yourself how many high-school students know anything about the authors of their physics textbook. Not many, I would guess. This means that most high-school students have acquired most of their knowledge of physics from the written testimony of people who are completely unknown to them. Can what they have acquired this way still be counted as knowledge? I certainly hope it can.

It is very likely a big mistake, then, to distinguish belief based on the mere authority of a testifier from *rational* (warranted, justified) belief. Testimonial beliefs are as rationally held as any beliefs. Unfortunately, there

---

14. C. A. J. Coady, *Testimony: A Philosophical Study* (Oxford: Oxford University Press, 1994), p. 6.

Introduction

is a traditional way of speaking that, if misunderstood, can obscure this insight. What I have in mind is the theological distinction between "reason" and "revelation" (or "faith"), conceived of as two different "sources" of knowledge or belief. Colin Gunton exemplifies how this distinction is typically used in modern theology:

> It is a truism that since the Enlightenment the question of revelation has bulked large in Christian theology because that movement . . . brought to the centre the epistemological dimension of belief. By tending to replace revelation by reason, or rather to displace it altogether, locating the source of revelation largely if not wholly in reason, it threw into question the historical basis of Christianity, and so opened up the modern debate about the epistemological basis of the faith.[15]

A similar-sounding distinction between "reason" and "faith" can be found, for example, in the First Vatican Council's *Dei Filius,* and in the writings of Saint John Paul II. While I agree with the substance of the message of the latter's encyclical *Fides et Ratio,* there is an obvious risk that the habit of contrasting "faith"/"revelation" with "reason" is taken to imply that "faith" is a *nonrational,* or at least a less rational, source of belief than is "reason."[16] The very terminology, taken by itself, can seem to assign to faith/revelation the unflattering role of being reason's "other." This is not how the First Vatican Council or John Paul II understood things. Many modern theologians and philosophers, however, have assumed that faith is distinguished from "reason" partly by the fact that it is constituted by, or includes, rationally *unjustified* beliefs, or beliefs that are not fully justified. This view represents, as I will now argue, a serious distortion of the traditional idea of the "twofold order of knowledge" as it is classically formulated by Saint Thomas Aquinas.[17]

Saint Thomas distinguishes between propositions that can be known by natural reason and the articles of faith — the latter being revealed to us by God.[18] This distinction is, however, not at all a distinction between

---

15. Colin Gunton, *A Brief Theology of Revelation* (Edinburgh: T & T Clark, 1995), p. 2; see also Colin Gunton, *Revelation and Reason: Prolegomena to Systematic Theology,* ed. P. H. Brazier (Edinburgh: T&T Clark, 2008).

16. John Paul II, *Fides et Ratio* [Encyclical Letter on the Relationship between Faith and Reason]: http://www.vatican.va/holy_father/john_paul_ii/encyclicals/documents/hf_jp-ii_enc_15101998_fides-et-ratio_en.html (accessed May 4, 2013).

17. Denzinger, *Compendium of Creeds,* §3015.

18. *ST* I, q. 2, a. 2.

the rational (knowledge) and the nonrational ("mere belief"). Instead, it is best understood as a distinction between two different *kinds* of knowledge, namely, between things known by *scientia* (and adjacent modes of cognition) and things known by testimony from God.

The paradigm case of *scientia*, for Aquinas, is knowledge generated by a certain kind of inference, namely, demonstrative syllogism.[19] A demonstrative syllogism is a valid deductive argument, which means that if its premises are true, then the conclusion is guaranteed to be true as well. Aquinas also recognizes a type of *scientia* whereby "immediate" propositions are known.[20] Immediate propositions are "cognized *(cognita)* or known *(nota)* by virtue of themselves (per se)" (p. 171).[21] This means that our justification for holding these propositions "consists in our being directly aware of the necessity of the facts they express" (p. 172). The "immediate" propositions constitute the foundations of *scientia*, the ultimate premises from which the demonstrations of other propositions proceed. "Aquinas claims that to have *scientia* with respect to some proposition *p* is to hold *p* on the basis of a demonstration the ultimate premises of which are propositions we are non-inferentially justified in holding" (p. 173).

The concept of *scientia*, defined in this way, has a very narrow application. Only axiomatic systems like geometry or logic qualify as *scientiae* in this very rigorous sense. Aquinas, however, admits that we can also have *scientia* in cases that do not fully fit the description above. He can, according to Scott MacDonald, "admit that paradigmatic *scientia* can be attained only in a priori disciplines such as logic and geometry, while allowing that we can correctly be said to have *scientia* (though not paradigmatic *scientia*) with respect to many other sorts of propositions" (p. 174).[22] Propositions about particular sensible objects can, for example, be said to constitute "immediate" propositions "for us," and therefore function as the founda-

---

19. The term *scientia* can mean both the process by which a certain type of knowledge is acquired and the product of that process, the knowledge itself.

20. *Sententia super Posteriora analytica,* 1.4.14. See Scott MacDonald, "Theory of Knowledge," in Norman Kretzman and Eleonore Stump, eds., *The Cambridge Companion to Aquinas* (Cambridge: Cambridge University Press, 1993), p. 168. Hereafter, page references to this essay appear in parentheses in the text.

21. Aquinas sometimes refers to this noninferential knowledge of "immediate" propositions as *intellectus*.

22. John Jenkins also argues that "the PA notion of *scientia* has a wider application than may initially seem" (John Jenkins, *Knowledge and Faith in Thomas Aquinas* [Cambridge: Cambridge University Press, 1997], p. 32).

tion of *scientiae*. Since such propositions cannot be known with complete certainty (we can be wrong about sensible objects), there is always a risk that the conclusions based on them will be false. This means that the kind of *scientiae* that are based on propositions about sensible objects can only approximate the paradigm cases of *scientia* — the latter being cases in which the conclusions are certain (pp. 174-78).

It is not unusual for commentators to take Aquinas's account of *scientia* to exhaust what he has to say about knowledge. If this understanding were correct, whenever Aquinas denies that we have *scientia* with respect to some proposition, we would have to understand that he is denying that we have *knowledge* of that proposition. However, *scientia* is not equivalent to our term "knowledge" (p. 162). We can see the glaring difference between Aquinas's account of *scientia* and a modern understanding of knowledge by the following example. I take myself to know that the earth orbits the sun. I guess that few would deny that this is a genuine piece of knowledge that I have. Aquinas would not, however, admit that it constitutes *scientia*. Why not? Because I only know that the earth orbits the sun because I have been told so by trustworthy authorities. That the earth orbits the sun is not an "immediate" proposition in Aquinas's sense, and I have not inferred that the earth orbits the sun from the relevant astronomical evidence. There are, of course, people who have done so and thus have *scientia* of the fact that the earth orbits the sun. The point is that I am not one of those people.

This example should make clear that most of my or anybody's knowledge does not qualify as *scientia* in Aquinas's sense, because most of what I know or anybody knows, we know on the basis of testimony. Aquinas would call the layman's secondhand knowledge of the earth's movement around the sun — about brains, historical events, and similar facts — *opinio;* but this does not mean that he would judge the layman's acceptance of these facts to be unjustified.[23] Aquinas discusses other modes of epistemic justification besides *scientia*. He recognizes, for instance, certain types of dialectical or probable reasoning as capable of justifying beliefs. More importantly, Aquinas admits that the testimony of *reasonable authorities* can provide epistemic justification (pp. 179-80). It is this type of

---

23. MacDonald writes: "When Aquinas's views commit him to denying that we have *scientia* with respect to some proposition or when he claims that we have no demonstration for that proposition, he should not be read as thereby denying that we know it or are justified in holding it" (MacDonald, "Theory of Knowledge," p. 180).

justification that makes belief in Christian doctrines reasonable. When the authority that testifies is God himself, the act of believing that testimony is an act of divine faith — *fides*. The propositions believed by divine faith (i.e., on the basis of God's testimony) are warranted to an excellent degree by the authority of God, who is the First Truth. Aquinas writes:

> The object of every knowing habit includes two things: first, that which is known materially, and is the material object, so to speak, and, secondly, that by which it is known, which is the formal aspect of the object. Thus in the science of geometry, the conclusions are what is known materially, while the formal aspects of the science are the means of demonstration, through which the conclusions are known. Accordingly if we consider, in faith, the formal aspect of the object, it is nothing else than the First Truth. For the faith of which we are speaking does not assent to anything, except because it is revealed by God. Hence the faith is based on the Divine Truth itself, as on the means.[24]

In the same sense as geometrical demonstration is the basis ("formal object") of geometrical knowledge, so the basis of our knowledge of the articles of faith is God's revelation: divine testimony. This is a very solid basis. "For although the argument from authority based on human reason is the weakest, yet the argument from authority based on divine revelation is the strongest."[25] We should not let the circumstance that faith requires grace obscure the fact that faith, for Aquinas, "rests on infallible truth" and thus is supremely rational.[26] (The question of how we can know that the Christian doctrines are proposed for our belief by *God* is another question to which Aquinas provides an interesting — though not, in my opinion, altogether satisfactory — answer.[27] (In this book we will see how contemporary philosophy of testimony can help us to improve on the answer.)

It is true that, for Aquinas, "imperfect cognition" *(imperfectio cogni-*

---

24. *ST* II-II, q. 1, a. 1.
25. *ST* I, q. 1, a. 8.
26. *ST* I, q. 1, a. 8.
27. There are different opinions about exactly what Aquinas's answer is. The naturalist interpretation claims that "credibility arguments," such as arguments from miracles, can justify the believer's acceptance of certain propositions as divinely revealed. A currently more popular interpretation claims that a supernaturally infused "light of faith" gives the believer nondiscursive knowledge that something is divinely revealed (Jenkins, *Knowledge and Faith in Thomas Aquinas,* pp. 185-97; Paul Macdonald, "A Realist Epistemology of Faith," *Religious Studies* 41, no. 4 [2005]: 373-93).

tionis) belongs to the very notion of faith.[28] He claims that the articles of faith are, by necessity, "imperfectly cognized" by us because we are not capable of "seeing" their truth in the sense of being compelled to accept it, either by finding it self-evident or by clearly seeing how it follows from something self-evident.[29] *Imperfectio cognitionis* is often translated as "imperfect *knowledge*." This is fine as long as we acknowledge that much of what we refer to as "knowledge" today would count as *imperfectio cognitionis* according to Aquinas's standards.

Aquinas's distinction between propositions known "by natural reason" and propositions known "by faith" does not, therefore, map onto the modern distinction between knowledge and "mere belief." Paul Macdonald has argued that faith, for Aquinas, "appears to qualify as knowledge according to some mainline standards of contemporary epistemology: it consists of true belief that is both appropriately justified and warranted."[30] It is, in any case, clear that Aquinas's denial that the doctrines of the Christian faith constitute *scientia* does not imply that belief in these doctrines is any less rational than the modern layman's belief in the findings of contemporary natural science. The modern idea that Christian faith has a less rational grounding than the things we normally call "knowledge" finds — as far as I can tell — very little support in the premodern Christian tradition as a whole. What Aquinas and the mainstream tradition distinguish between is knowledge based on divine testimony (or knowledge that depends on some other special, divine act) — "faith, theology" — and knowledge that does not depend on divine testimony (or on some other special, divine act) — "reason, philosophy."[31]

However, with the modern dichotomy of "reason" and "revelation" firmly in place, understood as a contrast between the more and less rational, it became an important task for theologians to explain how it could be "overcome." This was, of course, by the nature of the task, a steep uphill struggle. The most common strategy for meeting the challenge was to dissociate the concept of revelation from the traditional understanding

---

28. *ST* I-II, q. 67 a. 3.
29. "Now those things are said to be seen which, of themselves, move the intellect or the senses to knowledge of them" (*ST* II-II, q. 1, a. 4).
30. Macdonald, "A Realist Epistemology of Faith," 389.
31. The fact that Aquinas understands the distinction between faith and reason in terms of a distinction between grace and nature has no bearing on the question of faith's *rationality*. That faith is a supernatural gift does not entail that the propositions believed by faith lack justification.

of revelation as divine testimony. By abandoning the idea of revelation through divine speech-acts in favor of manifestational forms of revelation (God "showing himself" in experience or history), theologians made the idea of revelation look less offensive to "reason." If revelation only means that God "shows himself," then there is no necessity of relying on divine authority.

Manifestational conceptions of revelation have, of course, always been an important and legitimate part of the Christian tradition, and it is certainly valuable for theology to explore different models of revelation. The divine testimony model, furthermore, is liable to abuse (as are all models of revelation), and modernity's critical attitude toward it is not altogether unjustified. It is a mistake, however, to think that the divine testimony model is inherently antirational or offensive to reason. The truth is rather that the standard modern attitude toward the divine testimony model is based on a general and rationally indefensible *prejudice against testimony,* a failure to appreciate the global importance of testimony as a source of rational justification.

People are not, as the Western philosophical tradition has usually portrayed them, autonomous knowers. Knowledge is social in nature — or else a very rare phenomenon. A person's epistemic standing (whether she has knowledge of a certain proposition or not) often depends on the epistemic standing of other persons whose reports she relies on. In many cases, I am only rationally justified in believing that *p* if some other person whose words I trust is rationally justified in believing that *p*. This kind of epistemic dependence is not at all surprising considering that we are linguistic creatures whose ability to think rationally is largely due to language. Language is, as Wittgenstein made clear, inherently social. If our very ability to think rationally is dependent on an inherently social phenomenon, it would be surprising if knowledge were primarily the property of autonomous individuals. Yet this is how the post-Enlightenment philosophical tradition, until recently, has almost exclusively thought of it. And post-Enlightenment theologians have usually followed suit. They have assumed that believing things merely on the say-so of some other person cannot be fully rational. If it is not fully rational to rely on the testimony of other people, without seeking independent verification of what they say, then it must surely be unacceptable to understand the Christian revelation in terms of the category of testimony.

In this book I will go against the current of much contemporary theology and argue that the divine testimony model of revelation is not only

Introduction

rationally defensible but also that it (or some other form of propositional revelation) is hard to do without if theology is to constitute a coherent activity. I will also argue that having an adequate understanding of the nature of testimonial knowledge, and of our profound dependence on testimony, will make us much less inclined to dismiss the divine testimony model.

In chapters 2 and 3, I argue that neither any kind of mystical or transcendental experience, nor any awareness of God's "mighty acts" in history, can — by themselves — give humans knowledge of the existence of God.[32] This is because "God," as the Christian tradition understands the concept, refers to a necessary, personal being on whom everything finite depends for its existence. The nature of God is such that his existence cannot be proved by any kind of experience or intuition or by the occurrence of historical events, however remarkable. God's existence can only be known by humans if there is some very potent form of natural theology capable of establishing it (e.g., if the traditional theistic arguments hold water), or if God has chosen to share some of his knowledge of his own nature with us by communicating conceptually structured contents (i.e., propositions) to us. A potent natural theology or propositional revelation — these are, I will argue, the only two viable options.

The take-home message of chapters 2 and 3 is that those Christians who, unlike me, are skeptical of the possibility of a potent natural theology should think twice before they reject the idea of propositional revelation. The result of rejecting both propositional revelation and the viability of a potent natural theology will be a lapse into incoherence.

The term "propositional revelation" has, unfortunately, become something of a catchword in contemporary theology. It is usually associated with conservative evangelicalism, but it has also figured as a label for Neo-Scholastic views of revelation within twentieth-century Catholicism. Since I am a Catholic, there is a risk that this book will be perceived as taking the side of "Neo-Scholastic rationalism" against the "dynamic" and "sacramental" understanding of revelation represented by the *nouvelle théologie* and the Second Vatican Council. However, that would be a misunderstanding of this book's argument. My agenda is not to oppose the multifaceted and dynamic understanding of revelation of Vatican II; on the contrary, I believe that the doctrine of revelation expressed in documents such as *Dei Verbum* (the Second Vatican Council's constitution on divine revelation)

---

32. John Baillie, *The Idea of Revelation in Recent Thought* (New York: Columbia University Press, 1956), p. 62.

is very sound and fully compatible with the ideas advocated in this book. My limited knowledge of "Neo-Scholastic" thought on revelation, on the other hand, derives (I must sheepishly admit) mostly from reading its critics. Accordingly, I "know" that "Neo-Scholastic rationalists" think that "the whole idea of revelation begins with propositions and concepts and ends with propositions and concepts";[33] that they view revelation "largely as the issuing of divine decrees";[34] that they regard the Bible "principally as a collection of propositions, each of which can be taken by itself as a divine assertion";[35] and that the result of all this is that "the God of the Bible and the Gospel . . . [is] reduced to a *caput mortuum* of frozen abstractions."[36]

This sounds pretty dreadful to me (though I suspect that the descriptions may not be entirely fair). My own view of revelation is much better captured by one of Neo-Scholasticism's sharpest critics:

> A comprehensive view of Revelation, precisely because it is concerned with the whole man, is founded not only in the word that Christ preached, but in the whole of the living experience of his person, thus embracing what is said and what is unsaid, what the Apostles in their turn are not able to express fully in words, but which is found in the whole reality of the Christian existence of which they speak, far transcending the framework of what has been explicitly formulated in words.[37]

Like Pope Benedict XVI (then Cardinal Ratzinger), I do not think that revelation is only, or principally, about grasping propositions. I think that revelation is mainly about getting to know a person, Jesus Christ. Furthermore, I believe that coming to know Christ through revelation requires a graced transformation, which is effected by participation in the sacramental life of the church. Revelation, therefore, involves much

---

33. Anthony Towey, "Dei Verbum: Fit for Purpose?" *New Blackfriars* 90, no. 1026 (2009): 206-18; 209.

34. Joseph Ratzinger, "Revelation Itself," in *Commentary on the Documents of Vatican II*, vol. 3, ed. Herbert Vorgrimler (New York: Herder and Herder, 1969), p. 171.

35. Avery Dulles, *Models of Revelation* (Maryknoll, NY: Orbis, 1992), p. 48.

36. Fergus Kerr, *Twentieth-Century Catholic Theologians: From Neoscholasticism to Nuptial Mysticism* (Malden, MA: Blackwell, 2007), p. 10.

37. Joseph Ratzinger, "The Transmission of Divine Revelation," in Vorgrimler, ed., *Commentary on the Documents of Vatican II*, vol. 3, p. 181; quoted in Tracey Rowland, *Ratzinger's Faith: The Theology of Pope Benedict XVI* (Oxford: Oxford University Press, 2008), p. 52.

more than divinely asserted propositions. What I reject is the kind of reductionism that does not acknowledge any role for divine assertions at all. Ratzinger is not a reductionist in this sense. That "[r]evelation . . . is founded not *only* in the word that Christ preached" implies that revelation is *partly* founded in the word that Christ preached. "A comprehensive view of Revelation . . . embracing *what is said* and what is unsaid" is a view of revelation that embraces divine assertions as an aspect of revelation. Ratzinger's view of revelation seems (unsurprisingly) to reflect that of *Dei Verbum,* a document that, in Gerald O'Collin's accurate description, pictures revelation "primarily as God's self-revelation, which invites the personal response of faith, and . . . secondarily [as] the communication of truths about God and human beings that would otherwise remain unknown."[38]

There is no difficulty in viewing the divine revelation both as God's self-revelation and as God's communicating truths about himself. On the contrary, to view these two descriptions of revelation as incompatible is as absurd as to view *my* self-revelation as incompatible with the fact that I tell things about myself.

I "reveal myself" partly by asserting things about myself, things that "would otherwise remain unknown," partly by acting, and partly by simply being physically present to other people. If my self-revelation can have three different aspects, there can be no problem in conceiving of God's self-revelation as equally multifaceted. This is exactly how *Dei Verbum* conceives of it:

> This plan of revelation is realized by *deeds* and *words* having an inner unity: the deeds wrought by God in the history of salvation manifest and confirm the teaching and realities signified by the words, while the words proclaim the deeds and clarify the mystery contained in them. . . . Jesus perfected revelation by fulfilling it through his whole work of *making himself present* and manifesting himself.[39]

---

38. Gerald O'Collins and Mario Farrugia, *Catholicism: The Story of Catholic Christianity* (New York: Oxford University Press, 2003), p. 97. Hans Urs von Balthasar expresses a similar view of revelation: "We can . . . see that Christianity, as genuine revealed religion, cannot be a communication of knowledge, a 'teaching,' in the first place, but only secondarily. It must be in the first place an action that God undertakes, the playing out of the drama that God began with mankind in the Old Covenant" (Hans Urs von Balthasar, *Love Alone Is Credible* [San Francisco: Ignatius Press, 2004], p. 70).

39. Denzinger, *Compendium of Creeds,* §4202 and §4204.

The spirit of this book is not reductionist but anti-reductionist. The aim is not to restrict or reduce revelation to its intellectual element; rather, it is to recover one essential aspect of what Ratzinger calls a "comprehensive view of revelation," an aspect that too often tends to be dismissed or underappreciated today. Even among theologians who accept that revelation is partly propositional, there is a tendency to view this aspect as inessential and rather unimportant. This is a problematic attitude, as I argue in chapters 2 and 3.

In order to illustrate how widespread the negative attitude toward propositional revelation is in contemporary theology, I find it sufficient to point out that not even Ratzinger himself is altogether innocent of flirting with it. Some of his statements tend to contrast — unfavorably — propositional revelation with God's *self*-revelation:

> If one understands revelation as a certain number of supernatural communications that took place during the time of Jesus' public life and were definitively concluded with the death of the apostles, then faith, in practical terms, can be understood only as a connection to an intellectual construct from the past. But this historicist and intellectualist notion of revelation that has gradually developed in the modern period is thoroughly false. For revelation is not a collection of statements — revelation is Christ himself. *He* is the Logos, the all-embracing Word in which God declares himself and that we therefore call the Son of God.[40]

The claim that the "intellectualist notion of revelation" is "thoroughly false" is rather unfortunate, as is the claim that "revelation is not a collection of statements." Together they can be taken to entail that linguistic statements are not included under the concept of revelation at all. In the passage above, Ratzinger can too easily be understood to represent a reductionist view according to which "revelation" *only* refers to Christ "himself" and not also to his verbal teachings (the "supernatural communications that took place during the time of Jesus' public life"). This would, in itself, be a very peculiar position, since it separates Jesus "himself" from his public statements. One may wonder whether Jesus' *nonlinguistic* actions and the things that he suffers — such as his death and

---

40. Joseph Ratzinger, *On the Way to Jesus Christ* (San Francisco: Ignatius Press, 2005), pp. 81-82.

Introduction

resurrection — are part of Jesus "himself" or if they must also be excluded from revelation.

I do not think, of course, that Ratzinger should be read this way. On a generous reading, we can understand him to be saying that revelation is not primarily a collection of statements. Revelation is primarily a person — Christ — who (as an integral part of who he is) teaches and makes statements, but who cannot be reduced to his teachings or statements. Christ's teachings are, according to this more reasonable view, a part of revelation *because they are a part of Christ*.[41] Ratzinger goes on to say:

> This one Logos, of course, has communicated himself in normative words, in which he presents to us what is distinctively his. Yet *the Word* is always greater than *the words* and is never exhausted by the words.[42]

This book focuses on the idea that the Logos has communicated himself in normative words, without thereby denying that the Word is always greater than the words. The main purpose of this book is to show that the general idea of knowledge by divine, linguistic testimony is intellectually viable and need not be swept under the carpet in contemporary theology. I will primarily be concerned with the words of prophets and of Jesus himself as instances of divine testimony, and only secondarily with the Bible. The claim that the Bible itself — and not merely some of the prophetic

---

41. That this is a plausible interpretation of Ratzinger becomes clear when he, in a different context, emphasizes the "inseparability of person and work" in Christ (Joseph Ratzinger, *Introduction to Christianity* [San Francisco: Ignatius Press, 2004], p. 208). When it comes to Christ, there is, according to Ratzinger, "no private area reserved for an 'I' that remains in the background behind the deeds and actions" (p. 203). Jesus "coincides with his deeds," including his "teachings" (p. 205).

42. Ratzinger, *On the Way to Jesus Christ,* p. 82. Ratzinger, however, is not entirely clear about the relationship between asserted propositions in *Scripture* and revelation. He emphasizes the "non-identity" of "Scripture" and "revelation" (Karl Rahner and Joseph Ratzinger, *Revelation and Tradition* [Freiburg: Herder, 1966], p. 35). This view is, however, compatible with my claim that assertions found in Scripture are *part* of revelation (a part is not identical to that of which it is a part). Sometimes Ratzinger seems to have this part/whole understanding of the relationship: "Scripture *is* not revelation but at most only a part of the latter's greater reality" (Rahner and Ratzinger, *Revelation and Tradition,* p. 37). A reductionist view of revelation that denies that revelation is even partly constituted by divinely asserted propositions is, in any case, incompatible with the teaching of *Dei Verbum*. *Dei Verbum* declares that "everything asserted by the inspired authors or sacred writers must be held to be asserted by the Holy Spirit" (Denzinger, *Compendium of Creeds*, §4216). Assertions by the Holy Spirit (which *Dei Verbum* claims exist) are, if anything, part of revelation.

and dominical utterances recorded therein — constitutes divine speech encounters some problems that I do not claim to resolve completely in this book. The model for knowledge transmission that I defend is, however, applicable also to the Bible, and I will point to some general ways of dealing with the objections that a view of the Bible as divine testimony commonly encounters.

My argument in favor of the divine-testimony model draws heavily on the thinking of two philosophers. Chapter 4 presents and defends some of the central ideas in Nicholas Wolterstorff's analysis of divine speech, found in his magisterial work *Divine Discourse*. The divine-testimony model presupposes a literal understanding of the claim that God speaks, and a coherent and defensible account of divine speech-acts is thus essential for the model.

Chapter 5 recounts and defends John McDowell's understanding of how testimonial knowledge is justified. McDowell is one of the most interesting and influential philosophers writing today and one of those unusual figures who attempt to bridge the divide between the analytical and the continental philosophical traditions.[43] His account of testimonial knowledge belongs in the "anti-reductionist" camp, which means that it conceives of testimony as a sui generis source of knowledge. McDowell's thinking on the subject is unusually profound, however, and he traces many of the philosophical problems that pertain to testimonial knowledge back to certain deeply rooted (but nonnecessary) "Cartesian" ideas about the relationship between our minds and the world.

In chapters 6-8, I try to show, using the philosophical tools provided by Wolterstorff and McDowell, how divine testimony could give us "entrance into the horizons of God's own knowledge."[44] The main problem that needs to be confronted in this context is the question of epistemic justification. A person only knows that p if he is rationally justified/warranted in believing that p.[45] Can beliefs about God and salvation that are acquired

---

43. Marcus Willaschek, Preface to *John McDowell: Reason and Nature*, ed. Marcus Willaschek (Münster: LIT Verlag, 1999).

44. Avery Dulles, *The Assurance of Things Hoped For: A Theology of Christian Faith* (New York: Oxford University Press, 1994), p. 225.

45. Epistemic justification is a necessary condition for knowledge (as most philosophers agree). A notion that is often used interchangeably with justification is *rationality* (see Mikael Stenmark, *Rationality in Science, Religion, and Everyday Life: A Critical Evaluation of Four Models of Rationality* [Notre Dame, IN: University of Notre Dame Press, 1995], p. 19). However, some philosophers distinguish between justification and rationality, and some

Introduction

from divine testimony, mediated by human spokespersons and expressed in human language, be rationally justified? It is the main purpose of this book to show that they can.

---

between justification, rationality, and warrant (Alvin Plantinga, *Warranted Christian Belief* [New York: Oxford University Press, 2000]). There are a number of theories about what it means for a belief to be justified/rational/warranted, and about what constitutes knowledge. In this book I will use the terms "justification," "rationality," and "warrant" interchangeably and (at least initially) without committing myself to any specific epistemological theory. By a "justified (rational, warranted) belief" I will simply mean a belief that the subject is *rationally entitled* to hold.

CHAPTER 2

Revelation and Knowledge of God

David Kelsey writes (in 1975):

> There has been a widespread consensus in Protestant theology in the past four decades that the "revelation" to which Scripture attests is a self-manifestation by God in historical events, and not information about God stated in divinely communicated doctrines or concepts.[1]

At about the same time, and in a similar spirit, Ray Hart declares: "No proposition would gain wider acceptance than the following one: the *content* of revelation is not a body of propositions to be accepted as a condition of faith."[2]

More recently, Denys Turner says:

> Within theological circles in our times there can scarcely be a proposition less likely to meet with approval than that which, on 24 April 1870, the first Vatican Council decreed, "that God, the source and end

---

1. David Kelsey, *The Uses of Scripture in Recent Theology* (Philadelphia: Fortress, 1975), p. 32.

2. Ray Hart, *Unfinished Man and the Imagination* (New York: Herder and Herder, 1968), p. 80; quoted in Avery Dulles, *Models of Revelation* (Maryknoll, NY: Orbis, 1992), p. 48. More than thirty years later, Rowan Williams gives expression to a similar judgment when talking about "the kind of propositional account of revelation which very few contemporary theologians would accept, but which was once characteristic of wide areas of Protestant and Catholic theology alike" (Rowan Williams, *On Christian Theology* [Oxford: Blackwell, 2000], p. 131).

of all things, can be known with certainty from the consideration of created things, by the natural power of human reason."[3]

The view that revelation consists of "information about God stated in divinely communicated doctrines or concepts" (Kelsey), or that the content of revelation is "a body of propositions" (Hart) is often labeled "propositional revelation." Propositional revelation refers not only to the idea that God reveals by speaking (in the literal sense), but also to other possible modes of revelation, such as the one envisioned by John Locke. According to Locke, God reveals by directly transmitting true beliefs to some humans. This way of revealing counts as propositional revelation, but it is not a species of speaking.[4]

The view that the existence of God "can be known with certainty from the consideration of created things, by the natural power of human reason" (Vatican I) is known as *natural theology* — something that is currently experiencing something of a revival. It is important, however, to distinguish between the modest versions of natural theology that are gaining currency today and the very potent natural theology that Vatican I defines. What I call "modest" versions of natural theology do not claim to demonstrate (or even justify belief in) the existence of God. "God," as the Christian tradition uses the concept, refers to an infinite, perfectly good, omnipotent, and omniscient personal reality whose existence is necessary, and on whom everything finite is fundamentally dependent. A being that lacks any of these characteristics does not satisfy the concept of God.[5]

---

3. Denys Turner, *Faith, Reason, and the Existence of God* (New York: Cambridge University Press, 2004), p. 3.

4. Nicholas Wolterstorff, *Divine Discourse: Philosophical Reflections on the Claim That God Speaks* (Cambridge: Cambridge University Press, 1995), p. 27.

5. By claiming this, I do not substitute an abstract, philosophical concept of God for the God of Abraham, Isaac, Jacob, and Jesus Christ. On the contrary, classic Trinitarian faith clearly entails that God's existence is not contingent, and that everything finite is dependent for its existence on God (the doctrine of *creatio ex nihilo*). Omnipotence, omniscience, and perfect goodness are also divine attributes that few Trinitarian theologians would hesitate to ascribe to God. However, even if we bracket these latter attributes, the argument of the present chapter is not seriously affected. The argument only depends on the assumption that God is a personal reality on whom everything finite depends for its existence. If you are prepared to deny that these are essential characteristics of the Christian God, then you may stop reading now. The radical Heideggerian critique that all metaphysical conceptions of God are due to *Seinsvergessenheit* — the forgetting or ignoring of the "ontological difference" between Being and beings — is answered by Merold Westphal in "The Importance of Overcoming Metaphysics for the Life of Faith," *Modern Theology* 23,

Modest versions of natural theology typically argue for the existence of some kind of creator without claiming to establish that that creator is God, in the relevant sense. Sometimes modest natural theologians only argue that scientific facts about the natural world "resonate" very well with, or "fit," the Christian worldview, thereby giving it indirect support.[6] The difference between what I have referred to as "potent" and "modest" natural theologies is a difference between lines of argument that purport to generate knowledge of (or satisfactorily justify belief in) *God* and lines of argument that do not.[7]

Both the idea of "propositional revelation" and the claim that there exists a potent natural theology are, as the quotes by Kelsey, Hart, and Turner make clear, rather unpopular. Contemporary theologians do not seem to see any problem with rejecting both. Presumably, they think that there are other ways by which God could be known. Are there not, after all, a number of "nonpropositional" construals of divine revelation available on the theological market?

The problem with all "nonpropositional" accounts of revelation,

---

no. 2 (2007): 253-78. In order to claim that God has certain essential metaphysical attributes, one need not think of metaphysics as *foundational* in relation to faith and theology, or even as *independent* of faith. Westphal's "humble metaphysics," which is "not a preamble to faith but a reflection that arises out of faith" can also generate such claims (Westphal, "The Importance of Overcoming Metaphysics," p. 272).

6. See, e.g., Alister McGrath, *The Open Secret: A New Vision for Natural Theology* (Malden, MA: Blackwell, 2008), pp. 15-18; Alister McGrath, *A Fine-Tuned Universe: The Quest for God in Science and Theology* (Louisville: Westminster John Knox, 2009), pp. 27-28.

7. There are, however, construals of natural theology that do not portray knowledge of God as the result of inferential arguments. The idea that knowledge of God is generated noninferentially by a natural cognitive mechanism — a *sensus divinitatis* — is usually counted as a form of natural theology (see John Calvin, *Institutes of the Christian Religion* [Grand Rapids: Eerdmans, 1989], pp. 43-45; Alvin Plantinga, *Warranted Christian Belief* [New York: Oxford University Press, 2000], chap. 6). A related idea is that knowledge of God is "innate," a claim that, if taken literally, is untenable. Infants do not master the concept of God and hence cannot have beliefs or knowledge of God. The suggestion by, e.g., Calvin that knowledge of God is present "from [one's] mother's womb" is thus best understood to mean that "the capacity for such knowledge is indeed innate, like the capacity for arithmetical knowledge. Still, it doesn't follow that we know elementary arithmetic from our mother's womb. . . . [W]hat one has from one's mother's womb is not . . . knowledge of God, but a capacity for it" (Plantinga, *Warranted Christian Belief,* p. 173). In Plantinga's construal, the capacity for knowledge of God is the *sensus divinitatis*. However, Plantinga's theory of the *sensus divinitatis* presupposes a strong version of epistemological externalism, which in my view is problematic (see the next note).

however, is that they cannot explain how humans can be justified in believing that an infinite, necessary, perfectly good, omnipotent, and omniscient personal reality, on whom everything finite is fundamentally dependent, exists. Those accounts might certainly be able to explain how belief in a very powerful spiritual being who acts in history can be justified, but they cannot explain how we could justifiably conclude that this being is *omnipotent* and that everything finite is fundamentally dependent on it. This kind of belief can only, as I will argue, be justified on the basis of propositional revelation or a very potent natural theology.[8]

I am not implying that Christians, in order to be entitled to their faith, must possess some argument that can rationally persuade other people that God exists. Christians might be rationally justified in believing in God even though they do not have such an argument. One can surely be justified in believing that *p* even though one is incapable of rationally con-

---

8. Strictly speaking, this claim holds only given the rejection of strong versions of epistemological externalism. It is always possible to posit (e.g.) a reliable belief-producing mechanism that, under certain circumstances, produces the belief that God exists — a belief that will thereby, according to theories of this type, count as knowledge. But I will assume that knowledge is "a standing in the space of reasons" (to borrow a phrase from Wilfrid Sellars and John McDowell), and that knowledge therefore requires having *a reason* for what one believes. (Other things than beliefs — e.g., perceptual experiences — can constitute reasons, so the requirement that beliefs be supported by reasons does not generate an infinite regress (see John McDowell, *Mind and World* [Cambridge, MA: Harvard University Press, 1996]). A reason is something that the subject can come to be aware of by reflection alone — something that is within his "reflective reach" (John McDowell, "Knowledge by Hearsay," in *Meaning, Knowledge, and Reality* [Cambridge, MA: Harvard University Press, 1998], p. 418, n. 7). The claim that knowledge is based on reasons is thus incompatible with accounts of epistemic justification that construe justification as depending mainly on circumstances that are beyond the subject's reflective reach, such as the reliability of a certain belief-forming process, or the circumstance that one's cognitive faculties are "functioning properly in an appropriate epistemic environment according to a design plan successfully aimed at truth" (Plantinga, *Warranted Christian Belief,* p. xii). I do not think, however, that my "internalist prejudice" is very significant for the argument of chaps. 2 and 3 of this book. As far as I know, there are no externalist accounts of knowledge of God on offer that attempt to give an account of such knowledge without positing the occurrence of propositional revelation or the existence of a potent natural theology. Plantinga's account, which first comes to mind, posits both a potent natural theology (the *sensus divinitatis*) and propositional revelation through Scripture: "Christian belief is produced in the believer by the internal instigation of the Holy Spirit, endorsing the teachings of Scripture, which is itself divinely inspired" (Plantinga, *Warranted Christian Belief,* p. 290). For an account of the distinction between epistemological externalism and internalism, see William Alston, "Internalism and Externalism in Epistemology," in Hilary Kornblith, ed., *Epistemology: Internalism and Externalism* (Oxford: Blackwell, 2001).

vincing others that *p* is true, or probably true, or even that one is justified in believing that *p* is true. For instance, if Susan clearly saw a tiger at close range in the woods near her home, she is justified in believing that a tiger was near her home. Even so, she might not possess an argument that could convince her friends that a tiger was near her home, or even that she is justified in believing this.

What I am suggesting, then, is just that Christians are obliged to explain how it is *possible* for a controversial belief of the kind that they hold to be justified. This is a very modest requirement.[9] The tiger-spotter, Susan, can easily satisfy it, with respect to her tiger-belief, by appealing to perception. Her friends might not believe her when she says that she saw a tiger at close range, but they must admit that *if she did,* then her belief in the tiger's existence would be justified. They must hence admit that this belief is *conceivably,* or *possibly,* justified. On the other hand, if Susan had claimed that a tiger was near her home at a time when she herself was abroad, and if she could not explain *how* she could possibly know about the tiger ("I just know that it was there"), and if there is no independent evidence in favor of her claim, then anybody must admit that her epistemic situation is extremely problematic. It is not just problematic in the eyes of other people; it should seem problematic to Susan as well.

It is vital for Christians that we do not end up in this kind of situation, that is, saying, "Okay, it seems impossible to explain how anyone can know, or justifiably believe, that God exists, but I know it anyway."[10] This is why it is important for theology to be able to give a plausible account of how justified belief in the God of theism comes about. My claim in this book is that there are only two conceivable ways. One is if there exists some kind of potent natural theology à la Vatican I. The other way is if God has chosen to share his knowledge of his own nature with humans by communicating conceptually structured contents (propositions) to us. If we reject both these ways, we will be unable to answer this question: How is it possible for belief in God to be justified?

The main objective of this book is to show how a version of propositional revelation, the traditional story that God reveals some of his properties by testifying, can indeed explain how humans could justifiably believe

---

9. It should be considered a minimum requirement.

10. Appealing to a coherentist model of epistemic justification will not, as we will see (chap. 3), make the demand for an explanation less urgent.

Revelation and Knowledge of God

(in fact, know) that God exists. If it is correct that no *other* construal of divine revelation can explain this (which is my task in this chapter and the next to show), then many theologians will have a strong incentive to reconsider the traditional view. I will leave open whether there is any form of natural theology that can satisfactorily justify belief in the existence of God. Since many theologians reject this, the inquiry into what ("special") revelation on its own can justify takes on a great significance.[11]

2.1 Revelation, Propositions, and Personal Relations

"Revelation," as we normally use it, is an epistemic concept. To reveal some reality is to make knowledge of that reality available to a subject.[12] By drawing aside the curtains, I reveal the man who is hidden behind them. I thereby make knowledge of the man's presence available for an observer.

Why has God revealed himself (or aspects of himself, or information about himself) to humans? According to the Christian tradition, this is because God wants personal communion with humans. Personal relationships (unlike impersonal relationships) require knowledge. It is impossible for me to relate in a personal way to somebody or something without knowing (or justifiably believing) something about that person or thing. We can, of course, relate in *impersonal* ways to persons or things that we know nothing about. For instance, I can stand in the impersonal relationship of being two kilometers from the *Mona Lisa* without ever having seen or heard about the painting. But I cannot stand in a personal relationship — such as the relationship of loving, hating, fearing, or praising — to somebody or something without knowing something about that object or person.[13]

---

11. The distinction between "natural" and "revealed" knowledge of God (or between "general" and "special" revelation) is far from clear and can be understood in different ways (see Paul Helm, *The Divine Revelation: The Basic Issues* [Westchester, IL: Crossway Books, 1982]). For the purposes of this book, however, we can understand "natural" knowledge of God to be *knowledge that God exists, generated by theistic arguments, or by (something like) Calvin's* sensus divinitatis.

12. Some theorists take revelation to be a success-concept, e.g., Gunton, *A Brief Theology of Revelation* (Edinburgh: T & T Clark, 1995), p. 113; and Martijn Blaauw, "The Nature of Divine Revelation," *The Heythrop Journal* 50, no. 1 (2009): 2-12. According to this understanding, revelation has only taken place if knowledge has actually been transmitted. It is not enough that knowledge has been made available.

13. It may be true that one can *think* of an object without knowing or justifiably

Knowing — in the sense that we are talking about here — is a propositional attitude, that is, an attitude that a subject has to a proposition.[14] Propositions are what declarative sentences express.[15] For instance, "snow is white" and "Schnee ist weiss" are different *sentences,* but they express the same *proposition* (which means that propositions cannot be identified with sentences or any other linguistic items).[16] Propositions are commonly conceived of as the primary bearers of truth-values (i.e., they can be true or false). They are expressed by *that*-clauses (that snow is white, that spring will come, etc.). Assertions, commands, and questions are not propositions; they are speech-acts that do things with propositions. For example, a proposition is "*what* is asserted in the act of asserting."[17] Furthermore, propositions are not mental items. When I think that snow is white, and you also think that snow is white, our thoughts are not (token-) identical to each other (they constitute different mental particulars). Nevertheless, we both have the same proposition in mind, and this proposition is thus distinct from our thoughts.[18] Many philosophers think of propositions as

---

believing that it exists, if the object is picked out by a definite description. However, it is doubtful that these kinds of cognitive relationships to unknown, merely postulated objects deserve the name "personal."

14. The sense of knowing that is relevant in this context is knowing *that* rather than knowing *how*. In the latter sense, the knowledge referred to is a skill.

15. Not all declarative sentences express, when uttered or inscribed, propositions. The sentence "it's raining here now" does not express a proposition unless it is made clear from the context of utterance what place "here" and what time "now" refer to. This seems, at least, to be the standard view (but see Richard Swinburne, *Revelation: From Metaphor to Analogy,* 2nd ed. [Oxford: Oxford University Press, 2007], chap. 1, for a different view). Some philosophers deny that sentences can be said to express propositions. According to John Searle, only *speakers* express propositions by making utterances (Searle, *Speech Acts: An Essay in the Philosophy of Language* [London: Cambridge University Press, 1969], p. 29). There is, in general, a lot of controversy surrounding the notion of a proposition, and very little consensus is yet in sight. My short account of the notion above is only intended to point to some relatively common views. For an overview of current debates, see Matthew McGrath, "Propositions," in *Stanford Encyclopedia of Philosophy* (Summer 2012 ed.), ed. Edward N. Zalta: http://plato.stanford.edu/entries/propositions/ (accessed May 6, 2013).

16. Peter Geach, curiously enough, seems to go against the consensus here. He identifies a proposition with "a *form of words* in which something is propounded, put forward for consideration" (Peter Geach, "Assertion," *The Philosophical Review* 74, no. 4 [1965]: 449-65; 449 [italics added]).

17. Searle, *Speech Acts,* p. 29.

18. Whether propositions are mind-independent is another and more controversial question; see McGrath, "Propositions," section 7.

abstract objects, like numbers. The risk of this is that propositions are pictured as too "free-floating" with respect to the mundane world of objects and facts. For people who are not familiar with the philosophical notion of a proposition, it may be useful to think of true propositions as identical with facts, or states of affairs, while false propositions are merely possible states of affairs.[19] This is, in the view of many philosophers, an attractive understanding — though not without problems. However, we do not need to assume that this understanding is correct; we need only assume that propositions exist.

To know something entails being related to a proposition. "Many theologians," says John Lamont, "seem to feel that propositional knowledge is something different from direct knowledge of realities, and that there are forms of knowledge of reality that are non-propositional or non-conceptual, and even superior in some respects to propositional knowledge."[20] However, as Lamont goes on to point out, this view is mistaken. The object of knowledge always includes some proposition; it is never merely, say, a physical object. For example, to know a particular room — as we sometimes say — means to know it *as* a room, that is, to know *that it is a room* (or at least to know things about it, such as that there are chairs in it, or some other facts expressed in propositional form). As Lamont says, "It is not as if propositions, *instead* of realities, are the objects of propositional attitudes like knowing, believing, hoping, fearing, and so on: rather, it is in having propositional attitudes that we know realities, fear realities, and so on."[21] So I know a particular room *by* knowing propositions about it.[22]

We cannot know or entertain propositions without applying *con-*

---

19. McDowell, *Mind and World,* p. 27; John McDowell, "Singular Thought and the Extent of Inner Space," in *Meaning, Knowledge, and Reality;* Timothy Williamson, *Knowledge and Its Limits* (Oxford: Oxford University Press, 2000), p. 43.

20. John Lamont, *Divine Faith* (Aldershot, UK: Ashgate, 2004), p. 7.

21. Lamont, *Divine Faith,* p. 8.

22. The same insight is found in Aquinas, *ST* II-II, q. 1, a. 2; see also Helm, *The Divine Revelation,* p. 25. It is, however, lacking in many modern theologians, who misleadingly talk as if a revelation of *God* does not logically presuppose the revelation of propositions about God. Hordern, e.g., says that "[w]hat God reveals is not propositions or information — what God reveals is God" (William Hordern, *The Case for a New Reformation Theology* [Philadelphia: Westminster, 1959], p. 61). John Bailie has similar ideas: "Yet in the last resort it is not information about God that is revealed, but very God himself incarnate in Jesus Christ our Lord" (John Baillie, *The Idea of Revelation in Recent Thought* [New York: Columbia University Press, 1956], p. 28).

cepts. I cannot, for instance, think the proposition expressed by the sentence "snow is white" without having the concepts expressed by "snow" and "white"; a creature who does not have these concepts cannot think that snow is white. To think about something is to apply concepts. (Concepts, of course, are not words.)

If God wants personal communion with us, he must make sure that we know some propositions about him. The "must" here is the must of logical/conceptual necessity. It is conceptually impossible for somebody to have a personal relationship to some reality without knowing (or justifiably believing) some proposition about that reality. However, there are theologians who deny this, and who thus can conceive of revelation as a nonepistemic concept. They believe that revelation could mediate a personal relationship between humans and God without making knowledge of God available to humans. This view is mistaken, as I will argue in the next chapter. For now I will simply assume that revelation is an epistemic concept.

There may be a lot of true propositions about God that God could not let us know because we are incapable of grasping them. God may be incomprehensible in many respects. But if God is *totally* incomprehensible, that is, if there are no true propositions about God that we can grasp, then God cannot have personal communion with us. Furthermore, the Christian tradition holds that a proper personal communion between God and humans requires that humans recognize God *as* God. This does not just mean recognizing him as a very powerful and loving personal being. Being very powerful and loving is not sufficient for being God. God must, according to Christianity, be recognized as the unique "creator of heaven and earth," that is, a reality on which everything finite depends for its existence. How can humans acquire knowledge (or at least justified belief) that there *is* a personal reality on which everything finite depends for its existence? This is a question to which the Christian tradition should feel obliged to provide a plausible answer.

2.1.1 Propositional and Manifestational Revelation

Propositional revelation is usually contrasted with *manifestational* revelation. The difference between these two types of revelation has to do with the means of revelation. Nicholas Wolterstorff has helpfully characterized manifestational revelation as revelation where "the means of revelation is

... a natural sign of the actuality revealed."[23] When I draw aside the curtains and reveal the man standing behind them, the means of revelation is a natural sign of the reality ("actuality") revealed. The reality revealed is the man, or his presence, and the "natural sign" of this reality is the visual appearance of the man.[24] Likewise, if I reveal my disgust by grimacing, or if I reveal my anger by hitting somebody in the face, the means of revelation are natural signs of the realities revealed (the latter being, respectively, my disgust and my anger).

When the means of revelation is not a natural sign, the revelation is nonmanifestational. If I reveal that I am afraid by saying that I am afraid, the means of revelation is a conventional (and hence not a natural) sign, namely, a sentence. If God reveals by directly transmitting a piece of knowledge to the mind of some person, God's means of revelation is also not a natural sign.

Nonmanifestational revelation is, according to Wolterstorff, identical with what is commonly known as *propositional revelation.* Wolterstorff justifies this identification by pointing out that "non-manifestational revelation essentially involves known (or true and believed) propositions as the entities revealed" (p. 30). In nonmanifestational revelation, "the actuality revealed is [always] the actuality corresponding to some *thought* of the revealer, that is, to some proposition entertained by the revealer — and not just entertained but known" (p. 28).

The two examples of nonmanifestational revelation just mentioned (revelation by speaking and Lockean, direct-transmission-of-knowledge revelation) illustrate this.[25] One cannot reveal that p by asserting that p unless one has the proposition p in mind. And God cannot transmit knowledge that p to some person's mind unless God has the same knowledge. So in order for an agent to be capable of revealing something nonmanifestationally, he must think — or at some point have thought — the relevant proposition.

---

23. Wolterstorff, *Divine Discourse,* p. 28. Hereafter, page references to this work appear in parentheses in the text.

24. If we have a "direct realist" view of perception, we can understand the "natural sign" to be the man himself — or a visual presentation of him. A man, presented visually to a subject, is a natural sign of (the presence of) a man.

25. What I loosely call "revelation by speaking" is, strictly speaking, "revelation by assertion" or "assertoric revelation." Revelation by speaking can be both manifestational and nonmanifestational. If I say, "My dogs is sick," I reveal that I have poor knowledge of grammar by manifestation. I do this, however, by speaking.

This is not the case with manifestational revelation. It is possible to reveal that *p* manifestationally without ever having thought the proposition *p*. For instance, I can reveal that I have bad manners by behaving a certain way, even though the thought that I have bad manners may never have occurred to me. Manifestational revelation, therefore, does not *essentially* involve propositions entertained by the revealer.

However, the term "propositional revelation" is somewhat misleading. It can be taken to imply that propositions do not figure at all in manifestational revelation. But this cannot be true. Revelation is an epistemic concept: it has to do with knowledge, and knowledge is, or involves, a propositional attitude (an attitude toward a proposition). Propositions, therefore, necessarily figure in both propositional and manifestational revelation. God, or any agent, cannot make knowledge of some reality available to a subject except by making knowledge of some proposition available. So even though manifestational revelation does not essentially involve propositions *known by the revealer,* it still essentially involves propositions as *the entities revealed.*[26]

Wolterstorff distinguishes between two different senses of the verb "to reveal." According to one of these senses, "a condition of properly predicating 'has revealed X' of some agent is that someone actually has come to know X by means of the agent's disclosing it." According to another sense of "to reveal," however, "what's necessary is only that the agent make X *knowable* to appropriately qualified observers, not that anyone actually have come to know it by means of the disclosure" (p. 31).

This means that what an act of revelation reveals is something that some person either actually comes to know as a result of the revealing, or something that a person potentially *could* come to know, that is, something knowable. But, as we have seen, what is known or knowable is — or necessarily includes — propositions. To deny that propositions are revealed is to deny that revelation has to do with the transmission of knowledge.

Suppose that I step out from behind the curtain. In virtue of what does this act constitute an act of revelation? In virtue of making some knowledge available, and this means making some proposition, or propositions, known or knowable. The propositions made known or knowable

---

26. Wolterstorff shows, as far as I can tell, no awareness of the fact that propositions can be revealed manifestationally. Maybe this is because he has a different concept of propositions than the one I am working with. George Mavrodes, on the other hand, sees that "propositions can be revealed in ways other than by communication" (George Mavrodes, *Revelation in Religious Belief* [Philadelphia: Temple University Press, 1988], p. 119).

include, in this case, that *there was a person behind the curtain, Mats was behind the curtain, a tall person was behind the curtain, an unknown person was in the room,* and so on.[27] If (per impossible) my act of stepping out from behind the curtain did not make knowledge of *any* proposition available for a potential observer, then in what sense could that act be said to constitute a revelation?

It can be argued that the necessary involvement of propositions in both propositional and manifestational revelation makes the term "propositional revelation" inapt. There is some truth to this, and clarity might in fact be better served by simply using the term "nonmanifestational revelation." However, the term "propositional revelation" is too well established in theological discourse to be easily replaced. Another reason to keep the term is that in nonmanifestational/propositional revelation, propositions are the only kinds of entities revealed, which is not necessarily the case in manifestational revelation. For instance, when I reveal that my house is yellow by telling you that it is (which would be a case of propositional revelation), what I reveal is only a proposition about my house. I do not reveal my house (that is, I do not present the house itself to you). However, if I reveal that my house is yellow by pointing it out for you (which would be a case of manifestational revelation), I not only reveal that my house is yellow (a proposition about my house) but also reveal the house itself. In manifestational revelation, therefore, the entities revealed can (and often do) include more than just propositions, while in nonmanifestational revelation they include only propositions.[28] If God appears to a person in a mystical experience, or as the incarnate Son of God in Palestine two thousand years ago (which would be examples of manifestational revelation), then God reveals both some propositions about himself (propositions, as we remember, figure necessarily in any kind of revelation), but also something that is not a proposition, namely, *God himself*. It is, I think, not counterintuitive to use the established term "propositional revelation" for types of revelation in which only propositions — and nothing else — figure as the entities revealed.

Before we move on, there are two more significant differences be-

---

27. I have italicized the sentences (e.g., *there was a person behind the curtain*) in order to indicate that I refer to the *propositions* they express rather than to the sentences themselves. I follow this practice throughout the book.

28. It could be argued that the entities revealed by nonmanifestational means usually include *facts,* or states of affairs, as well as propositions. In my view, facts or actual states of affairs are, however, identical to true propositions.

tween propositional and manifestational revelation that we need to be aware of. Suppose that God reveals the proposition *that God loves her* to a subject by asserting it (which is a form of propositional revelation). Then God has already *conceptualized* the revealed proposition (cognized it by applying concepts, and expressed the result in words). The receiver of the revelation need not do that job. Similarly, if God directly transmits the belief that God loves her to the mind of a subject (also a form of propositional revelation), then it is God who has conceptualized the proposition that is the content of the belief (if not, it is hard to see how what God has transmitted can properly be described as a belief). However, if God *manifestationally* reveals that he loves a certain person — for instance, by making her feel his love in a mystical experience — then it is the receiver of that revelation who must conceptualize the relevant proposition *(that God loves her)* herself.

We can also formulate this same difference in terms of interpretation. When my friend reveals to me that he is nervous by suddenly twitching (a manifestational revelation), I both have to interpret his behavior (i.e., see it *as* a twitching), and conceptualize the proposition(s) that this behavior reveals (for instance, *that my friend is nervous*). However, when my friend reveals that he is nervous by saying, "I am nervous," I just have to interpret his behavior as an assertion of the proposition *I am nervous.* I do not have to conceptualize the relevant proposition, since my friend has already done that for me. As Wolterstorff puts it,

> Though interpretation is typically involved in the reception of propositional revelation as well as in the reception of manifesting revelation, there's less of it. The revealer has already interpreted the actuality revealed by way of formulating the proposition; now all we have to do is interpret what he does as the assertion of that proposition. (p. 29)

The content of manifestational revelations is also less specific than that of propositional revelations. If I suddenly burst out in a curse, I reveal several things by manifestation. I reveal that I know some curses, that I can speak, that I am angry, that I have a shrill voice, and so on. Knowledge of all these propositions is made available (to properly qualified observers) by my cursing. The observer (i.e., the recipient of the revelation) must not only conceptualize the propositions in question but also choose to focus on one or some of them as most relevant. The content of propositional revelations, on the other hand, is controlled by the intentions of the revealer to a much greater degree and is thus restricted to what the revealer finds relevant.

2.1.2 Misconceptions about Propositional Revelation

The theological literature abounds in confused ideas about divine propositional revelation. A common misconception is that divine assertions — if there are any — must be "timeless" and "unhistorical" in the sense that their interpretation requires no reference to specific times and places — or historical and cultural contexts.[29]

There are, of course, no assertions in human language that can be interpreted without reference to specific historical or cultural contexts, and proponents of propositional revelation have no interest in claiming that there are. In order to know which proposition (if any) a particular sentence expresses, and whether that proposition is being asserted or not, we need to know a lot about the conventional use of words at the time when it was uttered or inscribed. If the utterance was made long ago (as is the case with biblical utterances), this may require a good deal of philological and historical research (e.g., what does "Messiah" mean in first-century Judaism?). We must also know certain things about the context of utterance or inscription in order to determine the reference of various terms, as well as for determining the literary genre or type of discourse to which the utterance belongs. When we know all these things, we may be in a position to find out which proposition the relevant sentence expresses, and whether that proposition is being asserted or if we are merely invited to imagine it to be true, as in fictional texts. If the assertions in a biblical text are regarded as *divine* assertions, the same principles of interpretation must still be applied. The idea that God speaks (in the literal sense of "speaks") means that God uses a particular human language in order to perform speech-acts, and human languages are context-dependent in the sense just explained.[30] (Chap. 4 addresses the relationship between the speech-acts of the Bible's human authors and God's speech-acts.)

It might be objected that interpreting biblical assertions theologically

---

29. See Paul Helm, "Revealed Propositions and Timeless Truths," *Religious Studies* 8, no. 2 (1972): 127-36.

30. Helm suggests more ways in which the claim that revealed propositions are "timeless" and "unhistorical" can be understood; see Helm, "Revealed Propositions and Timeless Truths."

is not about finding out what they meant in their historical context, but rather what they mean "for us." For example, what does the claim that Jesus is the Messiah mean for us today? That question can be understood in different ways. One way is as a question about whether the idea of a messiah is credible for us today. Can we, who live in an age of electric light and wireless communication, really believe that there is such a thing as a messiah in the New Testament sense, or must we give a new content to that concept? Understood in this way, the question is not about how to interpret the New Testament claim about Jesus at all. It is, instead, a critical question about the epistemic status of the central idea that figures in that claim. In order to be able to ask whether the idea of a messiah in the New Testament sense is credible or must be revised, we must, of course, already have a decent understanding of the New Testament concept of the Messiah. The question about what Jesus' messiahship means for us today (understood as a question about credibility) is thus not an alternative to the question of what the claim meant in its historical context; the question about credibility presupposes that the historical question has been answered.

Another way of understanding the theological question is in terms of the *significance* of the claim that Jesus is the Messiah. What significance does it have for us today that Jesus is the Messiah? This is also not a question about interpretation. It is about the existential or moral consequences of the fact (if it is a fact) that Jesus is the Messiah. In order to ask this existential, or moral, question, we must already know a good deal about what the claim that Jesus is the Messiah means.[31]

It is sometimes argued, however, that the idea of propositional revelation excludes the asking of these and other kinds of questions altogether. If God has asserted that Jesus is the Messiah, there can be no critical scrutiny of the concept of the Messiah and no development of the meaning of that concept. Some have argued that propositional revelation is "static" in this sense.[32]

It is true that, if God has asserted something, it cannot turn out to be false. However, this does not entail that divine assertions and the concepts they contain cannot be critically evaluated. A person who believes that God

---

31. But it can be argued that one has not fully understood what it means for Jesus to be the Messiah until one has understood the existential and moral consequences of that claim.

32. John Polkinghorne seems to endorse this view when he criticizes the idea of "knowledge of the divine, mysteriously conveyed in the form of infallible propositions that are endowed with unquestionable authority and immune from challenge and critique" (John Polkinghorne, *Science and Religion in Quest of Truth* [London: SPCK, 2011], p. 18).

asserted that the world was created in six days can, without abandoning his belief in God or in propositional revelation, come to question whether what he *took* to be a divine assertion really *is* a divine assertion. If there is a solid scientific case against the claim that the world was created in six days, then the person has good reason to think that God has not asserted this (the reason being that God does not assert falsehoods). Therefore, such a person also has good reason to return to the biblical text in order to see whether there is a way of interpreting it that does not ascribe the false assertion to God. The fact that we are fallible when it comes to identifying divine assertions does not, of course, mean that we should never claim to know that something is divinely asserted. Science is fallible when it comes to identifying the causes of natural events; but this does not mean that scientists should never claim to know the cause of any natural event.

More importantly, it is possible to acknowledge something as a divine assertion and yet criticize a certain understanding of that assertion. To claim that God speaks (in the literal sense of "speaks") is to claim that God uses human language in order to say things. The concepts that God then uses are human constructs that are as such deficient and inadequate in many respects. This is why there is a constant need for conceptual development in languages. Concepts evolve, and new ones come into being when it is felt that the available ones do not carve up reality in a correct or useful way. The biblical concept of the messiah exemplifies this kind of development. In light of the narrative of Jesus' life, can the Old Testament concept of messiah be seen to reflect an inadequate — but not totally inadequate — understanding of what it means to be the Messiah? The Old Testament understanding is not totally inadequate since it contains many elements that are also essential to the concept of the Messiah (Christ) of the New Testament and the Christian faith, such as the kingship of the messiah and his descent from the house of David. In other respects, it can be seen as misleading, for example, with regard to its emphasis on political dominance rather than suffering obedience to God.[33]

When Jesus asserted that he was the Messiah, his disciples initially understood him in terms of the established, Old Testament concept. Only gradually, and as a result of their experience of Jesus' actions and passion,

---

33. I am, of course, simplifying here. There are certainly different understandings of the messiah in the Old Testament itself, e.g., with respect to the balance between royal, priestly, and prophetic elements in the messiah's mission, as well as with respect to the concept's eschatological connotations. It is only in a loose sense that we can talk about "the Old Testament concept of the Messiah."

did it become clear to them that the messiah concept had evolved into something new in the mouth of Jesus. They recognized, moreover, that the new concept was a faithful and logical — though somewhat unexpected — development of the Old Testament precursor.

Jesus' claim to be the Messiah is, according to Christian faith, a *divine* assertion.[34] To regard it as such is fully compatible with acknowledging that our understanding of it, and the concepts it contains, can develop and change. The New Testament itself testifies, as we have seen, to such a change. When God spoke (let us suppose) through the Old Testament prophets, he spoke in a particular cultural context with certain necessarily limited and thus sometimes inadequate linguistic and conceptual resources. The idea of a crucified Messiah would have appeared as a contradiction in terms in that context, and such an idea could thus not be expressed.[35] It was only through the life, death, and resurrection of Jesus (as retold by the early Christians) that a messiah concept compatible with crucifixion evolved.

This example shows that a view of revelation that posits divine assertions is not necessarily "static" and incompatible with critical scrutiny. If propositional revelation is "static," it is so only in the sense that it entails that God's revelation has, as one of its aspects, a determinate *cognitive content*. This means that our interpretations can get what God says more or less right. It might not always be easy to distinguish more or less correct interpretations from each other, but some *are* more correct than others. This is just another way of saying that God actually says something.[36] A person who is prepared to deny that God can make assertions with a determinate meaning is probably crediting God with less power than she (that

---

34. Jesus does not say, "I am the Messiah," but one can assert that one is the Messiah in other ways, for instance, by affirming a claim made by another person, as Jesus does in Matt. 16:16-17.

35. N. T. Wright says: "The crucifixion of Jesus . . . was bound to have appeared as the complete destruction of any messianic pretensions or possibilities he or his followers might have hinted at. The violent execution of . . . a would-be Messiah did not say to any Jewish onlooker that he really was the Messiah after all, or that YHWH's kingdom had come through his work. It said, powerfully and irresistibly, that he wasn't and that it hadn't" (N. T. Wright, *The Resurrection of the Son of God* [Minneapolis: Fortress, 2003], pp. 557-58).

36. The claim that a person can say something determinate by way of authoring a text is attacked by philosophers in both the continental and the analytical traditions, e.g., Jacques Derrida, *Positions* (Chicago: University of Chicago Press, 1981); W. V. Quine, *Word and Object* (Cambridge, MA: MIT Press, 1960), chap. 2. It is, of course, not possible to address this general issue here; for a defense of determinate content, see Wolterstorff, *Divine Discourse*, chaps. 8-9.

person) ascribes to herself. She probably believes that her own denial that God can assert something with a determinate meaning has a determinate meaning. If future historians were to interpret her denial as an affirmation, they would have got what she said wrong. This is just another way of saying that people actually *say* things.

Maybe the most common misconception about propositional revelation is that it is incompatible with the metaphorical and symbolic character of much biblical language. Avery Dulles expresses this view: "Revelation, according to the propositionalists, must impart some definite truth, or else it could not be believed. The powerful symbolism of the Bible, in their view, *must be fully translated into literal statements.*" Because Christ taught "by preference through parable and paradox," his teaching does not, according to Dulles, constitute "strictly propositional revelation." Dulles's general characterization of the "propositional model of revelation" makes a similar point:

> The Bible, in this approach, is viewed principally as a collection of propositions, each of which can be taken by itself as a divine assertion. In spite of the efforts made to prove the contrary, the Bible does not seem to claim such propositional infallibility for itself. Nor did the ancient and medieval exegetes, for the most part, hold to the narrowly literalistic view espoused by twentieth-century conservatives. The church Fathers and their medieval followers, by and large, were open to a great variety of allegorical and spiritual interpretations that went well beyond the literal meaning of isolated propositions.[37]

Dulles's mistake is to think that only *literal* speech can express propositions, and that propositional revelation hence entails a "narrowly literalistic view" of revelation. This is a misconception. A "propositional assertion," as John Lamont points out,

> is not the same thing as an assertion that uses words literally. Symbolic and metaphorical words and expressions can be used in assertions that are true or false, that can convey information, and that can be the objects of cognitive attitudes. This is true, whether or not it is always possible for the propositional content of assertions that contain symbolic or metaphorical words or expressions to be put in literal terms.[38]

---

37. Dulles, *Models of Revelation*, pp. 42 (italics added), 161, 48.
38. Lamont, *Divine Faith*, p. 9.

The sentence "Betty is an angel" is metaphorical, but it expresses — if the reference of "Betty" is fixed by the context of utterance — something that can be true or false and that can be the object of propositional attitudes such as belief. This can be seen from the fact that people can disagree about whether Betty is an angel. Somebody may say: "I don't believe that Betty is an angel. I saw how she laughed at a homeless person yesterday." "Betty is an angel," therefore, expresses a proposition, probably the same proposition that is expressed by "Betty is a very good person." This latter sentence may not have the same emotional coloring as "Betty is an angel," and it may not elicit the same associations. This, however, is not necessary for sameness of propositions. "Work makes you free" may not have the same emotional coloring and elicit the same associations as "Arbeit macht frei," but they do express the same proposition.[39]

There may be, as Lamont acknowledges, propositions that can *only* be expressed by metaphorical or symbolic speech. Perhaps the metaphor that God is our father is capable of expressing a proposition about God's relationship to us that cannot be conveyed by literal language. There is, in that case, no literal expression that says exactly what the metaphor "God is our father" says. Stanley Hauerwas has a more down-to-earth example: perhaps the metaphorical statement "It's the Taj Mahal" describes my aunt's hat in a more accurate way than any literal expression (such as "it's very ostentatious") is capable of doing.[40]

Avery Dulles also seems to believe that all the propositions that the Bible expresses must, according to the propositional model of revelation, constitute "revealed truths." He says: "Essential to the propositional model, in the form here considered, is the thesis that every declarative sentence in the Bible, unless the contrary can be shown from the context, is to be taken as expressing a revealed truth."[41]

However, propositions can be *expressed* without being *asserted* (claimed to be true). In a work of fiction, we are invited to entertain a number of propositions that the author does not assert. Dostoevsky, for

---

39. Swinburne treats this in *Revelation: From Metaphor to Analogy,* chap. 3. But he uses a different terminology. It seems that he uses the term "statement" for (roughly) what I call "proposition."

40. Stanley Hauerwas, *The Hauerwas Reader* (Durham: Duke University Press, 2001), p. 167. For a treatment of the cognitive importance of metaphor in scientific contexts, see Janet Martin Soskice, *Metaphor and Religious Language* (Oxford: Oxford University Press, 1985).

41. Dulles, *Models of Revelation,* pp. 48-49.

example, does not claim that there actually was a man called Raskolnikov who lived in St. Petersburg, and who killed an old woman with an axe. He only invites us to imagine this.[42]

The books of Jonah and Job in the Bible are pieces of fiction, and many of the propositions that the declarative sentences in these books express are not asserted — that is, not claimed (by the human authors, or by God) to be true. The view that "every declarative sentence of the Bible" is to be taken as "expressing a revealed truth" is therefore a caricature and not at all "essential to the propositional model."

A work of fiction as a whole can have a message, that is, make assertions about, for example, the conditions of human existence or morality. Such a message may not be identifiable with anything expressed by the individual sentences of the work. It may be impossible to capture the message in a single sentence or a small set of sentences. The message may even be such that it cannot be appropriately expressed in any other way than by telling a story.[43] This does not mean that it is "nonpropositional." Not all propositions can be expressed in literal or nonnarrative terms (remember "God is our father").

A text need not, of course, be fictional in order to have an overarching message. A historical (nonfiction) narrative can convey a message, as is often the case in the Bible.[44] Furthermore, historical narratives, as well as fiction, may contain messages on multiple levels. The Christian tradition has always felt that biblical texts have depths that cannot be probed by staying on the historical/literal level. Allegorical or spiritual interpretations have been seen as necessary for discovering the full meaning of texts. The insights acquired through such readings may or may not be capable of being stated succinctly in literal terms, but, as we have seen, this does not mean that they must be nonpropositional. Therefore, Dulles's remark

---

42. See Wolterstorff, *Divine Discourse*, p. 243.

43. The message of a literary work can be, for instance, that a certain attitude toward morality is untenable. It might be the case, however, that the attitude in question cannot be specified except with reference to a certain character in a certain narrative (e.g., "the attitude of Raskolnikov in *Crime and Punishment*").

44. What makes a text "historical" — as opposed to "fictional" — has very little to do with whether it is true or not. A historical account may be massively false, while a piece of fiction may be largely true. This does not alter their status as history and fiction, respectively. What determines the genre (history or fiction) is the illocutionary stance taken toward the content, that is, whether the author asserts or invites us to imagine something (see Wolterstorff, *Divine Discourse*, p. 243).

that "the church Fathers and their medieval followers . . . were open to a great variety of allegorical and spiritual interpretations" misses its mark.

Finally, there is the misconception that if revelation is, or includes, the transmission of propositional contents, then it cannot be inextricably linked with existential commitment and spiritual transformation. Keith Ward, for example, contrasts the view that revelation provides "information about the world" with the view that revelation is essentially transformative:

> Revelation functions as an evocation of a process of spiritual self-transformation. The revelation discloses the goal to which one is working and empowers one to pursue it. This is at a far remove from the provision of possibly useful information about the world. To regard it as a body of information which could be correctly recited . . . would be to misunderstand it wholly. The true believer is one who discerns at a certain point of historical existence the reality of God and who is personally transformed by the power of Divine love mediated at that point.

The critical reader will wonder how it is possible for revelation to "disclose the goal to which one is working" without providing any information about that goal. Furthermore, what could it mean to "discern . . . the reality of God" without acquiring the information that God is real? Can a person who is not prepared to assent to the proposition *God is real* be said to discern the reality of God?

Ward's dislike for the view that revelation includes a transmission of information (propositional knowledge) seems to have two different grounds. First, he seems to regard revelation as nonconceptual: "Its content cannot be conceptually pinned down, but always has the character of 'pointing beyond' to a form of acquaintance beyond finite name and form." This is a very problematic view, and we will return to it in chapter 3 for criticism. The other reason for Ward's dismissal of information-transmission in revelation is that "[i]nformation requires no existential commitment . . . it leaves the character of the subject untouched."[45]

Information might not require existential commitment, but what information is *about* may very well do so. The information that God exists does not deserve my or anyone else's existential commitment, but *God* does, and having information about his existence makes it much easier

---

45. Keith Ward, *Religion and Revelation: A Theology of Revelation in the World's Religions* (Oxford: Oxford University Press, 1994), pp. 276-77.

to be committed to him. Information, moreover, does not always "leave the character of the subject untouched." Information about the death of his mother may not, for example, leave a five-year-old child's character untouched.

Does the existential importance of a mother's death entail that we cannot meaningfully speak of *being informed* about events of this magnitude, or that knowledge of such events cannot, at any rate, be part of a "body of information which could be correctly recited" (Ward)? I would not think so. It might be true, of course, that a person who, in an emotionally detached way, "recites" information of this kind thereby shows that he has failed to grasp the significance of what he is talking about. It can also be argued that a person who has failed to grasp the significance of what God has revealed, or who has an emotionally detached attitude as to its content, cannot be said to be the recipient of divine revelation at all. But from this it only follows that the divine revelation encompasses more than information. It does not follow that revelation can ever take place without the communication of information.

Information, by itself, is often insufficient for personal transformation, and I agree with Ward that personal transformation is an essential function of the divine revelation. This means that revelation indeed is more than a transmission of information. The crucial point is that it cannot be less. If the goal of the transformation is something that the subject is supposed to consciously affirm and pursue, then information about that goal must somehow be involved in revelation. And there is absolutely no incompatibility between viewing revelation as life-transforming and as information-providing. When pressed, most theologians would admit this; but it is a truth that is apparently easily forgotten when caricatures and rhetorical overstatements come into play.

2.1.3 Conclusion

After this lengthy analysis of the role of propositions in revelation, it might be wise to summarize the points that will be most important for the argument of this book. The difference between manifestational and propositional revelation is not, as one might think, that propositions are involved in the latter but not in the former. Propositions are among the entities revealed in both kinds of revelation. In manifestational revelation, however, other things besides propositions are revealed (such as *God himself*). The difference between the two kinds of revelation has to do with the *means* of revelation, which in the case of manifestational revelation is a natural sign of the reality revealed. To reveal x by manifestation means to present something that naturally calls x to mind — such as x itself. Propositional revelation, on the other hand, is nonmanifestational, which means that something is revealed in a way that does not involve a natural sign. We need not dwell on exactly what defines a "natural" sign. Everybody agrees that linguistic entities (words, sentences) are not natural signs, and revelation through speaking is hence clearly a species of nonmanifestational (propositional) revelation. Another kind of propositional revelation is the kind that John Locke works with, namely, God's direct, supernatural communication of knowledge to the mind of some agent.

2.2 The Problem of Knowledge of God

The Christian tradition believes that it is important, as we have seen, for Christians not only to worship something that is in fact God, but also to recognize the object of their worship *as God*. To recognize the object of worship *as God* means to believe that what one worships is an infinite, necessary, perfectly good, omnipotent, and omniscient personal reality on whom everything finite is fundamentally dependent. How can Christians come to believe the proposition that a reality with the mentioned characteristics exists? One possible answer, of course, is cognitive error. The belief arises as a result of fallacious reasoning, or by some cognitive mechanism that does not have any propensity to produce true beliefs (such as wishful thinking), but which may happen to produce a true belief by pure luck.[46] However, explanations such as these are unacceptable from a Christian point of view since they entail that belief in God is unjustified. Christians must show that it is conceivable how belief in God can arise without the necessary involvement of cognitive error, and without this belief being the result of cognitive processes or mechanisms that do not have any propensity to produce true descriptions of reality. Can Christians meet this requirement? Strong and persistent voices within modern philosophy and theology argue that they cannot. The critics have usually focused on the (im)possibility of a potent natural theology.

---

46. George Mavrodes recognizes the category of "fallacious theology" in addition to "rational" and "revealed" theology (Mavrodes, *Revelation in Religious Belief,* p. 10).

2.2.1 Kaufman's Challenge

Many Christians through the centuries seem to have believed that it is possible to know, without relying on "special" revelation, that an infinite, necessary, personal reality on whom everything finite is fundamentally dependent exists. The existence of such a reality can, according to this view, be inferred from "naturally" knowable premises. A major reason why many theologians today are skeptical of this idea is that they believe that Immanuel Kant, once and for all, demonstrated its untenability.

It is seldom noted, however, that Kant acknowledges the possibility of a *modest* natural theology. The physico-theological proof can, Kant says, "lead us to the point of admiring the greatness, wisdom, power, etc., of the Author of the world, but can take us no further." This means that we might, at least in principle, be able to infer the existence of an Author of the world from the orderliness of the natural world. But an Author of the world is not the God of theism. An Author of the world could be a minor deity who has created things from preexisting matter, and whose existence is contingent. The knowledge that an author of the world exists is therefore "altogether inadequate to the lofty purpose which we have before our eyes, namely, the proof of an all-sufficient primordial being." The physico-theological proof cannot accomplish what it sets out to do, but is — as it turns out — secretly dependent on the cosmological proof, which, in turn, depends on the soundness of the ontological proof. Since the ontological proof is invalid, there can be no (theoretical) knowledge of the God of theism — or so Kant claims.

The impossibility of a potent natural theology is due to the nature of the being whose existence is to be proved. "The transcendental idea of a necessary and all-sufficient original being," says Kant, "is so overwhelmingly great, so high above everything empirical, the latter being always conditioned, that it leaves us at a loss, partly because we can never find in experience material sufficient to satisfy such a concept."[47]

Experience cannot, in other words, justify the application of the concept of a necessary and all-sufficient original being. This claim has some plausibility. It seems to be impossible to *perceive* that a necessary and all-sufficient being exists (arguments to this effect will be presented later). Perception by itself, therefore, cannot justify the application of

---

47. Immanuel Kant, *Immanuel Kant's Critique of Pure Reason,* trans. Norman Kemp Smith (New York: Palgrave, 1929), A 629, A 627, A621.

the concept. If it is also (as Kant argues) impossible to *infer* the existence of a necessary and all-sufficient original being, either by a priori reasoning (such as the ontological proof) or empirical reasoning (such as the physico-theological or cosmological proofs), then the theist is faced with a problem.

Gordon Kaufman thinks that Kant is right, and he argues that this has far-reaching consequences for theology. Echoing Kant, Kaufman says that the concept "God"

> intends to point to that which is in and under and behind all things everywhere and always, "the Creator of all things visible and invisible." Little wonder, then, that it does not correspond to anything we can directly perceive or know and that it must be constructed in the mind and through history by processes quite different from those which produce an ordinary concept.

"With a perceivable object, we put together our concept on the basis of abstraction and generalization from percepts; but if there are no direct percepts of God, how — and out of what — is this concept constructed?" Kaufman's answer is that "God" is an "imaginative construct," "created by the mind for certain intra-mental functions." "The only God we can know or respond to or take account of . . . is the God that we, with the help of a long tradition developing before us, construct in our imagination as the ultimate point of reference for all life and thought and reality."[48]

This means that the concept "God" plays a very different role in our cognitive economy than do concepts that apply to objective realities.[49] The function of the God-concept is to help us organize our experience. It is "the ultimate unifier of all experience and concepts."[50] The cognitive

---

48. Gordon Kaufman, *An Essay on Theological Method,* 3rd ed. (Atlanta: Scholars Press, 1995), pp. 30, 33.

49. Kaufman is a bit fuzzy about the status of the referent of the concept "God," and Paul Macdonald discerns a shift in Kaufman's thought on this matter (Paul Macdonald, *Knowledge and the Transcendent: An Inquiry into the Mind's Relationship to God* [Washington, DC: Catholic University of America Press, 2009], pp. 24-26). In his work *In Face of Mystery,* Kaufman says that "the word 'God' stands for something *objectively there,* a reality over against us that exists whether we are aware of it or not" (Gordon Kaufman, *In Face of Mystery: A Constructive Theology* [Cambridge, MA: Harvard University Press, 1993], p. 320). However, it seems as though we cannot predicate any specific properties of the "objective" referent, only of God as a "symbol" internal to the mind.

50. Kaufman, *An Essay on Theological Method,* p. 34.

Revelation and Knowledge of God

processes that produce belief in God are, in other words, not aimed at providing knowledge of a transcendent reality.

Alvin Plantinga has criticized Kaufman's contention that God cannot be an object of experience.[51] Plantinga points out that it is odd to assume that God, just because he is infinite, omnipotent, omniscient, all-sufficient, and so forth, cannot be perceived. Why could not an infinite God make himself *heard* by speaking from a burning bush, or bring it about that humans experience him in some other way, for instance, in some inner, mystical experience?

Plantinga's critique, however, misses Kaufman's point. It is true that an infinite, omnipotent God could make himself heard by speaking from a burning bush. So it is possible that Moses could hear the infinite God speak. But this is not the same as saying that Moses could hear *that* the infinite God speaks. One can hear the infinite God speaking from a burning bush without knowing (or being in a position to know) that what one hears is the infinite God. The interesting question, of course, is whether there can be experiences that can put the subject in a position to know that the object of experience is the infinite God. An experience that puts a subject in a position to know this must present something, for example, the mystical, inner presence of a loving and powerful spiritual being, *as* the presence of the infinite God. But to experience something as the presence of the infinite God means to experience something *as infinite.* But it is highly doubtful that infinity (and other theistic properties) can be represented in experiences.[52]

Plantinga also criticizes Kaufman's implicit assumption that "if nothing within our experience can be directly identified as that to which the term 'God' properly refers, then the term 'God' doesn't refer to anything, or at least it is problematic that it does."[53] Why believe this? Plantinga asks. Nothing within our experience can be identified with that to which the term "the Big Bang" refers. Does this mean that the term does not refer to anything at all, so that when we talk about the Big Bang we do not talk about an objective event that took place billions of years before there were any human minds? This seems to be a questionable conclusion. So why is the case different with "God"?

Maybe the difference between "the Big Bang" and "God," in this

---

51. Plantinga, *Warranted Christian Belief,* pp. 32-35.
52. I will argue this point in chap. 3.
53. Plantinga, *Warranted Christian Belief,* p. 33.

respect, is the following. Theoretical concepts in science, such as "the Big Bang," do not "correspond to any percept."[54] They are, however, inferentially linked to observational concepts and thereby given empirical meaning. However, the concept "God" does not have any (or at least not a sufficient number of) inferential links to observational concepts. Kant has (as Kaufman assumes) demonstrated that the existence of God cannot be inferred from experience. There is simply too much slack between experience and "God" for that concept to be injected with empirical meaning through inferential links to observational concepts.

This response to Plantinga (which is mine, but on behalf of Kaufman) presupposes, of course, that Kant really has shown that there can be no potent natural theology. I am not convinced that he has. The purpose of this and the next chapter, however, is to inquire into the consequences of rejecting both propositional revelation and a potent natural theology. I will not, therefore, quarrel with Kant about the possibility of a potent natural theology.[55]

---

54. Kaufman, *An Essay on Theological Method*, p. 30.

55. Kant seems to believe that it is possible to think and talk about God, despite the impossibility of having *knowledge* of God. He regularly refers to God in several works, and his famous dictum about "deny[ing] knowledge, in order to make room for faith" (Kant, *Critique of Pure Reason,* preface to 2nd ed., B xxx) seems to presuppose that we can think about God. Other philosophers and theologians, however, claim that Kant's philosophy entails that we cannot even think about God because our concepts are not applicable to God. The reason why our concepts are not applicable to God is that concepts, on the Kantian view, are rules according to which the mind synthesizes the manifold of experience and thereby constructs the phenomenal world. God, of course, is not a phenomenon constructed by the mind, but a *noumenon,* a "thing in itself," which as such is beyond the bounds of possible experience. Concepts are thus not applicable to God, as they are not applicable to any *noumenon.* The problem with this argument is that it presupposes the doctrine of transcendental idealism (understood in accordance with the traditional "two-worlds" interpretation), the idea that the mind constructs the phenomenal (i.e., empirical) world. This doctrine is extremely problematic, and many commentators view it simply as incoherent (see, e.g., Peter Strawson, *The Bounds of Sense: An Essay on Kant's 'Critique of Pure Reason'* (London: Routledge, 1966), p. 16; Plantinga, *Warranted Christian Belief,* p. 20). Strawson, however, argues that the doctrine of transcendental idealism can be disentangled from Kant's analytical argument in the *Critique of Pure Reason,* and that a Kantian criticism of "transcendent metaphysics" (discourse about God and other supersensible things) can be pursued on the basis of a simple "principle of significance" (Strawson, *The Bounds of Sense,* p. 33). This principle says that "there can be no legitimate, or even meaningful, employment of ideas or concepts which does not relate them to empirical or experiential conditions of their application" (p. 16). Unfortunately, Strawson does not tell us why we should accept this principle,

2.2.2 A Response to Kaufman's Challenge

Even if Kant was right about natural theology, Kaufman's conclusion would not follow. It is at least metaphysically possible to acquire a solid rational justification for belief in — and, therefore, knowledge of — the existence of God in the absence of a potent natural theology. In order to understand this possibility, consider the following analogy.

My mathematical skills are extremely limited. This means that I am not in a position to understand the scientific reasoning behind the theory of relativity. I am thus not in a position to check the soundness of this reasoning. Nevertheless, I know that the (relativistic) mass of an object increases as its velocity increases. How can I know this? Because other people, possessing abilities that I lack, have performed the relevant experiments and reasoning and concluded that the theory of relativity is true. One proposition entailed by that theory is that the mass of an object increases as its velocity increases. The people who are able to confirm that the theory is true, and that this theory entails that the mass of an object increases as its velocity increases, have then told people like me about their conclusions.

So there are propositions that I am incapable of knowing unless other people, with greater intellectual skills than I have, transfer their knowledge to me by means of linguistic communication.

Let us look at this example from the standpoint of Kaufman's ideas about knowledge. If I am left to my own devices, it is impossible for me to get to know the proposition that the mass of an object increases as its velocity increases. I cannot, of course, *perceive* that the mass of an object increases as its velocity increases, nor can I infer the truth of this proposition from facts that I can perceive. It is possible to infer the truth of the

---

which is suspiciously similar to the positivist "verifiability criterion" of meaning. The doctrine of transcendental idealism certainly explains *why* there can be no meaningful application of concepts to supersensible things, but then the doctrine itself is not credible. It is doubtful whether the Kantian corpus provides any other convincing reason to accept the "principle of significance." Alvin Plantinga writes: "It is exceedingly hard to see how to construct an argument . . . for the conclusion that we cannot refer to or think about God . . . from materials to be found in the work of Kant" (Plantinga, *Warranted Christian Belief,* p. 31). See also Nicholas Wolterstorff's criticism of Kant in "Is It Possible and Desirable for Theologians to Recover from Kant?" *Modern Theology* 14, no. 1 (1998): 1-18. The only serious challenge for theology to be found in Kant's work is, in my view, a certain challenge to the possibility of *knowledge* of God.

proposition from facts that I can perceive, but *I* am not capable of making these inferences.

However, my perceptions of the world include perceptions of the linguistic utterances of other people. Since I have perceptual access to these, and since I understand language, I am in a position to know the problematic proposition in question. Knowledge acquired by understanding what other people say or write is testimonial knowledge. Almost everybody agrees that a lot of the knowledge that any individual has is acquired from testimony. There are, however, different opinions about the status of testimony as a source of justification. Some claim that it is reducible to more basic sources, such as perception, memory, and inference. This means that when I acquire knowledge that p from testimony, my justification for believing p can be accounted for in terms of perception, memory, and inference only. Others claim, as we have seen, that testimony is itself a basic, or sui generis, source of justification. We will return to this debate in chapter 5. Whether or not testimony can be reduced to other sources of justification, it is agreed by most parties that testimony can confer knowledge. This is what is important in the present context.

There are plenty of examples of cases in which certain kinds of knowledge are *only* available, to some persons, by testimony. For instance, suppose Karl dreams that he is aboard the *Titanic* when it sinks. Being the subject of the dream, Karl has introspective knowledge of the fact that he dreams about the *Titanic,* and he may have access to this introspective knowledge through memory when he wakes up. But how can *we* acquire knowledge of the fact that Karl has dreamed about the *Titanic*? Only by way of Karl's testimony.

In this case, it is the peculiar, private nature of the fact known that makes it impossible for people other than Karl to know it except by testimony. But the earlier example about relativity theory concerned knowledge of a proposition about the objective, physical world, namely, *that the (relativistic) mass of an object increases as its velocity increases.*

It could be argued that the impossibility for me — and similar kinds of people — to know the latter proposition is not an impossibility *in principle*. I could, by hard training, develop my intellectual skills and become able to confirm the truth of the proposition without relying on testimony. Of course, since I am not Einstein, I would still be dependent on help from others in order to learn how to infer the truth of the proposition from publicly available evidence. Nevertheless, when my learning would be done, I would not be dependent on the testimony of others in order to know the truth of the relevant proposition. I would be capable of knowing it independent of testimony.

Maybe this is true for me (although I have my doubts). However, there are people with even more limited potential for learning higher mathematics than I, such as people with dyscalculia. For them, it *is* impossible to acquire the skills necessary to be able to check for themselves whether the theory of relativity is true or not. As long as they understand the concepts "mass" and "velocity," however, they can understand the proposition *the mass of an object increases as its velocity increases.* If I now know this proposition by testimony, even though I am now unable to check its truth for myself, then people with dyscalculia can also know it, though they are in principle unable to check its truth.

The consequences of denying that I (or people with dyscalculia) *can* know the relevant proposition are severe. If it is denied that I know that *the mass of an object increases as its velocity increases,* because it is impossible for me to check for myself whether this proposition is true, then we must say that whatever my school teacher communicated to me in physics class when he taught relativity theory, it was not knowledge. If this is true, I would have wanted to know that when I was still in school, so I could have skipped physics class.

This simple reasoning shows that it is conceivable — contrary to what Kaufman suggests — how we could acquire knowledge that the God of theism exists, even given the Kantian ban on natural theology. We could acquire it by testimony from God. If the God of theism exists, then he *knows* that he is God, that is, an infinite, perfectly good, omnipotent, and omniscient personal reality on which everything finite is fundamentally dependent. It seems to be at least metaphysically possible that God could communicate his knowledge of his own properties to people with more limited epistemic abilities — such as us.[56]

---

56. It might be objected that appeal to God's own testimony does not solve the problem, since the problem is that the concept "God" has no empirical content. *This* is why God cannot be an object of (theoretical) knowledge. The objection echoes Kant: "It would be absurd for us to hope that we can know more of any object than belongs to the possible experience of it or lay claim to the least knowledge of how anything not assumed to be an object of possible experience is determined according to the constitution that it has in itself" (Immanuel Kant, *Prolegomena to Any Future Metaphysics That Will Be Able to Come Forward as Science,* trans. James Ellington [Indianapolis: Hackett, 2001], p. 85). Kant's view on this matter is, however, very difficult to maintain. Electrons, neutrinos, and quarks are not "objects of possible experience," but most of us would admit that we can know a good deal about them. Plantinga's "Big Bang" objection to Kaufman (see above) is right on the money here.

We can obviously know the existence of entities that we cannot possibly experience by inferring their existence from circumstances that we *can* experience. Moreover, a

The idea that we could have a share in God's own knowledge of himself through testimony raises, of course, important questions. The idea requires that God speaks. Is it conceivable that God speaks? (By "speaking," I mean — here, as before — the activity of using linguistic signs in order to perform speech-acts. Of course, this can be made without the use of the vocal cords.) Could propositions linguistically communicated to us by God count as knowledge? Remember that if what God communicates to humans is to constitute knowledge, then the human recipients must be justified/warranted in believing it. So the question is not whether it is conceivable that God could bring it about that some proposition pops up in the head of some human. The question is whether humans can acquire *knowledge* of some proposition on the basis of God's testimony.

Before we embark on the project of showing that these and other questions can be answered in the affirmative, and that Kaufman's challenge to the possibility of knowledge of God can be met in terms of divine testimony, I will try to show that there are no "nonpropositional" (i.e., purely manifestational) construals of divine revelation on offer that are capable of proving Kaufman wrong. If we reject propositional revelation, together with the idea of a potent natural theology, then Kaufman's challenge stands. That Kaufman's challenge stands means that it is inexplicable how we could possibly have epistemic access to God as an objective reality. If this is inexplicable, then it follows that God is best thought of as an "imaginative construct," "created by the mind for certain intra-mental

---

person who is blind from birth can acquire knowledge of the existence of entities that she cannot possibly experience (such as colors) from other people's testimony. So testimony can provide people with knowledge of the existence of entities that they cannot possibly experience, and whose existence they cannot even possibly *infer* from circumstances that they can experience (the blind person probably cannot, if left to her own devices, infer that colors exist from things that she can experience, such as sounds, smells, tastes, and feels). If we want to cling to the view that any meaningful concept must have "empirical content," we can say that the concept "color" is injected with empirical content for a blind person through the testimony that she receives about the existence of colors from her sighted friends. The unattractive alternative to this would be to say that persons who are blind from birth cannot know that colors exist, no matter how many physics books they read. For general criticism of the modern idea that God "belongs outside or beyond a cognitive boundary, insulating God from the mind" (in its Kantian as well as other versions), see Paul Macdonald, *Knowledge and the Transcendent,* chaps. 1-2. Macdonald also engages theologians who, for theological reasons, argue for the cognitive inaccessibility of God with reference to God's transcendence.

functions."[57] I trust that this is a conclusion that many Christians would want to avoid.

Since I cannot review all important manifestational theories of revelation, I have made a selection based on Avery Dulles's classification of different "models of revelation."[58] I have selected a few theories that display features representative of all of Dulles's ideal-types (except the propositional one[59]). That way my discussion will be able to indicate the limitations of manifestational theories of revelation in general. Since there are some recent "postliberal" construals of revelation that are hard to fit into Dulles's classifying scheme, I have added a section that treats of them separately.

My review of contemporary models will not only show the limitations of manifestational theories of revelation; it will also show that some of the theories that are usually taken to be manifestational presuppose, in fact, the occurrence of propositional revelation (God literally speaking, or directly implanting conceptual contents in the minds of believers).

Note that the target of my attack is neither the idea of manifestational revelation in general, nor any specific variety of that idea. Manifestational revelation is, in itself, completely legitimate and has always been posited by the Christian tradition. Furthermore, I regard several of the manifestational models of revelation to be discussed below as appropriate, though partial, accounts of the Christian revelation. The target of my criticism in the following discussion is just the claim that revelation can be thought of as *exclusively* manifestational.

Although I will in the next chapter contrast manifestational theories of revelation with propositional ones, and will argue for the necessity of construing revelation as partly propositional, I do not regard all propositional theories of revelation as equally feasible. I do not, for example, defend the Lockean model of revelation, which has difficulties explaining how the divinely transmitted beliefs can acquire the status of knowledge.

---

57. Kaufman, *An Essay on Theological Method*, p. 30.
58. Dulles, *Models of Revelation*.
59. "Revelation as Doctrine."

CHAPTER 3

Theories of Revelation

In his classic book *Models of Revelation,* Avery Dulles classifies currently popular theories of revelation under five major headings, or "types," depending on "their central vision of how and where revelation occurs": *Revelation as Doctrine, Revelation as History, Revelation as Inner Experience, Revelation as Dialectical Presence,* and *Revelation as New Awareness.*[1] These types or models are intended to capture the main tendencies and indicate the principal issues in current debates about the nature of divine revelation. "Revelation as Doctrine" is Dulles's (somewhat misleading) name for propositional revelation. The other four models all claim to represent, in different ways, the contemporary tendency to portray revelation as manifestational. In this chapter I will discuss examples of each of the four manifestational models, and finally some postliberal views of revelation.

3.1 Revelation as History

The central idea of this construal of revelation is that "revelation occurs primarily through deeds, rather than words, and . . . its primary content is the series of events by which God has manifested himself in the past."[2] As George Ernest Wright says: "The primary means by which God communicates with man is by his acts, which are the events of history."[3]

---

1. Avery Dulles, *Models of Revelation* (Maryknoll, NY: Orbis, 1992), p. 27.
2. Dulles, *Models of Revelation,* p. 53.
3. George Ernest Wright, *God Who Acts: Biblical Theology as Recital* (London: SCM Press, 1952), p. 107.

The proponents of the revelation-as-history model claim, accordingly, that some historical events are divine acts, and that they can be identified as such. But how can those who witness the revelatory events (either directly or through the biblical witness) know that those events are divine acts? There are different answers to this question. According to some theologians, such as William Temple and Oscar Cullmann, a special divine help is necessary in order for us to be able to identify the events as acts of God. For Temple, only minds illumined by God can read the events aright.[4]

The meaning of Temple's claim is somewhat unclear. Either it is possible to infer from the relevant events (together with background knowledge) that it is God who acts in them, or it is not. If it is possible, then no divine illumination is, in principle, necessary in order for a sufficiently intelligent subject to be able to know that they are acts of God. If it is not possible to infer from the events (together with available background knowledge) that it is God who acts in them, then the "divine illumination" that makes knowledge of God possible must include a communication of extra information to the one whose mind is illumined. The illumination cannot just consist of an enhancement of our cognitive capacities. As Lamont points out, "No enhancement of cognitive capacities can enable them to go beyond what the evidence available to them can warrant them in believing; if a change to our cognitive capacities were to do this, it would not be an enhancement but a corruption of them."[5] If the illumination that Temple and others speak of includes the communication of information that is not inferable from the events themselves, then that illumination includes an element of propositional revelation. God must either *tell* the believer that *x is an act of God,* or he must implant knowledge to this effect in the believer's mind. (We will come back to this problem when discussing John Milbank's view of faith and revelation.)

Other proponents of the revelation-as-history model insist that the revelatory events can be understood to be divine acts without the help of supernatural illumination. For Wolfhart Pannenberg, "The events of

---

4. See Dulles, *Models of Revelation,* p. 54. Baillie's view is similar. Revelation is not merely in the objective events, and not merely in human minds, but "in the intercourse of mind and event" (John Baillie, *The Idea of Revelation in Recent Thought* [New York: Columbia University Press, 1956], p. 65). Part of God's revelation is his guidance of the human interpretation of historical events.

5. John Lamont, *Divine Faith* (Aldershot, UK: Ashgate, 2004), p. 12.

history speak their own language, the language of facts." God's "indirect self-revelation" in history is open for anyone to perceive.[6]

Pannenberg views reality primarily as *history,* a view he takes to be biblical, which he contrasts with the Greek understanding of reality as an eternal, cosmic order graspable by reason in the present. To understand reality as history means to understand it as something that "is always new and open to the future, which points in the direction of unforeseen possibilities and which can only be understood in the light of the ultimate future or the end of time."[7] Only at the end of history is reality complete, and then can be seen for what it is.

For the Israelites, Yahweh is the ultimate reality who reveals himself indirectly through his acts in history. Yahweh first appears as a "tribal God," a "numinous being" who proves himself to be a powerful agent by delivering the land promised to Israel. However, "[i]n the history of Israel, Yahweh had not proved himself to be a God for all men. . . . This proof will be made in the strict and ultimate sense only at the end of all history."[8]

Pannenberg connects the lordship (i.e., "God-hood") of God with salvation. "God," as the Christian tradition understands it, is a concept that designates "a power on which all finite reality depends," an "all-determining reality." However, in order to satisfy the Christian concept of God, the being on which everything depends must also be a personal being whose nature is love. This entails that the Christian God is a God who saves. "God cannot be at the same time loving and omnipotent (as one must suppose the all-determining reality to be) if he left his creatures to the powers of evil and destruction." This means that, strictly speaking, we do not know that God exists until the eschaton. "It is only in the event of final salvation that the reality of God will be definitely established."[9] In other words, "the thesis that God's deity is connected to his lordship over creation means that only the final salvation of God's creatures can ultimately demonstrate the assertion of God's existence."[10]

---

6. Wolfhart Pannenberg, "Dogmatic Theses on the Doctrine of Revelation," in Wolfhart Pannenberg, ed., *Revelation as History* (New York: Macmillan, 1968), pp. 132-53; 135.

7. Wolfhart Pannenberg, *Faith and Reality* (Philadelphia: Westminster, 1977), pp. 10, 17.

8. Pannenberg, "Dogmatic Theses on the Doctrine of Revelation," pp. 139, 134.

9. Wolfhart Pannenberg, *An Introduction to Systematic Theology* (Grand Rapids: Eerdmans, 1991), pp. 10-12.

10. Stanley Grenz and Roger Olson, *20th Century Theology: God and the World in a Transitional Age* (Carlisle: Paternoster Press, 1992), p. 191.

Theories of Revelation

What, then, about our epistemic situation in the present? Pannenberg's view is that belief in the existence of God is justified if we can present "a coherent account of the world as God's creation" that is able to make sense of our experience and knowledge, and that can compete favorably with rival interpretations of the world. An account of the world as God's creation must include an account of the final salvation, since "it is only in the eschaton that God's work of creation will be complete."[11] In order to justifiably believe that the Christian God is the "one true God," we must have reason to believe that history will end in salvation rather than in some other way. It is with respect to this claim that the resurrection of Jesus becomes important as an anticipation of the final salvation. "It is through the resurrection that the God of Israel has substantiated his deity in an ultimate way and is now manifest as the God of all men."

> The witness of the New Testament is that in the fate of Jesus Christ the end is not only seen ahead of time, but is experienced by means of a foretaste. For, in him, the resurrection of the dead has already taken place, though to all other men this is still something yet to be experienced.[12]

The resurrection of Jesus is thus an anticipation of the general salvation of all people, and as such a "pre-view" of the final destiny of the world.

It might seem that Pannenberg does not need to assume the occurrence of any propositional revelation. This impression, however, is misleading. Pannenberg's account of revelation clearly presupposes that God literally speaks to humans. "Israel experienced the self-vindication of Yahweh in the given events of its history largely as a confirmation of *words of promise or threat*. . . . One gains a revelation of God's deity in seeing the way in which he fulfills promises." So a given event can be seen for what it is, namely, an act of Yahweh, only because it fulfills a prior promise by God to Israel. "There is a circularity in this. The prophetic word precedes the act of history, and these acts are understandable as acts of Yahweh only because a statement coming in the name of Yahweh interprets them this way."[13] The bare fact that Pannenberg's God promises things and makes threats entails that God literally speaks to humans. To make a promise or a threat is to perform a speech-act.

---

11. Pannenberg, *An Introduction to Systematic Theology,* pp. 12-13.
12. Pannenberg, "Dogmatic Theses on the Doctrine of Revelation," pp. 142, 141.
13. Pannenberg, "Dogmatic Theses on the Doctrine of Revelation," p. 153 (italics added).

What does Pannenberg mean, then, when he says that "the revelation of God 'is open to anyone who has eyes to see' and does not need any supplementary inspired interpretation"?[14] What he means is that *we* need not rely on any supernatural help (direct communications from Yahweh) to be able to interpret the events of Israel's history as acts of God. By normal historical investigation, we know, for instance, that the Jewish culture of the first century CE was permeated by apocalyptic expectations and that those expectations were connected to the idea of a resurrection of the dead. The source of the apocalyptic expectations, furthermore, was a series of prophetic words alleged to be words of Yahweh, recorded in Scripture. Against the background of the existence of these passages in Scripture, and the expectations connected to them, Jesus' resurrection (assuming, with Pannenberg, that we can know that it really happened) takes on a significance it would not have had if these words and expectations had not existed.[15] The resurrection confirms the prophetic words. There is a God who will raise the dead. This is how the resurrection of Jesus can function as a "proof" of the deity of Yahweh.

Let us try to sort out the implicit logic of this "proof," which seems to be as follows. The fact that Jesus miraculously came back from the dead requires an explanation. The Israelite tradition provides such an explanation: there is a God who has promised to raise the dead, and he has now (partly) fulfilled his promise. This explanation would probably not be superior to other possible explanations (such as that Jesus was raised by the devil, or that Jesus was an extraterrestrial creature with very peculiar properties) were it not for the fact that the Israelite tradition had talked about a resurrection of the dead *prior* to the event of Jesus' resurrection. The fact that Jesus' resurrection fit so well with the expectations of the Israelite tradition is something that requires an explanation itself. In this situation, the best explanation of both Jesus' resurrection and the Israelite "prediction" of it seems to be that there really is a God who has raised Jesus, and who has communicated information about his own existence and his intentions to the Israelite community prior to the event of Jesus' resurrection.

Pannenberg's "proof" of the deity of Yahweh (which seems to be an argument-to-the-best-explanation) thus presupposes that information about what God is going to do in the future has been communicated by God to humans in the history of Israel. Information of this kind can only be

---

14. Wolfhart Pannenberg, *Systematic Theology*, vol. 1 (Grand Rapids: Eerdmans, 1991), p. 249.

15. Pannenberg, "Dogmatic Theses on the Doctrine of Revelation," pp. 141, 146.

communicated by revelations in which the medium is a nonnatural sign of the actuality revealed (the future raising of the dead by God). It is impossible for God to reveal that he is going to raise the dead in the future manifestationally, that is, by presenting a "natural" sign of the reality revealed. We could, of course, imagine that God gives a prophet a hallucinatory visual experience or a dream in which the dead arise from their graves. This would be a purely manifestational revelation (a vision of dead people getting up from their graves is, arguably, a natural sign of a general resurrection). Such an experience, however, would not by itself be sufficient to inform the prophet that it is *God* (a power on which all finite reality depends) who is responsible for the raising. Neither would the experience, by itself, tell the prophet whether the event is future or past. God would have to communicate this extra information in some other way, for instance, by implanting a belief in the prophet's mind with the content that God (a being on which all finite reality depends) is the agent behind the events in the vision, and that the events are in the future. But this extra information would have to be transmitted by means of some *nonnatural* sign, such as by words or by direct divine transmission of conceptual contents to the mind of the prophet.

While Pannenberg's account clearly entails that God has communicated propositions in a nonmanifestational way to humans in Israel's history, Pannenberg nevertheless denies that these communications deserve the title "revelations." The reason he denies this is that revelation is God's self-disclosure. To disclose something means to make knowledge of that reality available. But knowledge is not just true belief; it is (at least) *justified* true belief. A mere experience of hearing God speak can never, in Pannenberg's view, justify the belief that it is God who speaks. The experience could be delusional, or caused by the devil. This means that a "prophetic word" (received in religious experiences, visions, dreams, etc.) does not in itself constitute a revelation of God, since it does not confer knowledge of God. Something more is needed for revelation to take place. Pannenberg says:

> We can decide about the truth (or true meaning) of dreams, trances, or oracles only on the basis of their relation to our normal experience of the world and the self. This is true of prophetic sayings, too, to the extent that their truth, and their claim to divine origin, must be measured by whether what is prophesied comes to pass.[16]

---

16. Pannenberg, *Systematic Theology*, vol. 1, p. 234.

"Prophetic words" are not revelations unless they are confirmed by objective events. Since revelation is an epistemic concept — a concept having to do with the transference of knowledge — this view is quite reasonable, given Pannenberg's conviction that one can never acquire knowledge from a prophetic word without independent confirmation of its content. My aim here is not to critique Pannenberg but only to show that his theory includes divine linguistic (or quasi-linguistic) communication as an essential element. This is something that we can easily forget because of Pannenberg's emphasis on historical events. The main difference between Pannenberg's view of revelation and the traditional view is that Pannenberg refuses to grant the title of revelation to prophetic words as such. However, he is prepared to call linguistic or quasi-linguistic transactions between God and humans "preliminary revelation": "There are preliminary revelation . . . in the prophetic reception of the word and the vision of the apocalyptic seer."[17]

Let us imagine a revised version of Pannenberg's account that includes *only* revelation through historical events, such as the Exodus and the resurrection of Jesus. According to this revised account, God has not told any prophet anything, nor has he implanted any conceptual contents in the mind of any human. No "preliminary revelations" have taken place. Could the purely manifestational revelation that is allowed by this revised account justify belief in the existence of the God of theism?

It could not. If we can know (as Pannenberg assumes) that some of the spectacular events of biblical history — such as the resurrection of Jesus — really happened, then it would certainly be justified to hypothesize that a *very powerful agent* is at work in the history of Israel and Jesus Christ. Still, it would not be justified to conclude that this agent is "a power on which all finite reality depends." It is quite conceivable that a very powerful agent who is not a power on which all finite reality depends could have liberated Israel from bondage and raised Jesus from the dead. The conclusion that this agent is the God of theism is hence not warranted by the historical events taken by themselves. It is not true that the resurrection of Jesus (seen in the context of Israel's history and world history) constitutes a "proof" of the "deity of God."[18]

We must conclude that the historical events that Pannenberg focuses

---

17. Pannenberg, *Systematic Theology*, vol. 1, p. 247.
18. Remember that we stipulated that Yahweh had not communicated any conceptual contents to prophets and others in our hypothetical scenario, which means that no predictions of a messiah or of the resurrection would be floating around in Israelite culture.

on as genuinely revelatory cannot justify belief in the existence of the God of theism. Of course, if we have other, independent reasons to believe that there exists a power on which all finite reality depends — reasons provided, for example, by a potent natural theology — then we might be justified in identifying the agent active in Israel's history with the power on which all finite reality depends. It might be more reasonable to assume this identity than to hypothesize that *two* powerful agencies exist — the power on which all finite reality depends and the power that raised Jesus. A purely manifestational historical revelation, in combination with a potent natural theology, would consequently allow us to infer that it is the God of theism who is active in Israel's history. A purely manifestational historical revelation by itself, however, would not.[19]

3.2 Revelation as Inner Experience: Nonconceptual Experience

3.2.1 *Friedrich Schleiermacher*

Another theory of revelation claims that God makes himself known by merely "showing himself," that is, making his presence experienced, in some kind of "inner experiences." The question we are asking ourselves here is not whether such experiences are possible or could plausibly contribute to our knowledge of God, but whether revelation through these types of experiences could totally *replace* the idea that God reveals himself nonmanifestationally, such as by speaking. This has been a rather popular suggestion since the time of Friedrich Schleiermacher.

"What is revelation?" Schleiermacher asks in *On Religion: Speeches to Its Cultured Despisers.* He answers: "Every original and new intuition of the universe is one."[20] The concept of revelation plays, however, a rather

---

19. Pannenberg seems to deny that knowledge of God's existence is available by way of philosophical argument, as in traditional natural theology (Pannenberg, *Systematic Theology,* vol. 1, pp. 90, 106-7). However, he claims that there is an "explicit awareness of God," a "knowledge of the true God from creation" (p. 118). This knowledge is based on "the religious experience of God by means of a sense of the working and being of God in creation" (p. 117). I criticize the claim that religious experience, on its own, could provide knowledge of God's existence in sections 3.2 and 3.3 of this chapter.

20. Friedrich Schleiermacher, *On Religion: Speeches to Its Cultured Despisers* (Cambridge: Cambridge University Press, 1996), p. 49. Hereafter, page references to this work appear in parentheses in the text.

subordinate role in Schleiermacher's thinking. Our relationship to "the infinite" or "the whole" or "God" (which seem to be interchangeable terms for Schleiermacher) is, instead, characterized by him in terms of "religion" or "piety." There is a kind of experience that is not empirical, moral, or aesthetic, but *religious*. Religious experience is sui generis, and it is this kind of experience that mediates awareness of God. So revelation is replaced by, or identified with, religion, and the capacity for religion is a universal feature of human existence, just like the capacity for empirical and moral experience. Wilfred Cantwell Smith has pointed out that Schleiermacher's *On Religion* "would seem to be the first book ever written on religion as such — not on a particular kind or instance and not incidentally, but explicitly on religion itself as a generic something."[21]

In *On Religion,* Schleiermacher describes religion or piety as "intuition of the universe," or of "the infinite." The object or content of this intuition is rather indeterminate; it seems to be the relatedness of everything to an unlimited totality: "To accept everything individual as a part of the whole and everything limited as a representation of the infinite is religion." Sometimes the infinite is conceived theistically: "[T]o present all events as the actions of a god is religion; it expresses its connection to an infinite totality" (p. 25).

Intuition is a Kantian concept whose meaning in Kant's writings is debated. We can think of it here as *that whereby something is given to our awareness*. Through sensory intuition, for example, empirical objects are given. The term "intuition," therefore, suggests a relationship of the mind to some object. "All intuition proceeds from an influence of the intuited on the one who intuits, from an original and independent action of the former" (p. 24).

For Schleiermacher, intuition is not dependent on concepts. When something is intuited, it is given to our awareness in a way that is "immediate" and does not involve concepts. Therefore, religion, as a kind of intuition, is not to be identified with doctrines and beliefs, which are conceptually structured items. Religion "stops with the immediate experience of the existence and action of the universe, with the individual intuitions and feelings" (p. 26)

Schleiermacher describes religion not only as intuition but also as feeling (p. 29). The two characterizations can seem difficult to reconcile.

---

21. Wilfred Cantwell Smith, *The Meaning and End of Religion: A New Approach to the Religious Traditions of Mankind* (New York: Macmillan, 1963), p. 45.

Feelings, unlike Kantian intuitions, do not — as we normally conceive them — "give" objects to our awareness. For Schleiermacher, however, religion is both *affection* (feeling) and *revelation* (intuition). It is through feeling that the infinite is given to our awareness.[22]

In *The Christian Faith,* Schleiermacher characterizes the religious affection as a "feeling of absolute dependence" on a source or power distinct from the world. This feeling of dependence is what gives meaning to the word "God": "God signifies for us simply that which is the co-determinant in this feeling and to which we trace our being."[23] This means that the content of the concept "God" is derived from the immediate feeling of dependence. "God" signifies the "whence" of the feeling of absolute dependence.

Wayne Proudfoot has pointed out a fundamental problem with Schleiermacher's account of the religious affection or experience. On the one hand, Schleiermacher describes it as "an intuition of the infinite" or "a feeling of dependence." On the other hand, he claims that the experience is independent of concepts and thought. But these two claims are incompatible, according to Proudfoot.[24] A mental state cannot both be intentional — that is, be about or directed at some object, at least not an object such as "the infinite" — and at the same time be independent of concepts. To say that an experience or affection is about or directed at a certain object means, arguably, that the subject of the experience is aware of that object *as such,* which means that she must master the relevant concept. Therefore, the possibility of the experience seems to depend on the subject's mastery of a concept. It is true that an experience can be "directed at" an object in (roughly) the sense of being perceptually *caused* by that object in an appropriate way, even though the subject does not master the concept of it. For example, a subject who does not have the concept "horse" but who looks at a horse can be said to have an experience of a horse. However, such

---

22. In later editions of *On Religion,* Schleiermacher avoided speaking about "intuition" in the context of religion, because the term suggested that an addition of concepts was necessary ("Intuitions without concepts are blind"), and Schleiermacher wanted access to God to be unmediated by concepts (Michael Forster, "Friedrich Daniel Ernst Schleiermacher," in Edward N. Zalta, ed., *Stanford Encyclopedia of Philosophy* (Fall 2008 ed.), sect. 10: http://plato.stanford.edu/archives/fall2008/entries/schleiermacher/ (accessed May 13, 2013).

23. Friedrich Schleiermacher, *The Christian Faith,* ed. H. R. Mackintosh and J. S. Stewart (London: T & T Clark, 1999), pp. 16, 17.

24. Wayne Proudfoot, *Religious Experience* (Berkeley: University of California Press, 1985), p. 33. In what follows, I try to give Proudfoot's argument the strongest possible formulation, which means that my concern is not to recount his own version accurately.

a subject will not be aware of the horse *as* a horse. It is thus questionable whether the *intentional* object of the experience — the object that determines the subjective character of the experience — is correctly specified by means of the concept "horse."

This line of reasoning can be criticized, but it gains considerably in force when the object of experience is not a horse or some other physical entity, but "the infinite" or "dependence" (as in the "feeling of dependence"). Arguably, as I have admitted, one can be said to have an experience "of" a certain physical object simply by virtue of being perceptually related to it, without knowing what kind of object it is. It is much less clear what it could mean to have an experience of *the infinite* or a feeling *of dependence* without knowing what "infinity" or "dependence" are. "The infinite," for example, is not a particular object, distinct from other objects, which one can stand in a perceptual relationship to. To experience "the infinite" means, according to Schleiermacher, "to accept everything individual *as* a part of the whole and everything limited *as* a representation of the infinite."[25] According to this description, the experience clearly presupposes a conceptual capacity. To think of *x as* a *y* is to apply the concept of *y* to *x*.

In the case of the "feeling of dependence," it is hard to see how having it could be something different from *feeling that one is dependent*. The object of the feeling seems to be, or include, a proposition. The capacity to have an affective attitude toward a proposition presupposes the ability to think it. The feeling, hence, cannot be independent of thought.

Proudfoot writes:

> If reference to the concept of dependence and to an intentional object or codeterminant (i.e., "the infinite" or the " 'whence?' of the feeling of absolute dependence") is required in order to identify the distinctive moment of religious experience, then it cannot be independent of language or thought. In the absence of the concepts of cause and dependence . . . the consciousness of absolute dependence Schleiermacher describes would not be available.[26]

---

25. Schleiermacher, *On Religion,* p. 25 (italics added).

26. Proudfoot, *Religious Experience,* p. 32. William Alston has criticized Proudfoot's reasoning: "From the fact that we use concepts to identify something as of a certain type (How else?!), it does not follow that what we are identifying 'involves' concepts and judgments. . . . From the fact that we use a concept to pick out cabbages as vegetables, it does not follow that cabbages are, have, or use concepts or judgments" (Alston, *Perceiving God: The*

Problems of the kind that Proudfoot points out are the result of Schleiermacher's ambition to respect the Kantian restrictions on knowledge. Theoretical knowledge, according to Kant, requires the application of concepts to the deliverances of sensibility, that is, to experience. Concepts that have no possible application to experience — such as "God" — cannot figure in theoretical knowledge. Schleiermacher was convinced that Kant was right about this, with the consequence that he could not picture our access to God in terms of experience structured by concepts. In other words, our access to God could not be a matter of theoretical knowledge. However, Scheleiermacher was aware that Kant also posited a kind of experience distinct from empirical experience, namely, a direct awareness of freedom and the moral law. This awareness, which belongs within the domain of practical rather than theoretical reason, is not mediated by concepts, which means that it cannot generate (theoretical) knowledge. However, our moral awareness points to a very important aspect of reality and is, according to Kant, to be taken with utmost seriousness. The idea of an unmediated access to the moral law inspired Schleiermacher to explore an analogous possibility: What if there is, besides moral experience, another form of awareness that is not structured by concepts, namely, religious experience? The positing of a sui generis religious domain of experience could explain how we can have access to "the infinite," and it could thereby legitimate religion and religious discourse. Schleiermacher thus claims to have "located a point of access to God . . . which overcomes the restrictions Kant placed on theoretical knowledge without recourse to practical knowledge."[27]

A problem with this solution, as we have seen, is that it is very difficult to claim that experiences that are independent of concepts can be *about* things like "the infinite" or God. But even if we disregard this problem, the Kantian framework poses another serious difficulty for Schleiermacher. If the religious experience or feeling does not provide us with any *knowledge* of its intentional object, God, what distinguishes it from merely

---

Epistemology of Religious Experience [Ithaca, NY: Cornell University Press, 1991], p. 41). This critique misses its mark. Clearly, what Proudfoot means is not that we must use concepts in order to identify some affection as religious. His claim is that what *makes* an affection religious (according to Schleiermacher's characterization) is that it has a certain property (or properties) that is intrinsically connected to conceptual capacities, such as the property of having "the infinite" as its intentional object.

27. Bruce McCormack, *Orthodox and Modern: Studies in the Theology of Karl Barth* (Grand Rapids: Baker Academic, 2008), p. 25.

subjective intentional states, such as fantasies? Fantasies have intentional objects — they purport to be about things — but they do not provide us with knowledge of the things they purport to be about. In what way is Schleiermacher's religious experience different from fantasies?

In chapter 1, I argued that a personal relationship with God requires knowledge of God. Schleiermacher's attempt to circumvent this requirement is not very convincing.

3.2.2 Karl Rahner

Karl Rahner, like Schleiermacher, talks about an awareness of God that is not mediated by concepts and that is independent of thought and beliefs. This awareness is a "transcendental experience in which a person comes into the presence of the absolute mystery which we call 'God,' an experience which is more primary than reflection."[28] Rahner's transcendental experience is an experiential dimension that is always "co-present" in every experience and act of knowledge. The transcendental experience "belongs to the necessary and inalienable structures of the knowing subject itself" (p. 20).

The transcendental experience includes an awareness of oneself "as the product of what is radically foreign to [one]," that is, an experience of oneself as conditioned and reducible to what is not oneself (p. 29). But one's ability to see oneself *as* conditioned, finite, and reducible testifies to the fact that one is a *subject,* a being with an unlimited horizon of questioning. "A finite system cannot confront itself in its totality," that is, cannot put itself in question, but this is precisely what the human being can do (p. 30). "In the fact that he affirms the possibility of a merely *finite* horizon of questioning, this possibility is already surpassed, and man shows himself to be a being with an *infinite* horizon" (p. 32). So "transcendental experience is the experience of *transcendence*" (p. 20). The human "experiences himself as infinite possibility" (p. 32). However, since he also experiences himself as dependent and conditioned, the subject does not see himself as *creating* his own unlimited space or infinite horizon (p. 34). Rather, he experiences himself as being *open* to or oriented toward "the silent and uncontrollable

---

28. Karl Rahner, *Foundations of Christian Faith: An Introduction to the Idea of Christianity* (New York: Crossroad, 1978), p. 44. Hereafter, page references to this work appear in parentheses within the text.

infinity of reality" (p. 35). The movement of transcendence is "the infinite horizon of being making itself manifest" to the subject (p. 34).

This "infinite horizon of being" is God, and man's experience of this horizon is an experience of God. "We are oriented towards God. This original experience is always present" (p. 53). Not only is the experience of transcendence in fact an awareness of God. "There is present in this transcendental experience an unthematic and anonymous, as it were, knowledge of God" (p. 21). The transcendental experience of ourselves as grounded in and moving within an "infinite mystery" includes the experience of this mystery as *personal:*

> In its very constitution a finite spirit always experiences itself as having its origin in another and as being given to itself from another — from another, therefore, that it cannot misinterpret as an impersonal principle. (p. 75)

It is from this prereflective, nonconceptual awareness of ourselves as grounded in an infinite, personal mystery that the explicit, conceptual, "thematic" knowledge of God emerges. In metaphysical, theoretical reflection about God, "we are only making explicit for ourselves what we already know implicitly about ourselves in the depths of our personal self-realization."

> For this reason the meaning of all explicit knowledge of God in religion and in metaphysics is intelligible and can really be understood only when all the words we use there point to the unthematic experience of our orientation towards the ineffable mystery. (p. 53)

The classical proofs of God's existence are "the elaboration of a more original knowledge" — the transcendental experience of God (p. 68). "A theoretical proof for the existence of God, then, is only intended to mediate a reflexive awareness of the fact that man always and inevitably has to do with God in his intellectual and spiritual existence" (p. 69). So the explicit knowledge of God that emerges from theistic proofs is only a "reflexive conceptualization" of implicit, unthematic knowledge already had through the subject's transcendental experience of being related to an infinite mystery (p. 54).

Rahner's account of the transcendental experience is plagued by the same problem as is Schleiermacher's account of the religious feeling. How can an experience of oneself as oriented toward an infinite mystery be constitutively independent of concepts such as "infinity" and "mystery" (or "oneself")? But Rahner's account also suffers from another problem. He claims, in contrast to Schleiermacher, that the transcendental experience constitutes *knowledge* of God — a knowledge that is "prereflective" and nonconceptual, but which can be made explicit (turned into "real," conscious knowledge) by a process of "reflexive conceptualization." But by this claim Rahner succumbs, as we will now see, to what is commonly known as the "myth of the given."

The myth of the given, a phrase coined by Wilfrid Sellars, is the seductive idea that our beliefs can draw epistemic support from something that is "conceptually innocent," something that has no intrinsic connection to concepts and conceptual capacities, such as brute sensory events. Sellars's critique of this idea has been very influential and has shaped the thought of philosophers such as Donald Davidson, Richard Rorty, and John McDowell.[29] Before we can see how the critique applies to Rahner, I need to recount, very briefly, the basic ideas behind it. The easiest way to do so is by focusing on perceptual experience.

Our reasons or evidence for perceptual beliefs are, according to a common view, perceptual experiences. We believe things about the world on the basis of our perceptions of it. The relationship between our perceptual reasons (such as a certain visual experience of a house) and our beliefs (such as the belief that there is a house before us) is, like all rational relationships, *normative*. When we say that an experience is a *reason for,* or justifies, a belief, we are not just saying that the experience has caused us to have the belief in question (a hammer blow to the head might cause us to have beliefs, but it does not justify them). We are saying something more, namely that, given the experience, we *should (ceteris paribus)* have the relevant belief.[30] If we assume that an experience has

---

29. Sellars's criticism of the myth of the given is found in Willem DeVries, Timm Triplett, and Wilfrid Sellars, *Knowledge, Mind, and the Given: Reading Wilfrid Sellars's "Empiricism and the Philosophy of Mind," Including the Complete Text of Sellars's Essay* (Indianapolis: Hackett, 2000). Although Sellars's view has convinced many, there are of course dissenting voices: see Richard Schantz, "The Given Regained: Reflections on the Sensuous Content of Experience," *Philosophical and Phenomenological Research* 62, no. 1 (2001): 167-80; William Alston, "Sellars and the 'Myth of the Given,'" *Philosophical and Phenomenological Research* 65, no. 1 (2002): 69-86. For a response to Alston's criticism of Sellars, see Jay Rosenberg, "Still Mythic After All These Years: On Alston's Latest Defense of the Given," *Philosophical and Phenomenological Research* 72, no. 1 (2006): 157-73.

30. See Mats Wahlberg, *Reshaping Natural Theology: Seeing Nature as Creation* (Houndmills, UK: Palgrave Macmillan, 2012), p. 31.

a conceptually structured content — for example, the content that it appears to be a house over there — then it seems clearly intelligible how the experience can justify a belief about a house. The content of the experience can, since it is structured in terms of concepts such as "house," figure in inferences that aim to establish whether there is a house before me or not. However, if we think of experiences as items that lack conceptual articulation — for example, as brute sensory events — then it becomes unintelligible how there could be rational connections between them and the propositional contents of beliefs. It is, of course, still possible to posit *causal* connections between experiences and beliefs, but those are not, as such, rational (i.e., normative). Sellars's main insight is that only items that have a propositional form, in the sense of a conceptual structure, can constitute reasons. Nonpropositional items such as hammer blows, Ping-Pong balls, or brute sensory events cannot stand in normative relationships to anything, and thus cannot justify anything. To suppose that they can is to embrace the inconsistent view that Sellars called the myth of the given.[31]

Rahner, as we have seen, tries to describe, or interpret, the nonconceptual, transcendental experience in conceptual terms. For instance, he characterizes this experience as an *awareness of oneself as determined by foreign factors,* but also as an awareness of "infinite possibilities," an openness to an "infinite horizon." Rahner claims that these conceptual descriptions of the object or content of the transcendental experience are

---

31. Many philosophers who accept Sellars's critique of the myth of the given have assumed that the world's impact on our senses can only be conceived as "brute sensory events" and have concluded that sense experience is irrelevant for the justification of our beliefs about the world, leaving epistemological coherentism as the only viable model of epistemic justification. Thus Richard Rorty says: "[N]othing counts as justification unless by reference to what we already accept, and there is no way to get outside our beliefs and our language so as to find some test other than coherence" (Rorty, *Philosophy and the Mirror of Nature* [Princeton: Princeton University Press, 1979], p. 178). Donald Davidson: "[N]othing can count as a reason for holding a belief except another belief" (Davidson, "A Coherence Theory of Truth and Knowledge," in E. LePore, ed., *Truth and Interpretation: Perspectives on the Philosophy of Donald Davidson* [Oxford: Basil Blackwell, 1986], p. 310). John McDowell has convincingly argued, however, that it is possible to hold on to the view that sensory experiences can justify beliefs without falling into the myth of the given. However, this requires that we conceive of the world's impacts on our senses as already imbued with conceptual structure, which in turn requires that we conceive of the world *itself* as having the kind of structure picked out by concepts. McDowell's groundbreaking argument is found in his *Mind and World* (Cambridge, MA: Harvard University Press, 1996).

based on the actual character of the experience. In other words, the actual character of the transcendental experience is what controls, or governs, or justifies, these descriptions. Of course, conceptual descriptions cannot, according to Rahner, *completely* capture the content of the experience. After all, the experience is supposed to be an awareness of God. But some descriptions are presumably more correct than others. Otherwise, Rahner could equally well characterize the transcendental experience as, say, an awareness of a thirst for beer.

However, if the content of the transcendental experience lacks conceptual structure, it cannot, by itself, justify the choice of any particular characterization over any other. An experience that lacks conceptual articulation cannot, by itself, constitute or provide a reason for anything, and hence cannot provide the subject with a reason to conceptualize the experience in terms of God or "an infinite horizon" rather than, say, in terms of Mickey Mouse.[32] Since Rahner believes that the transcendental experience is both "conceptually innocent" and capable of justifying an interpretation — a piece of explicit knowledge — that mentions "God" or an "infinite horizon," it seems that he has succumbed to the myth of the given.[33]

---

32. For a different view, see Richard Heck, "Nonconceptual Content and the 'Space of Reasons,'" *The Philosophical Review* 109, no. 4 (2000): 483-523. The idea that perceptual experiences can "tell" us things about the world without having conceptual structure is defended by Heck and other philosophers in terms of "non-conceptual content"; see, e.g., Christopher Peacocke, *A Study of Concepts* (Cambridge, MA: MIT Press, 1992). John McDowell argues that the idea of nonconceptual content is a version of the myth of the given (*Mind and World,* lecture 3). In later writings McDowell has expressed a more nuanced view of the contents of perceptual experiences. He now claims that experiences have "intuitional" conceptual content rather than "propositional" conceptual content (McDowell, "Avoiding the Myth of the Given," in *The Engaged Intellect: Philosophical Essays* [Cambridge, MA: Harvard University Press, 2009], p. 269).

33. Henri de Lubac encounters similar problems as does Rahner in his account of our knowledge of God. De Lubac does not talk about a "transcendental experience" of God, but instead of an "idea" of God that is "previous to all our concepts" (Henri de Lubac, *The Discovery of God* [Grand Rapids: Eerdmans, 1996], p. 38). "The idea of God is mysteriously present in us from the beginning, prior to our concepts, although beyond our grasp without their help" (p. 39). "God must be present to the mind before any explicit reasoning or objective concept is possible . . . he must first of all be secretly affirmed and thought" (p. 54). The philosophical problems here are, as Fergus Kerr points out, considerable. "It is difficult to understand how God can be 'secretly affirmed and thought' prior to there being any of the judgment or concept formation which we normally mean by affirming and thinking" (Fergus Kerr, *Twentieth-Century Catholic Theologians: From Neoscholasticism to Nuptial Mysticism*

Theories of Revelation

Hitherto we have only talked about Rahner's account of "natural revelation." But the natural revelation is merely "the presence of God as question, not as answer" (*Foundations,* pp. 170-71). It "leaves God still unknown insofar as he becomes known . . . only negatively by way of his pre-eminence over the finite." But God wants a deeper communion with humans — he wants "the radical closeness of self-communication" (p. 170). This is where the "supernatural" revelation comes in. It constitutes God's personal self-communication and has the character of an event with two aspects, one transcendental and one historical. The transcendental aspect is the "inner self-communication of God in grace at the core of a spiritual person," which is offered "to all times and to all men" (p. 172). However, the transcendental revelation "must always be present as mediated in objective and reflexive knowledge" (p. 173). This mediation is the historical aspect of revelation.

> The attempt is made in every religion, at least on man's part, to mediate the original, unreflexive and non-objective revelation [i.e., the transcendental revelation] historically, to make it reflexive [i.e., the object of reflexive, conceptual thought] and to interpret it in propositions. In all religions there are individual moments of such successful mediation made possible by God's grace, moments when the supernatural, transcendental relationship of man to God through God's self-communication becomes self-reflexive. Through these moments God creates for man the possibility of salvation also in the dimension of his objectivity, his concrete historicity. (p. 173)

The interpretation of the transcendental revelation in conceptual terms can be more or less successful. "The prophet is none other than the believer who can express his transcendental experience of God correctly" (p. 159). The supernatural revelation is hence, like the "natural revelation," primarily constituted by a transcendental experience. The experience is given propositional expression in particular religions under the guidance of God and becomes "historical." The original experience of grace, however, is prereflective and independent of concepts and thought.

The nonconceptual character of the experience of grace creates, as we have already seen, the problem of how that experience can stand in

---

[Malden, MA: Blackwell, 2007], p. 79). Furthermore, since de Lubac thinks of our explicit knowledge of God as grounded in something nonconceptual, his account succumbs, like Rahner's does, to the myth of the given.

rational relationship to the conceptually structured propositions that are supposed to express it. Since it is God who, in cases of true or "pure" revelation, guides the subject's interpretation of the transcendental revelation, it may be thought that the problem of interpretation does not arise. Rahner, it might be thought, could just say that God makes sure that the subject chooses the right propositions, that is, those that are adequate to express the transcendental experience. But this does not solve the problem. The problem is what *makes* certain propositions adequate. This question is not answered by saying that God helps the subject choose propositions. If it just is the fact that God makes the subject choose certain propositions that makes those propositions adequate, then the transcendental experience itself drops out of the picture as irrelevant. Revelation, then, would not consist in a human interpretation of a transcendental experience, but would be better described in terms of God's directly communicating propositions to humans.

Revelation reaches its climax, according to Rahner, when its transcendental aspect and its historical, categorical aspect become inseparably united. In Christ, the content of the revelation (God as he communicates himself to humankind), the medium of revelation (the life of Jesus as God's self-expression), and the recipient of revelation (Jesus as a human being) have become "absolutely one." God's self-communication thereby becomes "revelation in an absolute sense" (pp. 174-75). God's self-communication and the "interpretation" of that self-communication in historical, categorical terms are now identical.

Rahner's assumption of the identity between God's transcendental self-communication and its historical embodiment in Jesus does not, however, help him to explain how humans other than Jesus himself can *know* that Jesus is identical to God. In order to be able to believe that Jesus is God (which means to accept him as the ultimate truth of one's life, as God's "ultimate word" [p. 227]), one must already have an implicit, unconscious understanding of the fact of the incarnation, brought about by grace. That this is necessary becomes clear when Rahner reflects about what a Christian can do in order to help somebody else enter the circle of faith:

> Basically a Christian can only do this: he can presuppose that an understanding ... is already present at the center of the listener's being, and he can express in a conceptual articulation for this person the understanding which is already present. If the listener also accepts the Christological assertion [i.e., that Jesus is Christ] explicitly, then

Theories of Revelation

the speaker has not really produced this understanding of faith in its original unity, but has only brought it to the conscious level of objective conceptualization. (pp. 231-32)

This means that Rahner, despite his appeal to the doctrine of the incarnation and the identity of the content and medium of revelation in Jesus, still needs to presuppose some kind of preexistent, nonconceptual knowledge of God (in this case, knowledge that Jesus is the God-man).

3.3 Revelation as Inner Experience: Conceptual Experience

We have briefly reviewed two theories that conceive of revelation primarily in terms of "inner experience," and that construe this experience as preconceptual and independent of language and beliefs. We have seen that these accounts display incoherences. Experiences cannot be both nonconceptual and intentional, and least not when the intentional object is supposed to be things like "the infinite," "the whole," "the universe," or "God." Schleiermacher and Rahner lack this insight. Furthermore, Rahner, who claims that the transcendental experience provides knowledge of God, is committed to the view that nonconceptual experience can justify knowledge. This is a version of the myth of the given. Schleiermacher avoids falling into this myth by denying that the religious feeling provides *knowledge* of God. However, he thereby deprives himself of any means to explain how the religious feeling can mediate a personal relationship between humans and God.

But what if God reveals himself in experiences that are more like normal perceptions? Normal perceptions — such as visual experiences of middle-sized physical objects — have conceptually structured contents, according to a common view.[34] We perceive things such as *that there is a house over there,* or *that the sky is blue.* Experiences with this kind of content can, unlike brute sensory events, conceivably justify beliefs.

The Christian tradition has a rich heritage of alleged mystical expe-

---

34. McDowell, *Mind and World;* Bill Brewer, *Perception and Reason* (New York: Oxford University Press, 1999). For criticism of this view, see M. G. F. Martin, "Perception, Concepts, and Memory," *The Philosophical Review* 101, no. 4 (1992): 745-63; Michael Tye, *Ten Problems of Consciousness: A Representational Theory of the Phenomenal Mind* (Cambridge, MA: MIT Press, 1995); Christopher Peacocke, "Phenomenology and Nonconceptual Content," *Philosophical and Phenomenological Research* 62, no. 3 (2001): 609-15.

riences of God. Could it be that such experiences constitute something like perceptual experiences of God? In that case, they may — like normal perceptions — make knowledge of their object available. In the same way as I can know that there is a house before me because I can see it, I could know that God exists because I can (mystically) perceive him.

Before we address this issue, I must make a clarification. Mystics sometimes claim to have heard God speak in mystical experiences. If such experiences are, in fact, veridical perceptions, they do not only constitute instances of manifestational revelation (God "showing" himself) but would also count as cases of propositional revelation (God telling something). Since my purpose here is to inquire whether purely manifestational theories of revelation can explain how justified belief in God is possible, I will not, in this context, consider experiences in which God speaks.

Suppose that a subject experiences an entity that is, in fact, God, but that the experience does not represent the entity *as* God. For instance, suppose that I have an experience in which it appears to me as if a very powerful and loving spiritual being is mystically present. Even if such an experience is veridical and the being who is thus presented to me is in fact God, the experience by itself still does not give me knowledge of God's existence. This is because "God," as Christianity — and theism in general — understands the concept, is not only a very powerful and loving being but also, and crucially, a being on whom all finite realities depend (just to mention one of God's unique and essential properties). In order for a mystical experience to be able, by itself, to provide knowledge of God's existence, the experience must represent (or present) the experienced object *as God,* that is, as a being on whom all finite realities depend (etc.). There seem to be strong reasons to believe, however, that no experience can do that.

Nick Zangwill has argued that, in order to represent something as God, an experience would have to represent the object experienced as omnipotent, omniscient, and all-good. But no experience could possibly represent "theistic properties" such as these, Zangwill argues.[35] In order to see that his claim is very plausible, we need only consider the possibility of experiencing (perceiving) some creature *as* omniscient, or all-knowing.

Normally, we do not regard it as possible to perceive that somebody knows that *p* unless she gives expression to this knowledge, for instance, by speaking. But suppose that it is possible, in mystical experiences, directly

---

35. Nick Zangwill, "The Myth of Religious Experience," *Religious Studies* 40, no. 1 (2004): 1-22.

to perceive that somebody knows that *p*. To know a proposition is to stand in a certain cognitive relationship — the knowing-relationship — to it. To perceive that somebody knows that *p* means, therefore, to perceive that the person stands in the knowing-relationship to *p*. It follows that, if one is to perceive that God is omniscient, one's experience must represent God as standing in the knowing-relationship to *all* true propositions. But this means that one's experience must represent all true propositions. Presumably, no experience can do that.

Furthermore, that God is omniscient entails that he has no false beliefs. So in order to perceive God as omniscient, one has to perceive the *negative* fact that God has no false beliefs. But it is extremely difficult to see how such a negative fact could be perceived. Presumably, we cannot perceive something like the "limits" of God's mind, and then scan the area inside those limits, in order to make sure that no false beliefs are present there. Likewise, in order to perceive that some being is omnipotent, we would have to perceive that there is nothing that this being cannot do. But that would mean to perceive the *absence* of things that it cannot do. It is quite inconceivable how such an absence could be perceived.[36]

William Alston is perhaps the most prominent defender of the possibility of experiences of the kind we are considering, that is, experiences in which God is directly perceived. But not even Alston contends that such experiences normally present God *as* God (i.e., as omnipotent, etc.) to the experiencing subject. "With rare exceptions one doesn't suppose that God presents himself as creator, three Persons in one Substance, the actor in salvation history, or even omnipotent, omniscient, and *a se*."[37]

> Though God may appear to one as good, powerful, and loving, He typically does not appear as *infinitely* good, powerful, or loving, or as possessing any other characteristics that are peculiar to God Himself. Hence we depend on the background theology and other aspects of the tradition for principles that lay down conditions under which what we are aware of is God. (p. 294)

So, in most cases, according to Alston, we are dependent on background knowledge in order to identify the object of our experience *as* God. "With mystical perception we have seen that a background system

---

36. Zangwill, "The Myth of Religious Experience," pp. 17-18
37. Alston, *Perceiving God,* p. 293. Hereafter, page references to this work appear in parentheses within the text.

of beliefs is drawn on for the support of the identification of the perceived object as God" (p. 300). This background system of beliefs can be derived from natural theology or public revelation. If we can know, from these sources, that an omnipotent and perfectly good being exists, then we might be able to infer that a being that is presented to our awareness, in a mystical experience, as very powerful and good, is the omnipotent and perfectly good being, God.

Alston's point is that, in order for us to be able to identify the object of a mystical experience as God, we are dependent on other sources of information besides mystical perception. We must rely on these other sources for the crucial information that there *is* a God who can possibly be encountered in mystical experience and recognized on the basis of certain criteria. Mystical perception does not provide this information, which means that the idea of mystical perception cannot explain how knowledge of God's existence is possible.

The other sources of information of God that Alston recognizes, such as natural theology and public revelation, provide mutual support for each other's credibility. Although no source of information about God is totally independent of the other sources, Alston says that, in the case of mystical perception, "the dependence on other sources is more obvious than in other cases" (p. 300).

> We have seen that MP [mystical perception] is limited in the range of beliefs it can effectively support. Except for the matters on which God has communicated messages in a direct perceptual manner, MP will not by itself give us the word on the essential nature of God. (p. 295)

Alston does not, so it seems, exclude the possibility that there could be experiences in which God is presented to the subject *as* God (omnipotent, etc.). But he admits that this is not normally the case, and he does not present any arguments in favor of the possibility for experiences to represent "theistic properties." At any rate, he does not base his contention that mystical perception can provide us knowledge of God on the assumption that experiences can present God *as* God. Rather, his main contention seems to be that, even though we are dependent on other sources of knowledge about God besides mystical perception in order to identify the object of our perception *as* God, such perceptions can nevertheless *contribute* to our knowledge of God. They can lend increased credibility to the beliefs produced by the other sources (natural theology and public revelation), and hence contribute to the credibility of the total case for Christian belief. Furthermore, mystical perception can provide information about God that no other source can provide, for instance, about God's will with respect to a particular individual.

So it seems that Alston does not have much to say about the possibility for perceptual experiences to represent something as God. Nelson Pike, however, argues explicitly for the possibility of "theistic experiences" — experiences that are "phenomenologically of God."[38] In order to exemplify such an experience, he quotes an informant figuring in William James's *Varieties of Religious Experience:*

> When all at once I experienced a feeling of being raised above myself, I felt the presence of God — I tell of the thing just as I was conscious of it — as if his goodness and his power were penetrating me altogether. . . . At bottom the expression most apt to render what I felt was this: God was present, though invisible; he fell under no one of my senses, yet my consciousness perceived him. (p. 117)

Scholars such as Ninian Smart,[39] W. T. Stace,[40] and J. William Forgie[41] argue that reports such as these are not to be understood as *phenomenological* reports (i.e., descriptions of the phenomenological content of an experience) but as interpretations of an experience that does not in itself have theistic phenomenological content. Pike, however, contends that an "identification element" — "It's God!" — is part of the phenomenological content of the experience. Pike does not deny that background beliefs are necessary in order to have a theistic experience. If the subject in the example above had not believed in the Christian God, "he would not have had a theistic experience" (p. 118). Pike's point, however, is that background beliefs are shaping the very phenomenological content of the experience

---

38. Nelson Pike, *Mystic Union: An Essay in the Phenomenology of Mysticism* (Ithaca, NY: Cornell University Press, 1992), p. 117. Hereafter, page references to this work appear in parentheses within the text.

39. Ninian Smart, "Interpretation and Mystical Experience," *Religious Studies* 1, no. 1 (1965): 75-87.

40. W. T. Stace, *Mysticism and Philosophy* (Philadelphia: Lippincott, 1960).

41. J. William Forgie, "Theistic Experience and the Doctrine of Unanimity," *International Journal for Philosophy of Religion* 15, no. 1 (1984): 13-30; Forgie, "The Possibility of Theistic Experience," *Religious Studies* 34, no. 3 (1998): 317-23; Forgie, "Pike's Mystic Union and the Possibility of Theistic Experience," *Religious Studies* 30, no. 2 (2008): 231-42.

rather than just figuring in subsequent interpretations of a more primitive given that lacks theistic content.

Concerning the question of how a subject can tell that the experience is *of God* (i.e., not that it is veridical, but that it is phenomenologically of God), Pike says that it need not be answered. There are many everyday experiences in which we just seem to become aware of the identity of some object — a coffeemaker, for example — without basing this recognition on a prior awareness of particular identifying marks or features (p. 144). "From a phenomenological point of view, my awareness of the coffee maker is not the product of an inference" (p. 142). It does not seem to me that I recognize my coffeemaker *as* a coffeemaker on the basis of a prior awareness of, for example, its "look" (the "look" being, say, a particular configuration of colors and shapes). "Phenomenologically, [the coffee maker's] look is not something from which my awareness of the coffee maker is *derived*" (p. 142).

Pike admits that, from an *epistemological* point of view, it might be reasonable to construe the perception of a coffeemaker as a two-stage process in which the identification of the coffeemaker is based on something more primitive that is given to our awareness (such as the "look" of the coffeemaker). However, this construal, which separates what is given from the act of identification, is a theoretical construal motivated by epistemological concerns. It is supposed to explain why we are more prone to make mistakes about the identity of a given object (is it a coffeemaker or a hologram of a coffeemaker?) than about the "look" of that object. This can be explained by a story that construes the "look" as immediately given, and the identification as a *judgment* that is based on the look.[42] However, such a story does not reflect the phenomenology of the experience.

> Although there may be epistemological reasons for restricting the content of perception to looks, feels, etc., and thus for striking a distinction, in principle, between *perceiving* an object and *recognizing* the object in question to be of some particular kind ... this distinction cannot be justified on phenomenological grounds. (p. 142)

Pike concludes that from a phenomenological point of view, as opposed to one that is epistemological/theoretical, an "identification

---

42. Such a construal is, however, not necessary. Even if we perceive the property of being a coffeemaker directly, we can still be more prone to make mistakes about such high-level properties than about "looks."

element" seems often to be part of the content of an experience, as opposed to being something that is added to the experience by a subsequent mental act.

However, Pike seems to conflate two different things here. It is one thing to say that it does not seem to a subject as if his recognition of a coffeemaker is based on a prior awareness of colors and shapes. This is a phenomenological observation about how the subject experiences *the act or process of recognition.* But we are not interested in how the subject experiences the act or process of recognition; we are interested in how he experiences the coffeemaker. The experience of how one recognizes a coffeemaker is, of course, a different experience from the experience of a coffeemaker. The first is an introspective experience of a mental act — recognition — while the second is an experience of a physical object (a coffeemaker). That the recognition of a coffeemaker does not seem to be divided into a prior awareness of colors and shapes and a separate act of identification does not entail that the experience of the coffeemaker includes anything beyond colors and shapes. It can, misleadingly, seem to the subject as if his recognition of a coffeemaker is direct, while in fact it is based on an awareness of colors and shapes.

There are at least two possible explanations for why a person experiences the act of recognition as direct. The first is that his experience of the coffeemaker has an identification element ("It's a coffeemaker") as part of its content, which means that his recognition of the object actually *is* direct. There is, however, another plausible explanation, namely, that the inferential process by which he recognizes a certain configuration of colors and shapes as a coffeemaker happens very fast. The act of recognition will then phenomenologically *seem* as if it is direct, even though it is not.[43] The phenomenological data that Pike appeals to do not help us decide between these two hypotheses.

So Pike's argument from the phenomenology of recognition does not support the idea that there can be experiences that are phenomenologically of God. Just because mystics sometimes experience the recognition of God as direct, it does not follow that their experiences of God must include an "It's God" identification element as part of their content. Since

43. Pike says, as we remember, that "a distinction . . . between perceiving an object and recognizing the object in question to be of some particular kind . . . cannot be justified on phenomenological grounds." This may be true. My point, however, is that Pike's phenomenological evidence cannot justify the claim that experiences contain "identification elements" as part of their contents either.

77

there are, as we have seen, rather strong arguments against the idea that an experience could present something *as* God to a subject, the idea must be regarded as very shaky at best. Moreover, perceiving high-level properties is something one learns. A small child cannot perceive that there is a garage in front of her, since she has not learned to identify garages. Learning how to identify garages takes time and training. It requires opportunity to practice. If this is the case with perceiving the property of *being a garage,* it should, a fortiori, be true of the property of *being God.* Mystics, however, often describe experiences in which God is directly perceived as unique or at least very rare. How can a perceptual skill that is supposed to detect the extremely high-level property of being God (or the very unusual "It's God" identification element) be learned almost instantly, while the ability to perceive normal properties — such as being a garage — takes time to develop?

In my view, the experiences of mystics are much better explained if we assume that what they (seem to) perceive are properties like goodness, power, plenitude, and love, rather than the property of being God. The mystic then *judges* that the experience is of God with the help of background beliefs about what God is like.

Alston laments:

> Those who report mystical perceptions are not concerned primarily with the needs of epistemologists. Typically they just announce that they were aware of God and leave us to figure out how they could tell. But in many cases we can see pretty clearly what they are taking as identifying characteristics.

The "identifying characteristics" can, according to Alston, be properties such as power, love, and plenitude, but they can also include certain subjective reactions caused by the experiences, for example, feelings of peace or awe. Alston concludes:

> The general point is that if the object presents itself as being or doing what it would be natural or reasonable to expect God to be or do, and/or if one reacts as one would expect to react to the presence of God, that supports the claim that it is indeed God Who is perceptually presented. This means that there is a heavy reliance on the background system of Christian belief at this point of perceptual belief formation.[44]

---

44. Alston, *Perceiving God,* pp. 97, 98.

Pike is not very interested in epistemological questions because his focus is on the phenomenology of experiences. But not even he seems to think that we could acquire *knowledge* of God on the basis of perceptions of God unless we were able to specify how the experienced object was identified *as* God. Pike says that "were the reporter [of an experience as of God] to go on to claim that the experience was veridical — that is, that God was, in fact, present — we might *then* insist that he specify criteria by which the identification was made" (*Mystic Union,* p. 120). If this is necessary, then knowledge of God can only be gained from mystical experiences with the help of a background system of beliefs, derived from other sources, which can supply the relevant criteria for identification of God. For instance, if one's background beliefs tell one that God is powerful and loving, then one can expect God to appear as powerful and loving if he reveals himself in mystical experiences. One could then identify God with reference to these criteria. But without any background system of (justified) beliefs about God, one would not know what properties to look for in the identification of God.

In this section I have argued against the idea that mystical perceptions of God can provide knowledge of God without the support of other sources of knowledge, such as public revelation or natural theology. This would require experiences in which God is presented to us *as God*. We have seen that this is a rather shaky thought at best. Alston does not defend it. Even Pike denies that experiences that are phenomenally of God could responsibly be taken as veridical unless the subject can specify how she recognized God as God.

My conclusion is that "mystical perception" probably cannot stand on its own feet as a source of knowledge of God. It is at least very doubtful that mystical perception can provide the subject with knowledge of the divine identity of the object of experience. I do not, of course, claim to have demonstrated the *impossibility* of acquiring this kind of knowledge experientially. My argument has not been intended to exclude the possibility of rare mystical experiences in which the normal boundaries of human cognitive capacities are transcended in a more or less miraculous way. Such experiences may, for all we know, exist; but against the background of the argument of this section, it is reasonable to conclude that a theology that relies *only* on such experiences for knowledge of God would have a very narrow and problematic base.

In summary, some theories of revelation as "inner experience" (such as Rahner's) deny that experiences of the transcendent have a conceptual structure but claim that they nevertheless can mediate knowledge of God. I have argued that this claim is incoherent. Other theories (e.g., Schleiermacher's) deny that religious experience mediates knowledge of God, but claim that it can nevertheless mediate a personal relationship with God. I have argued that this idea is incoherent as well. Finally, we have seen that "mystical perception" probably cannot provide knowledge that the God of theism exists.

3.4 Revelation as Dialectical Presence

Avery Dulles uses this label for the views of revelation represented by Karl Barth, Emil Brunner, and Rudolf Bultmann. These theologians (I will treat Barth and Brunner here) are very different from each other, and the habit of grouping them together under such headings as "dialectical theology" or "neo-orthodoxy" can be questioned. However, there are some interesting similarities among them when it comes to their views of revelation. They all emphasize that our relationship to God depends on revelation, and that revelation is God's speaking his Word to us, a Word that is identical to himself. The channel through which this Word — and hence God himself — meets us is, importantly, the Bible and church proclamation.

The dialectical theologians also insist that we not identify the Bible with revelation. The biblical word can be the medium of revelation, but it is not itself revelation. Indeed, commentators and critics often ascribe to the theologians mentioned above the radical view that revelation has nothing to do with "propositional knowledge." Dulles, for instance, characterizes their view this way: "While the written and spoken word are media of revelation, the content of revelation, for these authors, is not the conceptual meaning of the language."[45] Carl Henry thinks that Karl Barth "denied the propositional nature of revelation and thereby forfeited its objective truth-character."[46] For Brunner, according to Dulles, "the truth of revelation ... is not propositional; it ... is not information about something."[47] Stanley Grenz and Roger Olson claim that "the main point of Brunner's doctrine

---

45. Dulles, *Models of Revelation*, pp. 87-88.
46. Carl Henry, *God, Revelation and Authority,* vol. 3 (Wheaton, IL: Crossway Books, 1999), p. 432
47. Dulles, *Models of Revelation*, p. 88.

of revelation is that in it God does not communicate something about himself, but himself."[48]

According to many commentators, then, the dialectical theologians make a point of contrasting the idea that revelation is an encounter with God with the traditional view that revelation involves propositions about God. We have already seen that such a contrast is based on a misconception. We can only *consciously* encounter a reality by grasping propositions about it. An encounter with some reality that does *not* involve grasping some propositions about that reality is not an encounter that happens on the personal/conscious level. Encountering the surgeon's knife in a state of anesthesia is an encounter with a reality (the knife) that is not mediated by any grasp of propositions. But this is not an encounter that happens on the personal level. The subject certainly encounters the knife, but he does not do so *as* a subject. It is probably true that we encounter God on such a subpersonal level, too. If God exists, then even people who do not believe in God are sustained in being by God, and thus encounter God as a reality that suspends them in being. But this relationship to God is not one that takes place on a conscious level.

If the dialectical theologians deny, as many commentators claim, that we encounter God by grasping propositions about him, then the dialectical theologians are wrong. I am not at all sure, however, that this is the position of the dialectical theologians. Let us start with Brunner.

3.4.1 Emil Brunner

Brunner says that the Word of God is a person, Jesus Christ, and hence not identical to any human words. "[Jesus Christ] is not 'speech,' or a summary of sentences like the prophetic utterances. . . . He is quite different from a speech, namely, God Himself present, acting in His own Person."[49] "The fact that he is 'here,' that He has 'come,' that we may see and know Him in His action and His suffering, in His speech and in His being . . . this is the revelation, the self-manifestation of God" (pp. 15-16).

In order for humans to be able to perceive Jesus Christ *as* God's self-

---

48. Grenz and Olson, *20th Century Theology*, p. 81.
49. Emil Brunner, *The Christian Doctrine of God: Dogmatics,* vol. 1 (Philadelphia: Westminster, 1950), p. 23. Hereafter, page references to this work appear in parentheses within the text.

manifestation, they need the help of God himself, which he grants through the inner testimony of the Spirit. "The Spirit of God testified *in their hearts* that Jesus is the Christ" (p. 29).

> It was a new particular intervention of God which opened the eyes of Peter to the Mystery of the Messiah, so that he could then confess Him as the Son of the Living God. And the same process of revelation takes place wherever Christ manifests Himself to a human being as the living Lord and is received in faith. (pp. 19-20)

In order to encounter the living Lord, those of us who live at the present time need the biblical testimony. Biblical sentences, however, are not revelation.[50] Jesus himself, about whom the Bible testifies, and the inner testimony of the Spirit, which helps us see Jesus *as* God, are the objective and the subjective elements of revelation (p. 19).

This account of revelation is surely compatible with the claim that revelation includes a transmission of propositional knowledge about God. If Jesus is the self-manifestation of God, and if God helps us to this insight by means of the inner testimony of the Spirit, then God has (non-manifestationally) imparted knowledge of at least one proposition to us, namely, *that Jesus is God's self-manifestation.* If, on the other hand, the inner testimony of God has no propositional content, then it cannot be *about* anything, and hence not about Jesus, and it cannot ascribe some property to Jesus, such as his being God's self-manifestation. The proposition expressed by the sentence "Jesus is God's self-manifestation" is, of course, not identical to any biblical sentence, since propositions are not sentences.

There is, however, a misconception among certain theologians that propositions *are* sentences — and composed of words. Grenz and Olson, for instance, write about Brunner that he "wished to eliminate any immanence of revelation in human propositions — even divinely 'inspired' ones. To equate revelation with *human words* would deny its transcendent

---

50. Brunner seems to accept, however, that the speech of the prophets in the Old Testament was one form of revelation. "In the prophetic revelation the revelation of the Old Covenant attains its highest point; the prophetic teaching is the standard and characteristic form of this revelation" (p. 22). This is a form of revelation where God speaks in human words, which is, however, surpassed by the revelation in Christ. "Hence now the old is over and past, even the Old Covenant with all the forms of revelation proper to it" (p. 23). "The Word which has been formulated in human speech is now only revelation in an indirect sense; it is revelation as witness to Him" (p. 27).

quality over against everything finite."[51] Here Grenz and Olson seem to assume that propositions are words, or at least composed of words. But one can surely deny that human words are involved in the process of revelation while one accepts that propositions are revealed.

It seems to me that Brunner's account of revelation entails that God communicates propositional knowledge to humans, that the media of revelation (at least sometimes) are not natural signs of the actualities revealed, and that Brunner is thus committed to a form of propositional revelation as defined by Wolterstorff.[52] Furthermore, it seems that Brunner has no problem with this. He says:

> [B]efore there can be a legitimate human witness, speech about God, genuine, valid testimony to Jesus Christ, there *must* be a Divine testimony to Him, which makes use of human forms of thought and speech — and it is precisely this that is meant by the witness of the Holy Spirit "in" the human spirit. (p. 29)

"God stoops down to us when He Himself speaks to us in human speech, in the witness of His Spirit, who bears witness to the Son" (pp. 29-30). "Man experiences the working of the Holy Spirit as a real utterance of God in language and thought familiar to mankind" (p. 30).

It is true that Brunner distinguishes between doctrines and confessions of faith, and he claims that the development of doctrine takes place by moving away from the "Thou-relation" to God. This is a transition "from the personal sphere to the impersonal" (p. 38). The difference between confessions of faith and doctrinal statements is a difference of attitude: "Doctrine is no longer a spontaneous, personal response . . . to the Word of God, but already . . . reflective speech *about* God" (p. 38). But I have found no reason to think that Brunner sees the transition from confessions of faith to doctrine as a transition from the nonpropositional to the propositional.

So the most reasonable construal of Brunner's position is that it entails a form of propositional revelation: God literally speaks in human words, or implants certain beliefs (e.g., that Jesus is the Christ) in the believer's mind. The question of whether Brunner himself is always fully aware of the implications of his own position is not my concern here.

---

51. Grenz and Olson, *20th Century Theology*, p. 82 (italics added).
52. The Holy Spirit, who "testified in their hearts that Jesus is the Christ," could presumably not reveal that Jesus is the Christ by presenting a *natural* sign of this state of affairs. However, see my discussion of Barth at the end of the next section (3.4.2).

3.4.2 Karl Barth

God, according to Barth, reveals himself by speaking. Revelation is a "divine speech-act" that is identical to Jesus Christ, the Word made flesh.[53] Scripture and church proclamation are witnesses to and bearers of this divine speech-act, without themselves being revelation. Barth asks: "What does the revelation attested in Holy Scripture and proclaimed in preaching and sacrament say to me? What is revealed to me in it? 'God with us' is how we stated generally the content of God's Word."[54]

Scripture and proclamation can sometimes *become* God's Word (p. 110). This happens whenever God wants it to happen, and in such events revelation takes place. "The Bible is God's Word to the extent that God causes it to be His Word, to the extent that He speaks through it" (p. 109). When God speaks through the Bible and proclamation, Jesus Christ is himself presented to us through these media (p. 121). But "the Bible is not in itself and as such" revelation, and neither is church proclamation (p. 111).

God is also involved in our *reception* of revelation. This is the action of the Spirit. "God, the Revealer, is identical with his act in revelation [i.e., Christ] and also identical with its effect" (p. 296). As John Webster puts it, "In the work of Jesus Christ and the Holy Spirit, God is both the objective and subjective reality and possibility of revelation. Revelation and its reception proceed alike from the triune God."[55]

Barth unhesitatingly says that revelation provides knowledge of God (p. 187). The Word of God becomes knowable for humans as a result of revelation (p. 188). But what does that mean? Bruce McCormack claims that Barth's view of revelation-knowledge must be understood against the background of the Kantian tradition. When Barth in 1915 moved away from the Schleiermachian project, he wanted, according to McCormack, to "articulate a theological epistemology which would more fully integrate with theoretical knowing the special kind of knowledge proper to faith."

> Revelation, Barth now wanted to say, occurs within the realm of theoretical knowing. If it nevertheless remains a "special" kind of knowing

---

53. John Webster, *Barth,* 2nd ed. (London: Continuum, 2004), p. 55.
54. Karl Barth, *Church Dogmatics,* vol. I.1: *The Doctrine of the Word of God* (Edinburgh: T & T Clark, 1975), p. 160. Hereafter, page references to this work appear in parentheses within the text.
55. Webster, *Barth,* p. 62.

> . . . it is because it has its source in an act of God by means of which the human knowing apparatus described by Kant is "commandeered" . . . by God.[56]

So the knowledge involved in revelation must be understood as robust, "real" knowledge. Theoretical knowledge for Kant is, of course, propositional knowledge. The problem for Barth, who moved within the Kantian framework, is that God, as transcendent, is "unintuitable" and thus cannot be an object of theoretical knowledge. McCormack summarizes Barth's solution to this problem thus: "If the unintuitable God is truly to be known, God must make Godself intuitable." However, God must not make himself intuitable in such a way that he is transformed into a creature among others. Rather, God must make himself intuitable in such a way that "the unintuitability proper to God is not set aside" (p. 28).

It is not until later that Barth finds a way of working out this solution. The key is the doctrine of the incarnation, understood in accordance with a classical model of Christology. If the life of Jesus of Nazareth is God's life, then "his intuitability is God's intuitability" (p. 32). However, since there is no "divinization" of the human nature of Christ, "the life of Jesus does not *in itself* impart the knowledge of God. . . . In itself it is instead a riddle, a mystery, a veiling." "Thus," McCormack says, "God remains unintuitable even as God enters fully into intuitability. God remains unintuitable as the hidden, never directly to be recognized, Subject of the life of Jesus" (p. 33).

But this means that "a third element must be introduced." "The Holy spirit must make the veil transparent by giving us the eyes of faith to see that which is hidden beneath the surface" (p. 33).

The thing that concerns us here is how propositions figure in Barth's account of revelation. Wolterstorff says that, for Barth, "in Jesus Christ, *God* is revealed. Not something *about* God, or some aspect *of* God; but *God*."[57] Does this mean that revelation, for Barth, is not mediated by propositions? It cannot mean this if our knowledge about God is "within the realm of *theoretical* knowing," as Barth wants to say, according to McCormack. We can agree with Wolterstorff that revelation for Barth is God's self-revelation; thus, what is revealed is God himself. But this does not

---

56. McCormack, *Orthodox and Modern,* p. 28. Hereafter, page references to this work appear in parentheses within the text.

57. Nicholas Wolterstorff, *Divine Discourse: Philosophical Reflections on the Claim That God Speaks* (Cambridge: Cambridge University Press, 1995), p. 64.

exclude that the awareness/knowledge of God imparted by revelation has a propositional structure. We may know God *in and through* knowing propositions, as we indeed know all other realities. Thus there is no contradiction here.

When Jesus Christ is revealed to us through the media of Scripture and proclamation, this revelation has the character of an *event*. As we have seen, Scripture and proclamation are not in themselves revelation, but they sometimes mediate revelation. Does this event-character of (subjective) revelation contradict the claim that revelation has a propositional content? I cannot see that it does. Barth says that the Word of God must be acknowledged by the human hearer if revelation is to be achieved (p. 214). This acknowledgment is itself the work of God. Barth talks about "the free action of God in and by which He causes it to be true to us and for us here and now that the biblical word of man is His own Word" (p. 110).

> Subjective revelation can consist only in the fact that objective revelation, the one truth which cannot be added to or bypassed, comes to man and is recognised and acknowledged by man. And that is the work of the Holy Spirit.

Objective revelation is the fact that "'God was in Christ reconciling the world to himself.' The work of the Holy Spirit is that our blind eyes are opened and that . . . we recognise and acknowledge that it is so" (p. 239).

This means that the human subject's acknowledgment, which is necessary for subjective revelation, is also (like objective revelation) dependent on divine action. This is why revelation must have the character of event, since the necessary divine action is not something the human subject can possess and control. We acknowledge Christ as God only when God makes us do that. But this, of course, does not mean that the proposition expressed by "God was in Christ" is *true* only when humans acknowledge it as true. It is always true. (Barth says that "[i]t is true that God is with us in Christ . . . even if we ourselves do not perceive it" (p. 238). However, it is not true *for us* unless God causes it to be so. In other words, it is not within our own power to hold that proposition true, and hence not in our own power to know that proposition. (In order to know that *p*, one must hold *p* true.)

So revelation can be an event and yet have as its content propositions that are always true. Furthermore, it seems clear that the Spirit's "opening of our eyes" involves our coming to know certain propositions. About this event, Barth says that "what takes place at this point does involve a conviction, an opening up, an uncovering of the truth of objective revelation before the eyes and ears and in the heart of man. It means that he himself recognises it to be true and therefore regards it as true and valid for himself" (p. 238). Can one be convinced of something, or recognize something as true, unless what one is convinced of or recognizes as true has a propositional structure? No. Moreover, Barth says that when the human subject recognizes objective revelation to be true, "[i]t means that his *reason* apprehends it" (p. 238 [italics added]).

Therefore, Barth's account of revelation entails that propositions are revealed. This in itself does not mean, however, that Barth is committed to some form of *propositional revelation*. Propositions are among the entities revealed in *manifestational* as well as in propositional forms of revelation. What distinguishes manifestational from propositonal (nonmanifestational) revelation is the means of revelation. In manifestational revelation, the means of revelation is a natural sign of the actuality revealed, whereas the means in propositional revelation is not a natural sign. Revelation by speaking and "Lockean" revelation are, as we remember, prominent examples of propositional revelation.

Let us now see whether Barth is committed to acknowledging the occurrence of some form of propositional revelation. As we remember, God's Spirit reveals to us *that God was in Christ.* Can the Spirit reveal to us that God was in Christ by manifestation — that is, by "showing" us that God was in Christ? One would think not. Barth agrees, as we remember, that God remains "unintuitable" even as he is incarnated in Christ. Within the realm of history, only Christ's human nature can be perceived. However, to complicate matters, Barth also — according to McCormack — holds that the Holy Spirit can make the impossible possible. By giving us "the eyes of faith," the Sprit can make the "veil" transparent and allow us to perceive (intuit) Christ *as* God.[58] "At the end of the day," McCormack says, "Barth is still making an appeal to an exercise of the power of God to disclose to us something which is unintuitable to us."[59]

It is hard to argue against appeals to divine power. We should, however, be aware of the extremely problematic implications of Barth's view (if, indeed, it is his view). To perceive something *as God* means to perceive

---

58. To "perceive" or "intuit" Christ as God, in this context, means to have Christ's divinity *directly manifested to one* (through the Spirit's action of "making the veil transparent").

59. McCormack, *Orthodox and Modern,* p. 34.

that x is God. This, in turn, means to perceive that x has always existed and will always exist, that x exists necessarily, that everything else that exists is dependent on x, that x knows all true propositions, and so on.[60] When Barth claims (if he does) that the Spirit can make us perceive or "intuit" Christ as God, he presupposes the occurrence of a form of perception/intuition that he himself admits is inconceivable.

I do not know whether this really is Barth's view. Many commentators seem to assume that it is.[61] But Barth does not *need* to claim that the Spirit discloses the unintuitable God. An alternative and much less problematic view is that the Spirit, without "showing" us Christ's divine nature, gives rise to a conviction in us that "God was in Christ." The "eyes of faith" that the Spirit gives us can then be understood metaphorically as a new understanding of (belief about) Christ, imparted supernaturally to us by the Spirit, rather than as a capacity to paradoxically "intuit" God.

If Barth would subscribe to this latter view (which he may very well have done), he would be a proponent of propositional revelation. The means of revelation is, according to the latter construal, not a manifestation of the actuality revealed (Christ's divinity), and hence not a natural sign of it.[62] The means of revelation is, instead, either the direct, supernatural transmission of a proposition to the believer's mind (Lockean revelation) or a verbal assertion of a proposition about Christ by the Spirit, or something similar.

A fact that is worth remembering in this context is that most people's knowledge of Christ's human nature is not acquired from a direct confrontation with it. Jesus' human body was revealed manifestationally only to a limited number of people who lived in the first century.[63] We who live

---

60. This is at least necessary if the "intuition" of God is to be capable of providing us with knowledge of God without presupposing a problematic (from Barth's perspective) background knowledge about God's existence and about some "intuitable" properties that would allow us to identify him.

61. Avery Dulles, for instance, says that "for Barth, the Word and the Spirit, as complementary aspects of revelation, *manifest* God as triune" (Dulles, *Models of Revelation*, p. 92 [italics added]).

62. The term "natural sign" can be confusing in this context, since Christ's divine nature (which is the actuality revealed) is not a "natural" but a "supernatural" entity. However, a natural sign of Christ's divine nature is simply something that is naturally (i.e., without the prior establishing of a convention or the like) taken as a sign of Christ's divine nature. The direct manifestation (presence, mystically perceived appearance) of Christ's divine nature would hence (if such a manifestation were possible) be a natural sign of Christ's divine nature.

63. This is true also given the "real presence" of Christ in the Eucharist. Christ's body

today know about the existence of the human being Jesus of Nazareth on the basis of testimony only. If this is the case, then it seems unnecessary to insist that Christ's *divine* nature must be manifestationally revealed to all Christians, despite the fact that this is impossible "within history."

My conclusion is that Barth, according to the most reasonable construal of his view, is committed to some form of propositional revelation.[64] Whether Barth saw himself as thus committed is not our interest here.

3.5 Revelation as New Awareness

According to this model, "revelation occurs when human powers are raised to their highest pitch of activity." The product of revelation is not knowledge but a "new mode of human consciousness."[65] Gregory Baum writes:

> The Christian message is not information about the divine.... It is, rather, salvational truth; it raises man's consciousness; it constitutes a new awareness in man through which he sees the world in a new light and commits himself to a new kind of action.[66]

For William Thompson, "revelation primordially means our expansion of consciousness."[67]

It is rather obvious that if revelation only produces a new awareness through which we see ourselves and the world in a new light, then revelation does not make it possible for us to relate in a personal way to God. A new awareness of ourselves and the world is not, as such, an awareness of

---

is not *revealed* to us (*as* Christ's body) in the Eucharist. We receive something that appears not to be Christ's body, but we accept in faith that it is.

64. We saw in the introduction (chap. 1, n. 12) that Barth is reluctant to identify the word of God with any specific statements in human language, such as those of the Bible or human preachers. This makes it uncertain whether Barth can consistently claim that God *speaks* to humans — in the literal sense of "speaks." There are, however, other forms of propositional revelation besides revelation by speaking. So even if divine speech in the literal sense does not, in the last analysis, figure in Barth's doctrine of revelation, that doctrine can still contain elements of propositional revelation.

65. Dulles, *Models of Revelation,* pp. 98, 100.

66. Gregory Baum, foreword to Andrew Greeley, *The New Agenda* (Garden City, NY: Doubleday, 1973), p. 16.

67. William Thompson, *Christ and Consciousness: Exploring Christ's Contribution to Human Consciousness; The Origins and Development of Christian Consciousness* (New York: Paulist Press, 1966), p. 172.

God, unless God is nothing more than the world and the self, or "our expansion of consciousness."[68] A new awareness of the world and self might, of course, be *caused* by God. But if we are not made aware *that* it is caused by God, then the new awareness does not, in itself, help us relate to God on a conscious, personal level.

May it not be possible to infer, then, from the fact that one's consciousness has been extremely expanded, that God is acting on one's mind? I do not think so. It is difficult to see how an experience of having one's consciousness extremely expanded could justify the belief that the cause of the expansion is a personal reality on whom everything finite depends for its existence. Some additional premises are needed for us to arrive at this conclusion.

On the other hand, if God, simultaneous with bringing about an expansion of the subject's consciousness, also imparts the insight that this expansion is due to the action of God, or that this action constitutes God's self-communication, then God has in a supernatural way transferred knowledge of a proposition. We are then dealing with propositional revelation of the Lockean variety.

This criticism of the "new awareness" model will probably appear irrelevant to most of its advocates. The model's typical proponents do not conceive of God as a personal reality who can be disclosed as an object of knowledge and thereby figure as one pole in a divine-human personal relationship. God is "the horizon rather than the object" of human knowledge, experience, and relationality.[69] According to Paul Tillich, for example, most of our talk about God is symbolic, and "a real symbol points to an object which never can become an object."[70] Religious symbols "must

---

68. Gregory Baum seems to represent something like this position. He claims that every sentence about God may be translated into a sentence "dealing with human possibilities promised to man and changes of consciousness offered to him" (Gregory Baum, *New Horizon: Theological Essays* [New York: Paulist Press, 1972], p. 56). Compare Paul Tillich, who, in a similar spirit, recommends that we "translate it [the concept of God] and speak of the depth of your life and the source of your ultimate concern and of what you take seriously without reservation" (Tillich, *The Shaking of the Foundations* [New York: Charles Scribner's Sons, 1948], p. 57).

69. Dulles, *Models of Revelation*, p. 102. The view of God as "horizon" is compatible with the orthodox view of God as personal agent. Karl Rahner, for instance, thinks of God as "the infinite horizon of being" (Rahner, *Foundations of Christian Faith*, p. 34), but also as personal (pp. 71-75) and as an object of knowledge (pp. 51-70).

70. Tillich says that all statements about God except the statement "God is being-itself" are symbolic (Paul Tillich, *Systematic Theology*, vol. 1 [Chicago: University of Chicago

express an object [God] that by its very nature transcends everything in the world that is split into subjectivity and objectivity."[71] However, a dialog between God and a human community requires a God who is more than an "ultimate mystery beyond the relationship of subject and object."[72] It requires a personal God, and it seems that God, for Tillich, is not personal. God is merely the "ground" of the personal.[73] As Guy Hammond writes, "In what appears to be the main current of Tillich's thought, God is the ground of the personal in the sense of the power of actualizing self-transcendence and personhood in man, but he is not a personal center."[74]

Tillich and many other proponents of the "new awareness" model of revelation hence work within a theological paradigm that denies that revelation mediates and conditions a personal, mutual divine-human encounter in the sense that is relevant for this book.[75] Their understanding of this model is thus of little help when it comes to accounting for the possibility of this kind of encounter.

3.6 "Postliberal" Views of Revelation

"Postliberal theology" names a highly differentiated movement in contemporary Anglo-American theology. The term, which famously appeared in George Lindbeck's *The Nature of Doctrine,* was first associated with the so-called Yale School.[76] It can, however, be used in a much wider sense

---

Press, 1951], p. 239). It is not clear, however, whether he consistently clings to this view. Rowe claims that Tillich changed his mind on the symbolic status of statements about God (and especially the statement that God is being-itself) at least twice in print (William Rowe, "The Meaning of 'God' in Tillich's Theology," *The Journal of Religion* 42, no. 4 [1962]: 274-86, esp. 278-280).

71. Paul Tillich, "The Religious Symbol," *Daedalus* 87, no. 3 (1958): 3-21; 5.

72. Keith Ward, *Religion and Revelation: A Theology of Revelation in the World's Religions* (Oxford: Oxford University Press, 1994), p. 230. Ward classifies Tillich's view of revelation in the "revelation as inner experience" category.

73. Tillich, *Systematic Theology,* vol. 1, p. 245.

74. Guy Hammond, "Tillich on the Personal God," *The Journal of Religion* 44, no. 4 (1964): 289-93; 292.

75. However, nothing prevents theologians who emphasize a personal relationship with God from claiming that an essential *element* of revelation is the "expansion of human consciousness." It is possible to combine the "new awareness" model with other models of revelation, as exemplified by, e.g., the theologies of Karl Rahner and Vatican II.

76. George Lindbeck, *The Nature of Doctrine: Religion and Theology in a Postliberal Age* (Philadelphia: Westminster, 1984).

(as I intend it here) so as to include theologians such as John Milbank and the Radical Orthodoxy movement.[77] Postliberals have often been rather reluctant to talk about "revelation."[78] Some postliberal thinkers, however, have elaborated on the topic. Their views do not seem to fit naturally into any of Avery Dulles's models of revelation, which makes it necessary to treat them separately. I will review two postliberal views.

3.6.1 Ronald Thiemann

Ronald Thiemann claims that the concept of revelation belongs in the intratheological context of explaining and defending the notion of God's prevenience: the idea that "our thought and speech about God are not simply the free creations of human imagination but are developed in obedient response to God's prior initiative." A theory of revelation should attempt to solve problems connected to this idea, mainly the problem of how to account for "both the priority and relation of God to our linguistic framework." What a theory of revelation should *not* attempt to do is explain how Christian beliefs are justified. To conceive of revelation as an epistemological concept — part of an epistemological theory — is to commit the mistake of confusing rational justification and causal explanation.[79] This is a mistake that many modern theologians have made, according to

---

77. The ongoing influence of the Yale School has been likened to a river delta (Paul DeHart, *The Trial of the Witnesses: The Rise and Decline of Postliberal Theology* [Malden, MA: Blackwell, 2006], p. 45), and it is only in this sense — and from a bird's-eye perspective — that Milbank and the Yale School can be placed under the same rubric. Even though Milbank is critical of the Yale School in several respects (see John Milbank, *Theology and Social Theory: Beyond Secular Reason* [Cambridge, MA: Basil Blackwell, 1990], pp. 382-88), he seems nevertheless to perceive "post-liberal" as a term of positive appraisal: "Has there really been in this century, at least within Protestantism, *any* post-liberal theology? And would not such a theology have to challenge . . . the autonomy of philosophy, and articulate a *theological* account of what it is to be and to know in general?" (Milbank, Catherine Pickstock, and Graham Ward, eds., *Radical Orthodoxy: A New Theology* [London: Routledge, 1999], p. 22). Milbank clearly regards his own and Radical Orthodoxy's vision as more deserving of the label "post-liberal" than that of the Yale School.

78. Stanley Hauerwas, for instance, says that "the very idea that the Bible is revealed . . . is a claim that creates more trouble than it is worth" (Hauerwas, *A Community of Character: Toward a Constructive Christian Social Ethic* [Notre Dame, IN: University of Notre Dame Press, 1981], p. 57).

79. Ronald Thiemann, *Revelation and Theology: The Gospel as Narrated Promise* (Notre Dame, IN: University of Notre Dame Press, 1985), pp. 4, 6, 96, 43.

Thiemann. They have assumed that the purpose of a theory of revelation is to show how Christian beliefs are justified in terms of their "first cause" — their *origin,* or source — whether this first cause is conceived of as divine testimony confirmed by miracles (Locke) or universal religious experience (Schleiermacher). Thiemann identifies (and dismisses) theories of this type as "foundationalist."

Therefore, if we are interested in how Thiemann understands Christian beliefs to be justified, we should not look to his doctrine of revelation. Instead, Thiemann's answer to the question of epistemic justification is to be found in his commitment to a general philosophical theory, namely, *epistemological coherentism.* Coherence theories of epistemic justification claim that justification is a function exclusively of the relationship between beliefs, and that the relationship between our beliefs and something "outside" the web of beliefs — such as perceptual experiences — is irrelevant for justification. This is why, according to Thiemann, the project of trying to justify Christian beliefs by referring to their origin or source ("first cause") is doomed to fail.

Thiemann's philosophical presuppositions and commitments are problematic in several respects. It is not, for instance, the case that any epistemological theory that accounts for the justification of empirical beliefs in terms of their origin or source (such as experience) is guilty of confusing rational justification and causal explanation. John McDowell has shown that experience can — in fact, must — figure into the justification of empirical beliefs and that this view does not entail the confusion Thiemann points to. McDowell's criticism of the "unconstrained coherentism" of philosophers such as Richard Rorty and Donald Davidson uncovers the problems that plague the coherentist framework that Thiemann and some other postliberal theologians work within.[80]

However, a critique of Thiemann's coherentism and his other philosophical commitments is out of place here. The purpose of this chapter is to show that anybody who wants to argue that Christian beliefs are (or could be) justified must appeal to propositional revelation or a potent natural

---

80. For McDowell's critique, see John McDowell, *Mind and World,* esp. "Afterword, Part I." Examples of other postliberal theologians who work within a coherentist framework are Bruce Marshall, *Trinity and Truth* (Cambridge: Cambridge University Press, 2000); William Placher, *Unapologetic Theology: A Christian Voice in a Pluralistic Conversation* (Louisville: Westminster John Knox, 1989); Nancey Murphy, *Beyond Liberalism and Fundamentalism: How Modern and Postmodern Philosophy Set the Theological Agenda* (Valley Forge, PA: Trinity Press International, 1996).

theology. This contention also holds given a coherentist view of epistemic justification. In order to see that Thiemann and other theologians who work on the basis of coherentist presuppositions cannot avoid relying on propositional revelation or a potent natural theology, we must very briefly reflect on the nature of coherentist views of justification.

Coherentist theories of epistemic justification claim that a belief is justified if it is part of a coherent system of beliefs. The notion of coherence is defined in different terms by different theories. Everyone agrees, however, that coherence involves more than just logical consistency. According to Laurence BonJour, "coherence has to do with the mutual inferability of the beliefs in the system." Furthermore, "relations of explanation are one central ingredient in coherence."[81] These characterizations of coherence by BonJour would, I believe, be accepted by most coherence theorists.

We have seen that it could be possible to infer the existence of a very powerful spiritual being from the occurrence of certain remarkable historical events (for instance, the events of the history of Israel) and/or nonverbal religious experiences of various kinds.[82] It is not possible, however, to infer from the occurrence of such events and nonverbal religious experiences that the spiritual being is infinite, omnipotent, omniscient, perfectly good, and such that everything finite depends on it for its existence — that is, that this being is God. If remarkable events in history and religious experiences are our only reasons for believing in the existence of a certain powerful spiritual being (let us call him "SB"), then the following claim holds: A system of beliefs, A, which contains beliefs about SB to the effect that he is very powerful, very knowledgeable, and very good is necessarily *more* coherent than a system B, which is exactly similar to A in every respect, except that SB is also believed to be *God* in B. Why is A necessarily more coherent? Because the existence of a very powerful spiritual being can possibly be inferred from other beliefs (such as beliefs about historical events and religious experiences), while God's existence cannot. Since coherence has to do with the mutual inferability of beliefs, A is more coherent than B.

This means that there can be no coherentist justification of belief in

---

81. Laurence BonJour, *The Structure of Empirical Knowledge* (Cambridge, MA: Harvard University Press, 1985), p. 95.

82. By "nonverbal" religious experiences I mean experiences in which God merely manifests his presence and does not communicate by speaking.

God if God has only revealed himself *manifestationally* (by means of historical events and nonverbal religious experiences).[83] A person who has the beliefs of system B could easily revise that system so that it becomes identical with A, just by abandoning the belief that SB is God. Such a revision would make the system more coherent, and it seems to be what any reasonable coherence theory of epistemic justification must dictate.

However, if we suppose that the systems A and B contain beliefs to the effect that the powerful spiritual being *has spoken* (i.e., that some propositional revelation has occurred), then the situation may become different. Suppose that both systems contain the belief that SB has declared, "I am omniscient and omnipotent," and that the belief that it really is SB who has declared this is explanatorily integrated into the system as a whole. (This could be the case if, for instance, the declaration were to be accompanied by certain remarkable events that seem to elude explanation except in terms of the hypothesis that a powerful spiritual being has acted.) Then it is no longer *necessarily* the case that B is less coherent than A. The hypothesis that SB *is* omniscient and omnipotent might explain why SB has *said* that he is infinite and omnipotent better than the alternative hypotheses that SB is lying or mistaken. This might be true, for instance, if there is evidence for the morally good character and epistemic competence of SB, evidence that would make it unlikely that SB would lie or make unjustified claims. The explanatory power of belief in the trustworthiness of SB could, under these circumstances, significantly increase the coherence of the belief system as a whole. The belief that SB has spoken would also provide system B (which claims that SB is God) with an explanation of how knowledge about the "godhood" of SB has become available (namely, by testimony). No such explanation existed in system B in the previously imagined scenario in which SB only manifested his existence by historical events or nonverbal experiences. And "relations of explanation" are, as we remember, a central ingredient in coherence. In the scenario in which SB speaks, it is consequently possible for B to be at least as coherent as, or even more coherent than, A. What makes the difference between the two scenarios is belief in propositional revelation.

This shows that theologians who advocate a coherentist account of the justification of Christian beliefs cannot thereby avoid assuming the occurrence of some kind of propositional revelation (God speaking or implanting conceptual contents in the minds of believers). Unless they

---

83. Assuming that there is no potent natural theology.

assume the existence of propositional revelation, the belief that the spiritual being whom they worship is God will "hang in the air," significantly reducing the coherence of their overall system of beliefs.[84] Another way of integrating the belief in God into the system, of course, would be to posit the existence of a potent natural theology. But this is an option that Thiemann and other postliberal coherentists would probably find rather unattractive.

If we turn from these considerations about coherentist justification of Christian beliefs to Thiemann's intratheological, nonepistemological account of revelation, we find that the latter clearly entails that God speaks in a literal sense. Thiemann understands revelation in terms of the notion of "narrated promise." The narratives of the Gospels proclaim, according to Thiemann, God's promise to forgive sins, justify the believer, and give the believer eternal life. This is what a doctrine of revelation should focus on. The advantage of understanding revelation in terms of *promise* is that "the speech-act of promising provides a category which will allow a consistent conception of God's relation and priority to our framework of beliefs." This is because "promise is a relational category which requires both a speaker and a hearer but grants primacy in that relation solely to the one who promises."

It is clear that Thiemann does not use the concept of "promise" in a metaphorical sense. He describes it as a speech-act, and he portrays God as the subject of this speech-act. He asks whether it is reasonable "to designate as God's speech-act a pardon or promise uttered by a human speaker,"

---

84. Bruce Marshall proposes a version of epistemological coherentism according to which the biblical narratives that identify Jesus in Trinitarian terms have "unrestricted epistemic primacy" for the Christian community. This means that Christians are committed to rejecting all beliefs that are inconsistent with these narratives. "Believing the gospel ... necessarily commits believers to a comprehensive view of the world centered epistemically on the gospel narrative itself" (Marshall, *Trinity and Truth*, p. 118). Can Marshall's version of coherentism, structured by specifically Christian epistemic priorities, explain how Christian beliefs are justified without reference to propositional revelation? It cannot (or at least it *does* not). One question that the Christian community, on pain of incoherence, must be capable of answering is why it holds the narratives that identify Jesus to be true. According to Marshall, the answer that the Christian community actually offers to this question refers to the action of the Holy Spirit. This action is "epistemically decisive: from it ultimately stems our willingness to hold true the narratives which identify Jesus and the triune God.... The Spirit elicits our assent to these central Christian beliefs" (Marshall, *Trinity and Truth*, p. 209). In other words, God, through the Spirit, makes us accept certain propositions (explicitly stated or entailed by the narratives) as true. This is propositional revelation.

and he answers this question in the affirmative with reference to the notion of double agency. When the human speaker in a liturgical act declares the forgiveness of sins, "these words are to be taken as the speech of God every time they are spoken."[85]

Thiemann thus assumes that God speaks in much the same way as a president speaks through the utterances of his ambassador or secretary (more about the notion of double agency in chapter 4).

3.6.2 John Milbank

According to John Milbank, revelation is not to be understood in terms of God's putting "new . . . information about God and what God has done" before our minds.[86] It consists, instead, of an "intensification of human understanding," a "special illumination of the intellect."[87] There can thus be no dualism between reason and revelation. Revelation (or faith) is simply a strengthening of reason.

Milbank views the propositional model of revelation (God's putting "new information" before our minds) as a Neo-Scholastic invention. The traditional view is the one Milbank defends, which he claims to find in the church fathers and Aquinas:

> In the Church Fathers or the early scholastics, both faith and reason are included within the more generic framework of participation in the mind of God: to reason truly one must be already illumined by God, while revelation itself is but a higher measure of such illumination, conjoined intrinsically and inseparably with a created event which symbolically discloses that transcendental reality, to which all created events to a lesser degree also point.[88]

For Aquinas (whom Milbank claims to follow in this respect),

---

85. Thiemann, *Revelation and Theology*, pp. 110, 105, 106.
86. John Milbank, "Intensities," *Modern Theology* 15, no. 4 (1999): 445-97, 450.
87. Milbank et al., *Radical Orthodoxy*, p. 5.
88. *Radical Orthodoxy*, p. 24. The mere fact that our reason is dependent on divine illumination for its workings does not, of course, explain how we can *know* that this is so (and thus that God exists). Our reason is dependent on our brains for its workings, but this does not mean that anybody who can use his reason automatically knows that he has a brain. Therefore, the Augustinian, participatory framework that underlies Milbank's view of revelation does not by itself explain our knowledge of God. See also the end of section 3.7.

the paradigmatic scene of revelation ... is represented by the instance of prophecy. Here a supernatural supplement of infused cognitive light is inseparably conjoined with some extraordinary sensory vision, miraculous event, or at least novel historical occurrence. Since all these latter three may only, as finite instances, mediate the divine in the shape of an enigma, the visions which they offer are partial and can be disclosed in their meaning — and so fully seen — only through acts of discursive interpretation (beginning with the prophet himself), as essential for faith as for reason.[89]

Milbank's view of revelation has a superficial similarity to the views of William Temple and Oscar Cullmann, which we encountered at the beginning of this chapter. Temple and Cullmann claim that God reveals himself through historical events. However, in order to read these events aright — to be able to identify them as divine acts — we need a special divine assistance. Our minds must be illumined by God in a special way. We saw that this view leads to a dilemma: if it is possible to infer, from the relevant historical events and background knowledge, that it is God who acts in them (and hence that God exists), then no divine illumination is, in principle, necessary. If it is not possible to infer from the events and background knowledge that it is God who acts, the "divine illumination" must include a communication of "extra information" to the one whose mind is illumined, and this would amount to propositional revelation. Unless the illumination includes a communication of extra information, it would in reality constitute a *corruption* of our minds. For God to induce us to draw conclusions that are not warranted by the evidence would be for him to induce us to reason fallaciously. The beliefs that result from such reasoning would be the result of cognitive error. This is not acceptable from a Christian viewpoint.

Milbank seems to claim, however, that it *is* possible to infer from the occurrence of "miraculous events" or "novel historical occurrences" that it is God who acts in them. This, I take it, is the meaning of his claim, quoted above, that these kinds of events can "mediate the divine in the shape of an enigma" and that the "meaning" of these events (their being expressive of God's will) is available "only through acts of discursive interpretation." Why, then, is divine illumination of the intellect necessary in order to "read" the events aright, to disclose their divine "meaning"? This

---

89. Milbank, "Intensities," p. 450.

is probably because our intellect, in its present, fallen state, is incapable of making the relevant inferences (in Milbank's terms, to interpret the meaning of the events correctly). Therefore, revelation simply makes us better thinkers, better "scientists."

Is this a reasonable view? As we saw before, the occurrence of miraculous and unusual events can possibly warrant the conclusion that some powerful nonphysical agent is at work in them. This can be said to be the "meaning" of such events. Maybe, in some cases, we are helped to *see* this meaning by a special divine illumination of our minds. However, no event — no matter how unusual, profound, dramatic, or miraculous — can, by virtue of its unusual, profound, dramatic, or miraculous character, warrant the conclusion that the spiritual agent behind it is infinite, omnipotent, omniscient, and such that everything finite is dependent on him. To claim that an extraordinary event, as such, can wear this type of "meaning" on its sleeve is extremely problematic.

Milbank, however, has a reply to this criticism available, a reply that draws on his participatory, Neo-Platonic ontology. According to Milbank, the world cannot be understood except with respect to its transcendent ground, its creator. It cannot be understood as it is "in itself." Why not? Because the world only exists as it participates in God. It does not have its being intrinsically, but is essentially dependent, essentially "gift." To think truly about the world, which is what reason is all about, one must think of the world as grounded in, or participating in, its transcendent creator. If reason fails to grasp finite realities as intrinsically related to the creator, then reason will have failed to achieve real knowledge. This means that "all real knowledge involves some revelation of the infinite [God] in the finite."[90] Milbank says that, "were one to attempt to comprehend a finite reality not as created, that is to say not in relation to God, then no truth . . . could ensue, since finite realities are of themselves nothing and only what is can be true."[91] Knowledge of God is hence implicit in *all* real knowledge.[92] By knowing that grass is green, I implicitly know that God exists, even though this implicit knowledge may remain implicit unless God illuminates my intellect in a special way.

This means that the miraculous or unusual character of historical

---

90. Milbank et al., *Radical Orthodoxy*, p. 5.
91. Milbank, "Intensities," 449-50.
92. This has a basis in Aquinas's axiom that "all knowers know God implicitly in all they know."

events is not what gives such events a capacity to reveal God. What gives them this capacity is the fact that they participate in God. But this is true of *all* finite events and objects. All finite realities have, when truly comprehended, the capacity to reveal God.

Milbank's view on this subject is close to the First Vatican Council's. The Council insists that "God can be known with certainty from the things that were created." A difference between Milbank and Vatican I, however, is that the Council adds, "through the *natural* light of human reason."[93] For Milbank, only an intellect that has received a special divine illumination is capable of knowing God from the consideration of created things.

Milbank's view thus portrays divine grace as necessary for knowledge of God, while Vatican I seems to claim that God can be known to some extent without the assistance of grace. For our present purpose, however, this difference is less important than the fundamental similarity: both Milbank and the Vatican Council are extremely optimistic about the possibility for reason to know God from the consideration of created things. For Milbank, this knowledge is not merely "natural," since it depends on grace. Remember, though, that grace does not supply *new information* to the believer, according to Milbank. It just makes the believer capable of understanding the information about God *that is already there* — in the created realities themselves. The fact that Milbank does not conceive of knowledge of God as "natural" is not very important in this context. For Milbank, nothing is merely natural. Since the world is essentially "gift" — it only exists as it participates in God — there is no "pure nature," no realm that is independent of grace. A "natural theology" is thus an impossibility, if one means by that term a way of acquiring knowledge of God that does not depend on divine grace. The closest one can come to a natural theology within Milbank's ontological framework is his own claim that finite realities, when truly comprehended, reveal God.

The aim of this chapter is to argue that, as Christians, we cannot both dismiss propositional revelation *and* deny the existence of a potent natural theology. Since Milbank is as optimistic as Vatican I about the possibility to know God by considering created things, I will regard his view as equivalent to belief in the existence of a very potent natural theology. This means that I will not quarrel with him. My argument is primarily directed

---

93. Heinrich Denzinger, *Compendium of Creeds, Definitions, and Declarations on Matters of Faith and Morals*, ed. Peter Hünermann, 43rd ed. (San Francisco: Ignatius Press, 2012), §3004 (italics added).

at those who deny the world's ability to reveal God (i.e., to make available knowledge of the proposition *God exists*). Furthermore, I have sympathy for Milbank's view. I am inclined to think that one important aspect of revelation is the illumination of our minds. This illumination enables us to see a face behind the world. However, we can only recognize that face as the face of Christ — the Pancrator, the eternal Logos — because revelation also provides "new information."

Milbank's denial that revelation provides new information is, in itself, rather peculiar. One would think that the proposition that God will judge all humans at the end of time would count as a piece of "new information" that God has revealed. However, if revelation does not provide any new information, then it seems to follow that the proposition in question must be somehow implicit in the structure of the world itself, or in the unfolding of world history up to the present. It is just that we, in our present state, are not capable of extracting this implicit knowledge without divine help. One wonders what motivates this view when a much less strained alternative is available, namely, that God indeed gives us "new information" by speaking.

3.7 Conclusion

We have seen that Pannenberg's, Brunner's, and Barth's theories of revelation, which are usually taken to be manifestational, in reality include important elements of propositional revelation (or, in the case of Pannenberg, "preliminary" propositional revelation). This is also true of Ronald Thiemann. All the mentioned theologians either tacitly or explicitly assume that God either *tells* humans things or directly implants beliefs in their minds. The latter alternative does not mean that God implants sentences in their minds, but beliefs have a conceptually structured content, so the idea that God implants beliefs entails that God implants conceptually structured contents.

I have also argued, with respect to Schleiermacher and Rahner, that the idea of revelation as mediating an *awareness* of God without transmitting any *knowledge* is incoherent, and that nonconceptual experiences cannot mediate awareness of anything, or at least not of God. We have also seen that even if we actually perceive God by having conceptually structured "mystical perceptions" in which God is directly presented to us, such experiences can probably not (unless we already know, from other sources, that God exists) justify the claim that their object is God.

Finally, I have argued that theologians who adhere to coherentist conceptions of epistemic justification do not thereby escape the problem of explaining how we can know that God exists. They are also forced to posit either propositional revelation or a potent natural theology.

By thus having displayed the shortcomings of purely manifestational theories of revelation, and the extent to which some allegedly manifestational theories are in reality committed to assuming the occurrence of propositional revelation, I hope to have convinced the reader that it is worth taking a second look at the idea that God transmits knowledge of himself by speaking. The account of the latter idea that I am going to present has the advantage of being able to explain, independently of a potent natural theology, how the belief that God exists can acquire the status of knowledge. The account is also, I will argue, compatible with the Christian tradition's central convictions about the nature of Christian faith.

Before closing this chapter, there is one more question that needs to be addressed. What about the traditional Catholic idea of the *beatific vision*? Does the argument of this chapter entail that something like the beatific vision is impossible? Saint Thomas Aquinas says:

> Therefore some . . . held that no created intellect can see the essence of God. This opinion, however, is not tenable. For as the ultimate happiness of man consists in the use of his highest function, which is the operation of the intellect, the created intellect could never see God, it would either never attain to happiness or its happiness would consist in something else besides God, which is opposed to faith. . . . There resides in every man a natural desire to know the cause of any effect which he sees, and from this wonder arises in men. But if the intellect of the rational creature could not reach so far as to the first cause of things, the natural desire would remain void. Hence it must be absolutely granted that the blessed see the essence of God.[94]

The idea of a direct *vision* of God (in the sense of immediate and nondiscursive knowledge of God's essence) is not a mere historical curiosity. It has recently been ably defended by the analytical Thomist Paul Macdonald. Macdonald defends a Thomistic/Aristotelian view of perception, which he (quite correctly) finds similar to the view of perception proposed by analytical philosopher John McDowell. McDowell and Aquinas both claim

---

94. Aquinas, *ST* I, q. 12, a. 1. Hereafter, references to this work appear in parentheses within the text.

that the mind is, in a certain sense, "open" to the world in perceptual experience. To have a perceptual experience of an object or a fact is not to form a mental representation of that object or fact. Our minds are, instead, *conjoined,* or united, with the (formal aspects of) extramental objects or facts in experience. In Aquinas's words: "Two things are required both for sensible and for intellectual vision — namely, power of sight, and union of the thing seen with the sight. For vision is made actual only when the things seen is in a certain way *in the seer*" (*ST* I, q. 12, a. 2 [italics added]). For Aquinas, the paradigmatic case of intellectual vision or knowledge is the beatific vision, in which the intellect is united to and thereby "informed by" the ultimate cause and ground of all there is — the divine essence itself. In the supernatural state of beatitude, "the essence of God itself becomes the intelligible form of the intellect" (*ST* I, q. 12, a. 5). The beatific vision is, as the highest achievement and the ultimate perfection of the intellect, "content rich," which means that it has a kind of "suprapropositional" cognitive content.[95] We "see," in the beatific state (e.g.) *that God is perfectly good.* According to Macdonald "the blessed actually know or 'see' God's perfect goodness itself" (p. 157).

The faculty of seeing God, however, "does not belong to the created intellect naturally, but is given to it by the light of glory, which establishes the intellect in a kind of *deiformity*" (*ST* I, q. 12, a. 6 [italics added]). This does not mean that the supernatural capacity to see God is superadded to the mind. That capacity is, instead, an extension or perfection of our natural intellective capacities, a raising of them to their full potential (Macdonald, pp. 162-63). Macdonald compares the process by which God elevates our natural cognitive capacities through grace with the way the human animal is (naturally) elevated into a rational animal by being initiated into a culture — a process that is usually described as the acquisition of a "second nature." "In receiving the 'light of glory,' which strengthens and perfects their natural intellective capacities, the blessed are initiated or habituated into a glorified set of intellective capacities in accord with their *deified* second nature — what I now want to call their *glorified second nature,* or *supernature*" (p. 160).

The idea of the beatific vision, as proposed by Aquinas and explicated by Macdonald, can seem to be incompatible with an important conclusion

---

95. Paul Macdonald, *Knowledge and the Transcendent: An Inquiry into the Mind's Relationship to God* (Washington, DC: Catholic University of America Press, 2009), p. 158. Hereafter, page references to this work appear in parentheses in the text.

of this chapter. I have argued against the idea that some kind of experience, by itself, can put us in a position to know that the object of the experience is God. The idea of the beatific vision, however, is the idea of precisely this kind of experience. Macdonald's account of the beatific vision, moreover, is not simply an appeal to divine power and the miraculous. His account sketches, in general but intelligible terms, the basic cognitive mechanism behind the experience.

It is important to remember, however, that Aquinas and Macdonald do not talk about the human mind in its current, embodied state. The possibility to have the very essence of God conjoined or united to one's mind in such a way that God himself becomes "the intelligible form of the intellect" is not a possibility for the human being in this life. Since God is immaterial and the human soul embodied, God cannot become the intelligible form of the intellect (*ST* I, q. 12, a. 11). "On Aquinas's view, no living human person in his or her current truncated cognitive state can 'see' the essence of God; consequently there can be no direct knowledge of the essence of God in this life" (Macdonald, p. 172). Since the argument of the present chapter is only about the limitations of human cognition in its current embodied state, there is no incompatibility between accepting this argument and accepting the possibility of a beatific vision of God according to the model of Aquinas/Macdonald. Both Saint Thomas and Paul Macdonald are in full agreement with my claim that knowledge of God in this life must be discursive, mediated by natural theology and/or propositional revelation. Aquinas says:

> Man's ultimate happiness consists in a supernatural vision of God, to which vision man cannot attain unless he be taught by God. . . . Now man acquires a share of this learning, not all at once, but little by little, according to the mode of his nature. And every one who learns thus must believe, in order that he may acquire science in a perfect degree. . . . Hence, in order that a man arrive at the perfect vision of heavenly happiness, he must first of all believe God, as a disciple believes the master who is teaching him. (*ST* II-II, q. 2, a. 3)

The idea here is that the human intellect is "perfected by a distinct disposition or habit of mind . . . that the blessed acquire and hence receive from God through something like education, imitation, training, and practice — that is, through submitting themselves to *divine pedagogy*" (Macdonald, p. 161). The training process whereby we acquire a "glorified second nature" is analogous to that whereby we acquire our "normal" second nature as rational animals, which also happens through education, training, and practice. For Aquinas, there is thus no question of "seeing" God's essence in the next life without first *believing what God says,* as an apprentice believes the master. John Jenkins summarizes Aquinas's view on the matter:

> In this life, we must submit ourselves to divine instruction and accept God's revelation in the assent of faith so that we may attain perfect apprehension in beatitude, just as students accept the teachings of a master in the acquisition of merely human *scientia*. . . . The docility and obedience which sacred doctrine requires, then, are comparable to those required in the acquisition of any *scientia*.[96]

Could we understand the process whereby we are prepared for the beatific vision as a series of increasingly clear "glimpses" or "foretastes" of the divine essence rather than as an education process that essentially involves propositional revelation? It is hard to see why anybody who is sympathetic to a Thomistic theory of cognition would want to opt for this perceptual construal of the process. Either the divine essence is the intelligible form of my intellect, or it is not. If it is, then I am in the beatified state and have the beatific vision. If it is not, then there is an epistemic distance between my intellect and God. Knowledge of God must then come about *indirectly*. What could it mean, within the Thomistic framework, to receive "glimpses" or "foretastes" of the divine essence? Could it mean to have God's essence *temporarily* become the intelligible form of one's intellect, and then subsequently to withdraw from it? Or could it mean to have a *part* of God's essence become the intelligible form of one's intellect? The coherence of these suggestions is questionable, and they seem, in any case, much more plausible as descriptions of rare mystical experience than as accounts of how God normally effects spiritual growth in Christians.

The claim that there is an epistemic distance between our intellects and God in this life should not be confused with the false claim that there is an *ontological* distance. Aquinas is clear that "the light of natural reason itself is a participation of the divine light" (*ST* I, q. 12, a. 11). There is, accordingly, a very intimate ontological relationship between our intellects and God, according to Aquinas. This circumstance, however, is completely compatible with the existence of a great epistemic distance, an impossi-

---

96. John Jenkins, *Knowledge and Faith in Thomas Aquinas* (Cambridge: Cambridge University Press, 1997), pp. 68-69.

bility to know God's essence in this life. A simple analogy can make this clear. There is a very intimate ontological relationship between a person's intellect and her brain. Without the brain, there is no intellectual activity (at least in this life). This fact, however, does not entail that a person must necessarily be capable of *knowing* that her intellect has anything to do with the brain. Many people throughout history have been ignorant of the dependent relationship between intellect and brain, and that ignorance was probably more or less incurable during the early phases of human history (even though speculative hypotheses could of course be formulated). This shows that the ontological dependence of our intellects on God is compatible with the existence of a great epistemic distance.[97]

---

97. Aquinas makes a similar point in *ST* I, q. 12, a. 11, ad. 3.

CHAPTER 4

Divine Speech

In the preceding chapter I reviewed the main manifestational alternatives to propositional revelation. The general conclusion of that review was that no purely manifestational model of revelation, or combination of such models, is capable of giving a satisfactory explanation of how Christians can come to know or even justifiably believe that there is a personal reality on which all other realities depend for their existence. This lesson has an important corollary: If the Christian revelation does not include some form of propositional (nonmanifestational) revelation, and if there is no potent natural theology, then Christians do not know that God exists. They are not even justified in *believing* that God exists.

One possible response to this state of affairs is fideism: So what if belief in God is not justified? This attitude may appear acceptable for those who have uncritically accepted the modern identification of faith with "unjustified belief" and the related dichotomy of "faith" and "reason." For most thinkers in the Christian tradition, however, faith is rational, and while Christian belief has frequently been denied the status of *scientia,* it has usually been assigned a status equivalent to knowledge.

Another way of responding to the conclusion of the foregoing chapter is to put one's hope in a potent natural theology. Theistic proofs — the main form of natural theology — have a venerable tradition, and the dismissive attitude toward them in much modern theology seems seldom to be based on thorough rational evaluations. The fact remains, however, that few of the theologians who advocate manifestational models of revelation have any faith in theistic proofs. Those who dismiss propositional revelation usually dismiss theistic proofs as well.[1]

The foregoing chapter was partly intended as a wakeup call for theologians and others who are inclined to think that natural theologies (with claims to potency) as well as propositional revelation are dispensable and that theology can rely exclusively on manifestational models of revelation. If we are to avoid fideism, this is not the case. We must posit some form of natural theology or propositional revelation.

The rest of this book will provide an opportunity to reconsider the viability of propositional revelation in its traditional form — what I have referred to as the *divine testimony model*. This model of revelation can, as I will attempt to show, be given a credible explication in terms of insights from contemporary philosophy of testimony. Understood in the right way, the divine testimony model is not at all an embarrassment to the contemporary theological mind.

Before I can present my version of the model, I need a couple of tools. First, I need an analysis of what it means to say that God speaks. God is not a physical entity, so it is not immediately clear in what sense God could be said to speak. Second, I need an understanding of what is involved in testimonial knowledge — that is, knowledge acquired by hearing the linguistic utterances of other persons. The latter is the topic of the next chapter, where I will present and defend John McDowell's anti-reductionist view of testimonial knowledge.

The most helpful recent philosophical discussion of the idea that God speaks is Nicholas Wolterstorff's widely acclaimed book *Divine Discourse*, in which he approaches divine speech from the perspective of Austinian speech-act theory.[2] In what follows, I will present and explain some of

---

1. The only credible alternative to theistic proofs in natural theology seems to be the idea of a *sensus divinitatis* (see chap. 2, n. 7). Alvin Plantinga is the masterful explorer of this route. If one is prepared to accept Plantinga's strong epistemological externalism, then his theory in *Warranted Christian Belief* may satisfy one's demand for a reasonable account of Christian knowledge of God (Plantinga, *Warranted Christian Belief* [New York: Oxford University Press, 2000]). It is not uncommon, however, for theologians who dismiss propositional revelation and theistic proofs to be very skeptical of Plantinga's model as well.

2. Wolterstorff claims that "contemporary speech-action theory opens up the possibility of a whole new way of thinking about God speaking: perhaps the attribution of speech to God ... should be understood as the attribution of *illuctionary actions*" (Nicholas Wolterstorff, *Divine Discourse: Philosophical Reflections on the Claim That God Speaks* [Cambridge: Cambridge University Press, 1995], p. 13). However, I agree with Michael Levine

Wolterstorff's central ideas and connect the issue of divine speech to the question of the Bible's status.[3]

4.1 Locutionary and Illocutionary Acts

Austin's fundamental insight is that to speak is to do things with words.[4] To utter or inscribe a certain sentence is (in Austin's terms) to perform a *locutionary* act.[5] But usually, when I perform a locutionary act, I also thereby do something else, for instance, assert, command, ask, promise, or request something. These latter acts are called *illocutionary* acts — speech-acts.

What is the relationship between locutionary and illocutionary acts?[6] It is obviously not causal. My act of uttering the sentence "I promise to do *x*" does not *cause* another act — the promising. Rather, my uttering the relevant sentence *counts as* my promising to do *x* in much the same way as flipping on the left-side blinker of a car counts as signaling a left turn. Uttering a certain sentence (in certain circumstances) and flipping on the left-side blinker count as, respectively, a promise and the signaling of a left turn, because certain social conventions about the meaning and use of words and traffic signs are in place.

When one performs an illocutionary act, one acquires a certain *standing*. By flipping on the left-side blinker I take on the standing — the status — of someone who has signaled a left turn. This standing is *normatively ascribed* to me, which means that people should treat me as somebody who has this standing. That people should so treat me is,

---

that the distinction between locutionary and illocutionary acts has "always been implicitly recognized" (Levine, "God Speak," *Religious Studies* 34, no. 1 [1998]: 1-16; 9).

3. The purpose of this chapter is to present and defend *one* way in which the idea that God speaks can be rendered philosophically credible. Of course, there might be other ways of doing so that are also compatible with the general argument of this book.

4. John Searle's version of speech-act theory is similar to Austin's. For differences between Austin's and Searle's theories, and how they affect Wolterstorff's argument, see Maarten Wisse, "From Cover to Cover? A Critique of Wolterstorff's Theory of the Bible as Divine Discourse," *International Journal for Philosophy of Religion* 52, no. 3 (2002): 159-73; 169-70.

5. Wolterstorff's use of the term "locutionary act" differs a bit from Austin's, for whom such an act consists of using words with a certain sense and reference, and not just of inscribing or uttering words, as for Wolterstorff (Wolterstorff, *Divine Discourse*, p. 304, n. 1).

6. What follows builds on chap. 5 of *Divine Discourse*.

of course, compatible with people failing to actually treat me so. The standing is not only normatively ascribed to me; it is also a *normative standing,* since the standing consists in — is constituted by — one's having certain rights and duties. For instance, by signaling a left turn, I have a (prima facie) duty to turn left soon, and I have the right to be treated in a certain way by others. If I fail to live up to the obligations that my act brings with it, I am blameworthy, and so is the person who fails to treat me as my standing requires.

Analogously, because I have *promised* that I will do x, the normative standing of having promised to do x is normatively ascribed to me. This means that the person who hears my promise *should* treat me as one who has promised to do x. The standing I have acquired consists in my having the prima facie obligation to do x. Likewise, by *asserting* that p, I acquire the normative standing of one who has asserted that p. This means that people have a right to hold me to my word, and that I have a right to be taken at my word. Speech-acts, however, can be malformed. For example, if I assert that p without believing that p, then I have done something I should not have done. If a hearer has good reason to believe that a certain speech-act is malformed, then the speech-act in question is "undercut." This means that the usual rights and obligations that accrue to speakers and hearers upon the performance of the speech-act do not accrue to them in that particular case.

In summary, to speak is not, essentially, to express one's inner self (even though one often does this by speaking) or to influence an audience in a certain way (though speech also often does that). It is, in essence, to take up a *normative stance* in the public domain.[7] It is to acquire rights and responsibilities.[8]

4.2 Double-Agency Discourse

To produce discourse (i.e., to *say* things) is, as we have seen, to perform illocutionary acts — that is, to take up normative standings, such as that of

---

7. Wolterstorff, *Divine Discourse,* p. 93.

8. Wolterstorff argues at length that God could acquire the rights and responsibilities of a speaker. For criticism of his argument, see Philip Quinn, "Can God Speak? Does God Speak?" *Religious Studies* 37, no. 3 (2001): 259-69; 260-65. See also Wolterstorff's response: Nicholas Wolterstorff, "Response to Helm, Quinn, and Westphal," *Religious Studies* 37, no. 3 (2001): 293-306.

having asserted that *p*.⁹ One can, however, perform such acts by means of words without actually uttering or inscribing those words. For example, the president can, by signing a letter that her secretary has written, make the letter a medium of her own discourse. If the letter reads, "Change the bill, or I will veto it," this counts as the *president's* issuing a threat. The threat is *her* speech-act, not the secretary's, even though it is the secretary who has inscribed the sentences that count as the threat. The president need not have dictated the very words of the letter to the secretary in order for the letter to be the medium of her discourse. In fact, she need not have said anything at all to the secretary about the contents of the letter. It might have been the case that the secretary knew what the president wanted to say without having to be told; nevertheless, the letter becomes the medium of the president's discourse by virtue of her act of signing it. But the president need not even sign the letter in order to say something via the letter. She can deputize the secretary to sign it for her. In such a case, the secretary's inscribing the president's name on the letter *counts as* a case of the latter's signing the letter. The basic phenomenon we are dealing with here is what Wolterstorff calls "double-agency discourse." In this type of discourse, one person's locutionary acts count as another person's illocutionary acts.

It is possible to deputize a person to *speak in one's name.* An ambassador, for instance, is a person who speaks in the name of the head of the state. When the president deputizes an ambassador to speak in her name, the president acquires the rights and responsibilities of having issued the threats, warnings, promises, and so on that the ambassador issues on her behalf. These threats, warnings, and promises may be formulated in words that reflect the personality of the ambassador rather than that of the president. The ambassador, on the other hand, might not even think that it is appropriate to issue the threats that he issues on the president's behalf.

To speak in somebody's name is not, as Wolterstorff points out, the same as delivering a *message* from that person. When S merely communicates a message from P, then P has already performed the illocutionary acts (threatening, promising, asserting, etc.) that are contained in the message. S merely delivers the message, that is, he *reports* what P has already said. If S, on the other hand, is deputized to speak in the name

---

9. This section examines chap. 3 of *Divine Discourse.* Hereafter, page references to this work appear in parentheses in the text.

of P, then S's utterances themselves constitute speech-acts by P. S's utterances are not reports of what P previously said, but they count as S's saying certain things in the present. In practice it is not always possible to distinguish between these two phenomena, which tend to "shade into each other" (p. 44). However, there is an important logical difference. When S communicates a message from P, then P does not speak in the present; P has merely spoken in the past. When S speaks in the name of P, then P is speaking in the present.

Double-agency discourse can also take other forms. Instead of merely making another person's locutionary acts the medium of one's own discourse, one can make another person's illocutionary acts — that person's *discourse* — the medium of one's own discourse.

Suppose that S delivers a speech in which he expresses his opinion on some matter. It is then possible for P to *appropriate* S's discourse by saying, "Those are also my views." In doing so, P is speaking by means of S's discourse. Compare this to the case in which a secretary writes a letter that the president signs. The secretary, in this scenario, has not *said* anything (performed any illocutionary acts). He has only inscribed words. In the case of P and S, however, S has also spoken (produced his own discourse).

Wolterstorff calls attention to an important distinction between two phenomena that often tend to get confused, namely, the degree and mode of *superintendence,* on the one hand, and *authorization,* on the other (p. 41). A discourser who uses the text or utterance of another person as a medium for her own discourse can exercise different degrees and modes of superintendence over the medium. On one end of the continuum are cases such as when the president dictates every word of a text to a secretary. Further down the line are cases in which the president merely indicates to the secretary the substance of what she wants to be said, or the secretary might even know, by himself, what the president wishes to say. In the latter case, the mode of superintendence is very indirect. The president's influence on what the secretary writes is due to her having spent time with him in the past. In the extreme case, the discourser's degree of superintendence over the medium is nil. One might, for example, find a postcard with a catchy slogan that one sends to a friend, thereby saying something to her. Even in such a case, the postcard constitutes the medium of one's discourse in virtue of being *authorized.* "To authorize a text is in effect to declare: let this text serve as the medium of my discoursing" (p. 41). In the case of the postcard, the authorization consists in the act of signing the card and sending it to a friend.

4.3 Possible Ways for God to Speak

Against the background of this general framework, we can imagine several possible ways in which God could speak by means of audible or written sentences. If God has deputized a prophet to speak in his name, then it is God who is the author of that speech. This means that the locutionary acts that the prophet performs count as illocutionary acts by God. God speaks by means of the prophet's utterances.

If a prophet merely delivers a message from God, then God must first have spoken to the prophet. God need not, indeed, have spoken the very *words* of the message to be delivered. However, the idea of delivering a message from God presupposes that God has already performed some speech-acts that constitute the message to be delivered. However, if the prophet speaks in the name of God, then the prophet's utterances themselves constitute the speech of God, and we need not postulate some prior speech-act by God in which God communicates to the prophet the content of what he wants to have said. It is sufficient if God has authorized (deputized) the prophet to speak for him. God would, one may presume, also want to influence or supervise what the prophet utters in his name in some way or another, but this can conceivably be done without God's speaking to the prophet (though the Old Testament often claims that this is how the prophet knows what to say). The Christian tradition talks about "inspiration." In order to inspire somebody to utter something, one need not speak to that person. Inspiration could, presumably, take many forms, leaving more or less freedom for the prophet to shape the message according to his own capacities and preconceptions.

Another possible way for God to speak is by appropriating the *discourse* of humans. If we are to understand biblical texts such as the Wisdom books and the Psalms as media of divine discourse, then this seems to be the right model to adopt (p. 51). These books cannot be understood as messages delivered by God, or as prophetic speech in the name of God. Often the structure of these books is that of human beings addressing God rather than the other way around.

By declaring them to be the media of his discourse, God could appropriate the human discourse of texts such as the Psalms. This would be analogous to the case in which somebody finds a postcard with a catchy slogan and sends it to a friend, thereby making the speech-act on the card the medium of her own discourse. What the sender of the card would thereby be saying is not necessarily the same thing as what the card itself (or its original author) says.

It is conceivable that the different books of the Bible could constitute media of divine discourse by virtue of having been brought together by God to form *one* book. God would then count as the author of this new book. It is well known that inserting a text into a new context can significantly change its meaning. Bringing together different books by different human authors is thus a very significant act, a way of saying something beyond what the human authors of the different books were saying.

In order for the books of the Bible to become media of divine discourse, God must *do* something that counts as his appropriating of these books. Wolterstorff suggests that "the event which *counts as* God's appropriating this totality [the biblical books] as the medium of God's own discourse is presumably that rather drawn-out event consisting of the Church's settling on this totality as its canon" (p. 54). It is likely, of course, that God would also want to influence the actual writing of the biblical texts to some degree. It is not divine inspiration, however, that makes the texts into a medium of divine discourse; it is divine appropriation.

Let us sum up. God could, conceivably, speak in several ways. One possibility is that God speaks immediately to people in religious experiences. Those people can then pass on what God has said to them to others. But God could also speak by means of the utterances of humans. God could deputize some humans to speak in his name (about certain topics, under certain conditions). If so, some of the speech-acts of these humans will *constitute* God's speech. Both of these models of divine speaking seem to figure in biblical descriptions of prophecy. The prophet either communicates a message, previously spoken directly to the prophet by God, or the prophet speaks in the name of God.

A third way in which God may speak is by authorizing the (written) discourse of humans. With the help of this model, it is possible to understand the Bible itself as divine discourse and not only as containing records or reports of divine speech-acts, previously performed by prophets and other divine spokespersons. God is, according to this construal, the author of Scripture, which means that when one reads the Bible, one is directly confronted with divine speech.

4.4 Biblical Interpretation

John Lamont has distinguished between "direct" and "deistic" conceptions of divine speaking. According to a deistic conception, "God conveys the Christian message by speaking to an initial group, which is (roughly) made up of the prophets and the apostles. Those who do not belong to this initial group . . . learn about the Christian message by hearing the reports of members of this initial group. . . . They do not hear it through hearing God himself when he speaks." According to the "direct" view, however, "God himself speaks to everyone who has Christian faith, not just an initial group."[10] "Direct" divine speaking is, according to Lamont's conception, not incompatible with God's using humans as instruments for his speech. Rather, to conceive of God's speaking as direct is to conceive of it as something that directly confronts believers of all times.[11]

Direct speaking could, conceivably, take place by God's speaking privately to believers of all times in mystical experiences. But God's direct speech could also be publicly available. Lamont distinguishes between three conceptions of God's direct, publicly available speaking. One is the Protestant model (the scriptural view), according to which the Bible constitutes God's speech. The traditional Catholic model (the magisterial view) also claims that the Bible is God's speech; however, it adds that to believe God when he speaks involves not only believing what the Bible says, but also believing "those propositions which the Church teaches as dogmas of faith, although the Church's teaching is not itself divine speaking" (p. 165). We need not consider exactly what this means and entails here. The third model, the ecclesial view, claims that "God speaks in the Church's teaching, and believing God consists in believing the Church when she teaches" (p. 163). Since the Bible is (the principal) part of church teaching, the Bible is God's speech in this model, too.

The third model introduces a way of construing divine speech that we have not considered above. God could be speaking in the church's doctrinal teaching, which is the view recommended by Lamont. It has a

---

10. John Lamont, *Divine Faith* (Aldershot, UK: Ashgate, 2004), pp. 150, 151. Hereafter, page references to this work appear in parentheses within the text.

11. Lamont seems to restrict the deistic view to the claim that the "initial group" receive propositions straight from God without the involvement of any human instruments or intermediaries (John Lamont, "Stump and Swinburne on Revelation," *Religious Studies* 32, no. 3 (1996): 395-411; 406). However, it would also be compatible with the deistic view that the initial group receives divine speech through human intermediaries.

foundation in the idea that the church is the body of Christ. According to Lamont, the church fathers insisted that the union between Christians and Christ was a real union of being. And "if the Church is in a real sense Christ's body, it follows that the Church's actions are Christ's actions" (p. 174). "If you do something through your body, you do that thing yourself; it is a basic action."[12] This also applies to the activity of speaking and teaching.

For the purposes of this book, we need not take a stand on whether God's speech is best construed in accordance with the scriptural (Protestant), the magisterial, or the ecclesial view. All three views agree that Scripture is authored by God. As we have seen, Wolterstorff has provided a way of understanding what the latter claim could mean. The texts of different human authors could have been appropriated by God and brought together into one book, which would thereby constitute the medium of divine discourse.

The conceptual distinction between the idea of divine influence (superintendence) and that of divine authorship puts us in a position to answer a common objection against the claim that the Bible is authored by God. The objection is that if God is to count as the author of the Bible, he must have overridden and superseded the normal human faculties of those who wrote the biblical texts (p. 23). This idea is (rightly) regarded as unattractive, since different biblical texts are clearly the products of different personalities, styles, and cultural/historical contexts. But there is no need to claim that the human writers of the Bible were mere puppets. God could speak directly through the utterances/discourses of humans without suspending the will and mind of those persons, just like a president can speak through an ambassador without having to suspend his mind and will (p. 25).

There is another objection commonly leveled against the claim that the Bible is authored by God, namely, that the Bible contains falsehoods and morally reprehensible views. Therefore, the objection goes, it could not have been authored by an omniscient and perfectly good God. Both Wolterstorff and Richard Swinburne offer resources for answering this objection.[13] Wolterstorff addresses the problems that it points to in terms of a hermeneutical method for determining and distinguishing between which

---

12. Lamont, "Stump and Swinburne on Revelation," p. 407.
13. Richard Swinburne, *Revelation: From Metaphor to Analogy*, 2nd ed. (Oxford: Oxford University Press, 2007).

elements in a particular biblical text are to be ascribed to, respectively, the human and the divine author (*Divine Discourse,* chaps. 11-12).

According to Wolterstorff's method, the first step (the "first hermeneutic") in finding out what God is saying by means of a biblical text is to find out what the human author of the text is saying.[14] To do so means to read the text in order to "discover what assertings, what promisings [etc.] . . . are rightly to be ascribed to the author on the ground of her having set down the words that she did in the situation in which she set them down" (p. 93). Hypotheses about the intentions of the author are indispensable in this context, but the goal of interpretation is not to determine what the author *intended* to say, but what she actually said — which speech-acts she actually performed. To know this, we must know the illocutionary stance of the text. In fictional works, the author does not *assert* the things she writes; she simply invites the reader to imagine them. Asserting and inviting to imagine are two different illocutionary stances, implied by different literary genres. Therefore, in order to find out what the human author of a biblical text is saying, we need to know the genre of the text.

The "second hermeneutic" aims at finding out what God is saying by means of the appropriated human discourses in the Bible. This hermeneutic proceeds on the assumption that the Bible is *one* book, authored by God, an assumption that affects how one chooses among different possible interpretations of particular sentences. If a sentence is viewed as part of a larger unit, it is reasonable to choose an interpretation of it that makes it consistent with the other sentences of the unit.

A fundamental principle for interpreting what an author says by means of an appropriated text is that unless evidence to the contrary surfaces, the stance and content of the appropriating discourse (God's, in this case) is the same as that of the appropriated discourse (the human author's). Sometimes, however, it is improbable that the appropriating discourse intends to say what the appropriated discourse says. In such cases it is legitimate to assume that the appropriating discourse has a different illocutionary stance than the appropriated discourse (e.g., that the appropriating discourse does not assert what the appropriated discourse asserts). To be able to reason about such probabilities, one needs background convictions about the author of the appropriating discourse. This

---

14. The very idea that one can find out what an author is saying by means of a text is frequently questioned today, but Wolterstorrf defends it against attacks from Ricoeur and Derrida (Wolterstorff, *Divine Discourse,* chaps. 8-9).

means that "we do our interpreting for divine discourse with convictions in two hands: in one hand, our convictions as to the stance and content of the appropriated discourse and the meanings of the sentences used; in the other hand, our convictions concerning the probabilities and improbabilities of what God would have been intending to say by appropriating this particular discourse-by-inscription" (*Divine Discourse*, p. 204). So we need background convictions about God in order to do the job, just as we need background convictions about human authors to interpret for human authorial discourse (p. 221).[15]

Wolterstorff points out a number of "patterns" along which one may legitimately depart from the default position of identifying the content and stance of God's discourse with that of the human discourser's. Sometimes, for example, it will be necessary to alter the "rhetorico-conceptual structure" of the human discourse in order to arrive at something that could plausibly be construed as the appropriating divine discourse. Texts in which the human author addresses God belong in this category. When the psalmist says "Have mercy on me, O God," we cannot interpret this as *God's* saying "have mercy on me, O God."

Sometimes it will seem reasonable to make a distinction between the main point of a discourse, and a way of making that point, and attribute the main point of what the human author is saying to God, but regard the particular way in which the human author makes this point as of merely human significance (p. 209). For instance, when the psalmist praises God's majesty by saying that God has established the world so that "it shall never be moved," the psalmist himself or herself probably made the literal assertion that the world shall never be moved. But since the assertion is false, we must separate the main point (praise of God's majesty) from the way the author makes this point, and only ascribe the former to God. This method of interpretation takes care of some of the cases in which the Bible seems to assert falsehoods.

Swinburne makes a similar point by distinguishing between what *statement* a sentence or text expresses and the *presuppositions* in terms of which it is expressed.[16] Suppose I say, "The man drinking a martini is very cheerful," thereby intending to refer to a particular man at a cocktail party,

---

15. The risk, of course, is that the bible becomes a "wax nose" — something we can interpret as saying whatever we want it to say. Wolterstorff addresses this worry in chap. 13. For criticism, see Levine, "God Speak," pp. 11-13; Wisse, "From Cover to Cover?"

16. Swinburne, *Revelation: From Metaphor to Analogy,* chap. 2. Hereafter, page references to this work appear in parentheses within the text.

who is not actually drinking a martini but a similar-looking drink. Nevertheless, it can be argued that the sentence expresses a true statement, namely, that the man in question is cheerful, even though reference to him is made by way of a false description. Swinburne argues that where the public criteria of a particular culture "make it clear to what reference is being made — in the sense that others in that context would agree about which object is being referred to — then the fact that the reference is made by means of a false description does not affect the truth-value of what is said" (p. 28). So when Roman historians say things about "the divine Augustus," we need not judge that what they say is false, even though we know that there is no such person as the divine Augustus. Since it is extremely difficult, if not impossible, to make statements that do not depend on the presuppositions of any particular culture, and since all cultures presumably have some false beliefs, it is not strange if God's revelation is expressed in terms of the (sometimes false) presuppositions of a particular culture (pp. 98-106). Swinburne argues that the most convenient way for God to communicate a message would be to formulate it in terms of the presuppositions of one specific culture (p. 105). If this is so, an interpreter inhabiting a different culture that does not share those presuppositions must distinguish between the (cultural-relative) presuppositions of the message and the divine message itself.[17]

Another possible way to depart from the stance and content of the human discourse in order to discover divine discourse is to interpret the human author's *literal* discourse as *metaphorical* divine discourse. When the psalmist blessed those who would take Babylonian infants and smash them against the rock, he was probably intending this to be taken literally. However, the church has seldom ascribed the blessing spoken by the human author to God. The content of the psalm is, more reasonably, construed as a strong metaphorical expression of God's opposition to whatever opposes God's reign (*Divine Discourse,* p. 212). This way of interpreting for divine discourse takes care of some of the cases in which the Bible seems to advocate morally reprehensible views.

Another interpretive pattern is to interpret a text as transitive discourse divided between human and divine author. Transitive discourse

---

17. Stump criticizes Swinburne on the grounds that, even if statements with false presuppositions can be true, it can nevertheless sometimes be blameworthy to knowingly make such statements. See Eleonore Stump, "Review of *Revelation: From Metaphor to Analogy,* by Richard Swinburne," *The Philosophical Review* 103, no. 4 (1994): 739-43; 740-41. See also Lamont's response to Stump in Lamont, "Stump and Swinburne on Revelation," pp. 400-401.

is discourse that says one thing by saying something else. For instance, by telling a story I can convey a moral point. In some cases, it seems reasonable to assume that God discourses transitively by means of biblical texts. The human author of the Song of Songs sings a love song, which the divine author appropriates as an allegory for the love between God and Israel. Or the human author writes a historical narrative, which the divine author appropriates in order to make a point — a point that may not be the same as the one made by the human author (*Divine Discourse*, p. 214). For instance, when the bellicose narratives of the book of Joshua are read as being authored (appropriated) by the same divine subject who speaks through the Gospel narratives, then the message that this divine author wants to convey in the book of Joshua will perhaps have to be understood as different from the message of the human author(s).[18]

4.5 Where Does It All Start?

In order for God to bring about that some prophet speaks in his name, or that a human text becomes a medium of divine discourse, it seems that God must, at some point, perform some *locutionary* act. God must *immediately* do something that counts as an act of deputizing or appropriating. God must "causally bring about events *generative* of divine discourse" (p. 117).

One way this could happen would be by God causing religious experiences. If God causes a person to have an experience in which it seems to her that God deputizes her to speak in his name, then this would constitute an act of deputizing. It would do so no less than if Stephen Hawking would cause his voice generator to utter, in the appropriate context, the words "I want you to speak in my name."[19]

Could there be other ways for God to generate discourse? Wolterstorff says, as we remember, that "the event which *counts as* God's appropriating this totality [the biblical books] as the medium of God's own discourse is presumably that rather drawn out event consisting of the Church's settling on this totality as its canon" (p. 54). Merold Westphal objects to this:

18. See Wisse, "From Cover to Cover?" pp. 171-72, for a critique of the idea that God speaks in a transitive way by means of biblical texts.

19. The question of how the subject of the experience can *know* that it is God who speaks in the experience is irrelevant in this context. The important thing is that it actually is God who causes the experience.

Divine Speech

[T]he act of a human entity, the Church, can hardly count as the divine act of appropriation. One might, of course, construe the "rather drawn out event" in question as a divinely deputized or appropriated speech act, but this would only begin a regress in which the question would again arise as to where the deputizing or appropriation is to be found.[20]

So it seems that we are still forced to posit, at some point, something like religious experiences in which God speaks immediately to people, that is, without borrowing locutionary acts performed by humans. However, it could be argued, contra Westphal, that this is not necessary after all. Suppose that God intervened in the normal course of nature to cause the Sea of Reeds to part. It seems perfectly appropriate, in that case, to say that this event *is* an act of God. If a material event (the parting of the sea) can properly be said to be an act of God by virtue of having been caused by God in a special way, then why could not a social event, such as the church's settling on its canon, constitute an act of God by virtue of having been caused by God in a special way? If it was, say, the subtle influence of the Holy Spirit that caused the church eventually to fix a certain canon, then it seems appropriate to say that this "rather drawn out event" constitutes the divine act of appropriation.

But things are not quite that simple. The act of appropriating somebody's discourse is an illocutionary act. Such acts are, as we have seen, essentially acts by which one takes up a normative stance in the public domain. If God's act of influencing the church to settle on a certain canon is a secret act — "behind the scenes," as it were — then it is not an act whereby God takes up a stance in the public domain.[21] So it seems that God must bring it about that at least some people are *aware* that the church's decision about the canon constitutes an act of a single invisible agent, distinct from the agents who are collectively and visibly involved in the decision-making.[22]

20. Merold Westphal, "On Reading God the Author," *Religious Studies* 37, no. 3 (2001): 271-91; 277.

21. Can a divine act of deputizing that takes place in a private religious experience really be said to be a public act by God? In the sense of "public" that is relevant here, it can. A very "private" conversation between two people (one of them whispering something in the ear of the other, say) consists, of course, of speech-acts. If people can speak privately with each other and still be said to take up public stances, then God can do so, too. "Public," in the present context, simply means that *somebody* is aware of what is happening.

22. God need not bring it about that people recognize his act — the church's decision about the canon — as an act of *God* (a being who is infinite, almighty, etc.). God can take

However, God could bring about such awareness in other ways than by causing religious experiences. Miraculous events, like the parting of the Sea of Reeds, or the bodily resurrection of Jesus, are events that could possibly function as divine "signatures," or authorizations. Why can the causing of events such as these (supposing that they happened) count as God taking up a stance in the public domain while his secret, providential influence on the canonization process cannot? The reason is that miraculous events, in certain contexts, will be interpreted as public acts of some invisible agent, while collective decisions by a social body such as the church probably will not be, at least not without further reason. Why did a fire start at the exact moment when Elijah asked Yahweh to consume his sacrifice (1 Kings 18)? The interpretation that lies closest to hand (supposing that the episode really happened) is that the fire was started by a conscious agent who responded to Elijah's invocation, and who thereby wanted to authorize Elijah as his prophet. God's causing of a certain miracle in a certain context thus can, conceivably, constitute a *communicative* act by God in the same way as raising an eyebrow in a certain context can constitute a human communicative act.

It can seem that all divine acts of authorization, even acts such as the causing of inner religious experiences, must constitute "miracles" in the sense that God, when acting in the world, must suspend the normal course of nature. But there is no reason to believe this. It is conceivable that certain religious experiences could be preordained by God as part of his eternal plan. The relevant experiences could then be said to be (indirectly) caused by God in virtue of having been preordained by him.[23] And even if God intervenes in history, he need not necessarily do this by suspending or violating the laws of nature. There are, as many have argued, possible ways for God to influence the world while respecting the integrity of natural

---

up a stance in the public domain without letting anybody know that he is God, in the same way as Obama can take up a stance in the public domain by, say, ordering a pizza, without letting anybody know that he is Obama.

23. Wolterstorff argues, however, that it is very likely that the events generative of divine discourse "cannot all be the consequence of God's implementation of a plan formed at creation — highly likely that many if not most of the purported episodes of divine discourse are the result of direct intervention on God's part" (Wolterstorff, *Divine Discourse*, p. 123). Wolterstorff's view on this subject contradicts, as Paul Griffiths points out, a strong strand of the Christian tradition, according to which God's acts are all part of an atemporal divine plan that unfolds in history (Paul J. Griffiths, "Book Review of *Divine Discourse: Philosophical Reflections on the Claim That God Speaks*, by Nicholas Wolterstorff," *Anglican Theological Review* 78, no. 3 [1996]).

laws.[24] In my view, however, there is nothing inherently problematic with the idea that God sometimes acts in such a way that the normal operations of nature are suspended. Nothing that we have learned from science contradicts this idea.[25]

In this chapter I have only dealt with the *meaning* of the claim that God speaks, leaving the epistemological question completely aside. How can we *know* that a certain prophet speaks in the name of God, or that a certain text has been appropriated by God? Is it even possible to know things like this (supposing that divine speaking really occurs)? The following two chapters will present an extended answer to the epistemological question. In order to be in a position to understand that answer, however, we need yet another tool. We need an adequate understanding of what is involved in testimonial knowledge.

---

24. E.g., Robert Russell, "Special Providence and Genetic Mutation: A New Defense of Theistic Evolution," in Robert Russel, William Stoeger, and Francisco Ayala, eds., *Evolutionary and Molecular Biology: Scientific Perspectives on Divine Action* (Notre Dame, IN: University of Notre Dame Press, 1999); Thomas Tracy, "Particular Providence and the God of the Gaps," in Robert Russel, Nancey Murphy, and Arthur Peacocke, eds., *Chaos and Complexity: Scientific Perspectives on Divine Action* (Notre Dame, IN: University of Notre Dame Press, 1996); Arthur Peacocke, *Theology for a Scientific Age: Being and Becoming — Natural, Divine, and Human* (Minneapolis: Fortress, 1993), chap. 9, and pp. 206-12.

25. For arguments to this effect, see Wolterstorff, *Divine Discourse,* pp. 123-26; see also Keith Ward, "Believing in Miracles," *Zygon* 37, no. 3 (2002): 741-50.

CHAPTER 5

Knowledge by Hearsay

5.1 Reductionism and Anti-Reductionism

Can a person acquire *knowledge* that *p* simply by hearing and understanding the words of another subject who asserts that *p*? There are voices within both Western and Eastern philosophy that deny this. John Locke, for instance, says:

> For, I think, we may as rationally hope to see with other Mens Eyes, as to know by other Mens understandings. . . . The floating of other Mens Opinions in our brains makes us not one jot the more knowing, though they happen to be true.[1]

Jonathan Barnes says this:

> No doubt we all do pick up beliefs in that second hand fashion, and I fear that we often suppose that such scavenging yields knowledge. But that is only a sign of our colossal credulity: . . . [it is] a rotten way of acquiring beliefs, and it is no way at all of acquiring knowledge.[2]

We may, following Frederick Schmitt, call the denial that beliefs acquired by hearsay can constitute knowledge *strong individualism*.[3] This

---

1. John Locke, *An Essay Concerning Human Understanding,* ed. P. H. Nidditch (Oxford: Clarendon Press, 1975), 1.4.
2. M. F. Burnyeat and Jonathan Barnes, "Socrates and the Jury: Paradoxes in Plato's Distinction between Knowledge and True Belief," *Proceedings of the Aristotelian Society, Supplementary Volumes* 54 (1980): 193-206; 200.
3. Frederick Schmitt, "Socializing Epistemology: An Introduction through Two Sam-

view is extremely difficult to countenance. It seems to entail that I do not know who my parents are, or even that humans have parents, that there was a World War II, and so on.

A more plausible position is the one that Schmitt refers to as *weak individualism,* which can be considered to be the received view in Western epistemology.[4] This view says that beliefs acquired through testimony *can* constitute knowledge, but that "a hearer is not epistemically justified in accepting... another's testimony unless she has (inductive or *a priori*) reasons, ultimately not themselves based on still further testimony, for regarding the testimony she confronts as credible."[5]

David Hume is probably the first to give written expression to this position in the West. He admits that testimony can transmit knowledge. "There is no species of reasoning more common, more useful, and even necessary to human life, than that which is derived from the testimony of men, and the reports of eye-witnesses and spectators." However, our *justification* for testimonial beliefs "is derived from no other principle than our observation of the veracity of human testimony, and of the usual conformity of facts to the reports of witnesses."[6] This means that beliefs gained from testimony are, ultimately, justified (when they are justified) on the basis of inductive reasoning: I have personally observed that what people (or certain types of people, or a particular person) say (about certain topics) has, in most cases, turned out to be true. From these observations I can construct an inductive argument that supports the general principle that what people (or certain types of people, or a particular person) say (about certain topics) is usually true. Armed with something like this general principle, I can then argue from further observations of what people say to the probable truth of their claims even in cases when I do not have the opportunity to check out the truth of their claims for myself.

Weak individualism is a form of *reductionism* with respect to testimony, since it claims that any justification/warrant that beliefs acquired

---

ple Issues," in *Socializing Epistemology: The Social Dimensions of Knowledge* (Lanham, MD: Rowman and Littlefield, 1994), p. 5.

4. C. A. J. Coady, "Testimony, Observation and 'Autonomous Knowledge,'" in B. K. Matilal and A. Chakrabarti, eds., *Knowing from Words* (Dordrecht, the Netherlands: Kluwer Academic, 1994), p. 225.

5. Sanford Goldberg, *Anti-Individualism: Mind and Language, Knowledge and Justification* (Cambridge: Cambridge University Press, 2007), p. 143.

6. David Hume, *An Enquiry Concerning Human Understanding and Other Writings,* ed. Stephen Buckle (Cambridge, UK: Cambridge University Press, 2007), p. 98.

through testimony have is reducible to nontestimonial sources of justification, such as perception, memory, and inference.

> Reductionists about testimony hold that, if testimony is to be vindicated as a source not merely of belief, but of knowledge [which entails warrant/justification], our epistemic right to believe what others tell us must be exhibitable as grounded in other epistemic resources and principles — perception, memory and inference — which are regarded by them as both more fundamental, and less problematic.[7]

Hume's theory of testimony is a schoolbook example, since it entails a "reduction of testimony as a form of evidence or support to the status of a species... of inductive inference."[8]

Until recently, the epistemology of testimony has not received much attention in the West. "The ideal seeker of knowledge in Western philosophy, at least since Locke, is a lonely figure. He does his job single-handed, finding out facts about his environment by direct observation, deducing, generalizing."[9] Hume was the first in the West to seriously address the question of the epistemic status of testimony. It is significant that he did so in the context of discussing the credibility of miracle reports. The reductionist view of testimony seems to be motivated by a desire to liberate the subject from dependence on authority and by the search for cognitive autonomy. J. L. Mackie, for instance, has argued that some form of Humean reductionism with respect to testimony is important for an empiricist concept of "autonomous" knowledge.[10]

What, then, is the alternative to reductionism? Well, testimony could be regarded as an *irreducible,* or sui generis, source of epistemic justification, in the same way that perception, inference, and memory are. If *anti-reductionism* with respect to testimonial knowledge is correct, then a satisfactory justification for believing that *p* can be that one has been told that *p*. This kind of justification should not (according to anti-reductionism) be understood as reducible to or reconstructible as an inferential justifi-

---

7. Elisabeth Fricker, "Telling and Trusting: Reductionism and Anti-Reductionism in the Epistemology of Testimony, a Critical Notice of Coady 1992," *Mind* 104, no. 414 (1995): 393-411; 394.

8. Coady, "Testimony, Observation and 'Autonomous Knowledge,'" p. 226.

9. B. K. Matilal and A. Chakrabarti, introduction to *Knowing from Words*, p. 1.

10. J. L. Mackie, "The Possibility of Innate Knowledge," *Proceedings of the Aristotelian Society,* new series 70 (1969-70): 245-57.

cation starting from premises such as "S asserted p" and "S usually speaks the truth" (or "people are usually correct about these kinds of things"). Instead, we should acknowledge that the phrase "I was told that p" denotes an equally legitimate and irreducible reason to believe that p as the phrase "I saw that p."

The case for anti-reductionism is largely driven by the failures of reductionist theories. C. A. J. Coady has, for example, pointed out a fatal weakness of the Humean reductionist project.[11] According to Hume, we trust testimony because observations "of the conformity of facts to the reports of witnesses" have shown it to be reliable. But what does Hume mean by "observations"? If he means my own *individual* observations "of the conformity of facts to the reports of witnesses," then it is extremely questionable whether the observations in question can support the claim that testimony is generally reliable. After all, it is only the truth of a very few of my testimonial beliefs that I have been able to confirm myself on the basis of direct observation. The evidence that these observations constitute cannot license the conclusion that testimony *in general* is reliable. If, on the other hand, by "observations" Hume means the common experience of mankind, then his account is viciously circular. I have access only to *other* people's observations by trusting their testimony. As Schmitt puts it, "We rely on testimony for most of the beliefs that would have to serve as the nontestimonial basis of the induction to the reliability of testimony."[12] So it seems that I must already assume that testimony is reliable in order to get access to the evidence that is supposed to prove the reliability of testimony. The mistake Hume makes, according to Coady, is to presume that "since we sometimes discover by observation and experience that some testimony is *unreliable* . . . then we must discover the general *reliability* of testimony by the same method."[13] But this conclusion does not follow.

Michael Dummett, another anti-reductionist, has argued that there is a very strong analogy between memory and testimony. Memory, according to Dummett, "may be said to be the testimony of one's past self."[14] The prospect of being able to account for the justification of testimonial beliefs merely in terms of other (nontestimonial) sources of justification is, according to Dummett, as bleak as the prospect of being able to account for

11. Coady, "Testimony, Observation and 'Autonomous Knowledge,'" pp. 227-29.
12. Schmitt, "Socializing Epistemology," p. 12.
13. Coady, "Testimony, Observation and 'Autonomous Knowledge,'" p. 246.
14. Michael Dummett, "Testimony and Memory," in Matilal and Chakrabarti, *Knowing from Words*, p. 252.

the justification of memory beliefs in terms of other sources of justification, such as perception and inference. Dummett writes:

> Try the experiment of building up a stock of knowledge from a base consisting only of what you know from present observation and present ratiocination, prescinding, at the outset, from all that you remember. At the first stage, admit only those memories which, on the basis only of what you presently know, you have a particular reason for supposing to be reliable. At later stages, if you ever reach a later stage, admit only such memories as you have, at that stage, reason to rely on. It is plain that the outcome of this exercise will be to leave you reckoning yourself to know practically nothing at all.

He goes on to point out that "the same applies to the experiment of building up a stock of knowledge from what you know of your own knowledge, that is, independently of anything you have been told."[15] So if we do not admit testimony as a sui generis source of justification alongside perception, inference, and memory, then skepticism follows.

Elisabeth Fricker, who is maybe the most prominent contemporary representative of reductionism, admits that Coady and other anti-reductionists are right about the impossibility of justifying all of one's testimonial beliefs on the basis of nontestimonial ones (or nontestimonial sources of justification). A "global reduction" of testimonial knowledge is thus unattainable. However, this does not spell the end of the reductionist project, according to Fricker. She contends that "justifying testimony by the reductionist route does not . . . require showing that the blanket generalisation 'Testimony is generally reliable' . . . can be non-circularly empirically established."[16] It is sufficient if the reductionist can show that a hearer can, on a particular occasion, acquire evidence sufficient to warrant her in taking a particular speaker to be trustworthy with respect to a certain assertion. Fricker calls the claim that this is possible *the local reductionist claim,* and contends that a hearer can have a sufficient justification for taking a particular speaker to be trustworthy (on a particular occasion, with respect to a certain assertion) without appealing to a blanket generalization about the general trustworthiness of testimony.

Fricker characterizes the issue between reductionism and anti-

---

15. Dummett, "Testimony and Memory," pp. 261-62.
16. Elisabeth Fricker, "Against Gullibility," in Matilal and Chakrabarti, *Knowing from Words,* p. 134.

reductionism in terms of the necessity or nonnecessity of accepting as basic the following normative thesis:

> On any occasion of testimony, the hearer has the epistemic right to assume, without evidence, that the speaker is trustworthy, i.e., that what she says will be true, unless there are special circumstances which defeat this presumption.[17]

Fricker refers to this thesis as the "PR principle" (for "presumptive right to trust") and claims that

> testimony as a source of knowledge reduces to other sources just if the status as knowledge of beliefs gained through testimony can be explained (as an instance of perception plus our normal forms of inductive and deductive inference) without postulating such an original PR principle.[18]

So the issue that divides reductionists and anti-reductionists, according to Fricker, is whether we have a general presumptive right to trust — or not.

Leslie Stevenson describes the difference between Hume's and Thomas Reid's views in similar terms. "Reid's position is that any assertion is creditworthy until shown otherwise; whereas Hume implies that specific evidence for its reliability is needed."[19] Reid postulates the existence of two principles, built into our cognitive nature. One principle is a propensity to speak the truth (lying requires more skill than telling the truth), and the other is a "principle of credulity," "a disposition to confide in the veracity of others, and to believe what they tell us."[20] Reid seems to regard the principle of credulity as not merely a descriptive claim, but as a principle that has implications for how we *ought* to reason.[21] Corresponding to the principle of credulity, there is a "first-principle" of reasoning that says "that there is a certain regard due to human testimony in matters of fact, and even to

---

17. Fricker, "Against Gullibility," p. 125. Richard Swinburne advocates a similar principle, which he calls the Principle of Testimony; see (e.g.) Richard Swinburne, *The Existence of God,* 2nd ed. (Oxford: Oxford University Press, 2004), p. 322.

18. Fricker, "Telling and Trusting," p. 399.

19. Leslie Stevenson, "Why Believe What People Say?" *Synthese* 94, no. 3 (1993): 429-51; 433.

20. Stevenson, "Why Believe What People Say?" p. 433.

21. See also C. A. J. Coady, *Testimony: A Philosophical Study* (Oxford: Oxford University Press, 1994), pp. 125-26.

human authority in matters of opinion."[22] Although this "first principle of reasoning" cannot be directly proved to be valid, it must nevertheless be considered reasonable, since its denial has severe consequences. Hume, on the other hand, demands that we justify our reliance on the words of others by some inductive argument. Ideally, such an argument would yield a blanket generalization such as "testimony is generally reliable."

Observe that a Humean "blanket generalization" is a *descriptive* thesis, supposed to be empirically established. Hence it is not to be confused with the *normative* PR principle that Fricker ascribes to anti-reductionists, according to which we have an epistemic right to trust others. The point of postulating a right to trust is to explain how we can (normally) be justified in believing what others say without having an empirical justification for the blanket generalization "testimony is generally reliable."

Fricker rejects the PR principle as "an epistemic charter for gullibility" ("Against Gullibility," p. 126). She claims that a hearer must have "adequate grounds to know that her informant was trustworthy" in order for her testimonial belief to be justified. The justification of testimonial beliefs is, in other words, inferential — that is, mediated by knowledge of the speaker's trustworthiness. However, this only applies to mature hearers of testimony. Fricker distinguishes between a "developmental phase" and a "mature phase." During the former phase, consumers of testimony cannot be expected to critically assess the trustworthiness of speakers. We must thus assume that, during this phase, something like a presumptive right to trust applies. "Simply-trusted testimony plays an inevitable role in the causal process by which we become masters of our commonsense scheme of things." However, the commonsense scheme includes the insight that testimony is often *not* to be trusted, and when we are masters of this scheme, we realize that "our belief in what others tell us should always be governed by our monitoring of them for trustworthiness." The presumptive right to trust does not, in other words, apply to mature speakers. This does not mean that a mature speaker must, in retrospect, justify all the beliefs that he has acquired from testimony during his developmental phase. This would be to demand a global reduction of testimonial knowledge. However, "acknowledging my general and irredeemable debt to past testimony, I may nonetheless want to trust no new informants unless I have grounds to believe them trustworthy" ("Telling and Trusting," pp.

---

22. Thomas Reid, *Essays on the Intellectual Powers of Man,* ed. James Walker (Cambridge: John Bartlett, 1852), p. 395.

403-4). Fricker claims that we often have grounds for believing particular informants, on particular occasions, to be sincere and competent about the subject matter they talk about. We need not know anything about the reliability of testimony *in general* in order to be able to justify our judgments about the trustworthiness of particular speakers on particular occasions.

How, then, do we acquire evidence sufficient for determining the trustworthiness of particular speakers? We do this by theorizing about the best explanation of the speaker's utterance. A hearer of some testimony must "engage in a piece of psychological interpretation of her informant, constructing an explanation of her utterance as an intentional speech act" ("Telling and Trusting," p. 405). This means that the hearer must piece together at least a fragment of a psychological theory of the speaker, which renders it comprehensible why she made the assertion she made. Whether the speaker's assertion is to be trusted will be "fall-out" from this theory ("Against Gullibility," p. 149). Within this interpretative exercise "sincerity is the default setting" ("Telling and Trusting," p. 405). This means that if we do not see any signs of deception or insincerity, we may assume that the speaker is sincere. Competence may also be assumed as the default setting, but only with respect to subject matters that commonsense psychology licenses us to expect competence about. When we construct the theory of the speaker, we use background knowledge from commonsense psychology. This background knowledge is dependent on past testimony, but this is not a problem for Fricker, who is not committed to defending a global reduction of testimonial knowledge.

If the interpretive activity results in an explanation of the speaker's behavior that does not ascribe insincerity or lack of competence to her, we have empirical evidence for her trustworthiness. Inference-to-the-best-explanation reasoning yields empirical knowledge, and the hearer's judgment about the trustworthiness of the speaker can, therefore, count as empirically based. The hearer has *grounds* to believe that the speaker is trustworthy. Fricker is careful to emphasize that the "default-settings," according to which sincerity and competence (within a restricted range of subject matters) can be assumed if evidence to the contrary is lacking, are "precepts within the task of constructing a psychological theory of the speaker, not a dispensation from engaging in this task" ("Against Gullibility," p. 154). This is the difference between Fricker's default settings and the PR thesis. According to the latter, we do not need to theorize about the speaker in order to have the right to believe her.

Christopher Insole has criticized Fricker because of the work done by the distinction between a developmental and a mature phase in her theory, and on account of her use of the "default-settings." With respect to the latter, Insole complains that it is hard to see "why it is supposed to be more perspicuous and coherent to give default settings a pivotal place in supposedly *reductive* accounts, rather than explaining the force of default settings as due to an irreducible epistemic value in testimony." Because the default settings are essentially evaluative, they cannot be construed as reducible to evidence from memory, perception, and reason. Instead, they seem to be principles that tell us "how to respond to and filter such evidence."[23] "No amount of non-testimonial evidence can support the evaluative ... status of these default positions."[24] It lies very close at hand to assume that the default settings apply *because of* the irreducible status of testimony.

Fricker's attempt to rescue the reductionist project is, in my view, rather unconvincing. Since our theorizing about the trustworthiness of particular speakers crucially depends on the legitimacy of our appealing to the default settings, and since Fricker has not shown how the legitimacy of our appealing to the default settings can be empirically grounded, it seems that Fricker does not succeed in giving even a "locally" reductive account of testimonial knowledge.

5.2 John McDowell's Anti-Reductionism

It seems to me — as well as to many contemporary specialists in the philosophy of testimony — that anti-reductionism with respect to testimonial justification has the upper hand in the current debate. The reductionist project is confronted by difficult problems, and anti-reductionism can seem to be the only viable option. But it is difficult to shake off the feeling that there is something peculiar about the idea of a "presumptive right to trust." What is the basis of such a right? Anti-reductionists imply that if a reduction of testimonial justification to other — more basic — sources of justification is impossible, then it follows that belief in testimony must be reasonable, that is, prima facie justified — *by definition*.[25] The very concept

---

23. Christopher Insole, "Seeing Off the Local Threat to Irreducible Knowledge by Testimony," *Philosophical Quarterly* 50, no. 198 (2000): 44-56; 53-54.

24. In a similar vein, Matthew Weiner argues that Fricker's default settings must be explicated in terms of an "acceptance-principle," which is basically equivalent to the PR principle (Weiner, "Accepting Testimony," *Philosophical Quarterly* 53, no. 211 [2003]: 256-64).

25. Stevenson, "Why Believe What People Say?" p. 430.

of testimony entails that testimony can be prima facie trusted. The hard question, however, is how the reasonability of trusting testimony can be a matter of definition. How can understanding a concept confer an epistemic right of this kind on one? Until this question is answered, it is difficult not to view anti-reductionism with suspicion.

There is, however, a version of anti-reductionism that altogether avoids making reference to a presumptive right to trust, and that thus bypasses the above-mentioned problem. This version of anti-reductionism suggested by John McDowell is, in my view, the most credible and profound understanding of testimonial knowledge available. But, in order to understand McDowell's account of testimonial knowledge, we must first consider his view of knowledge in general.

Knowledge is, in McDowell's words, a "standing in the space of reasons."[26] The "space of reasons" is a logical space of normative relations. It is the logical space we move in when we do not just ask what *causes* a subject S to believe the proposition *p*, but instead ask whether it is *reasonable* for S to believe that *p*, that is, whether S *ought to* believe that *p*. That knowledge is a standing in the logical space of reasons means that S, in order to know that *p*, must be *rationally entitled* to hold that *p* is true. S must, in other words, have a *justification*, or reason, for believing that *p*.[27]

According to the standard use of the term "knowledge," knowledge entails truth. This means that whether a person S knows that there are three cars in the parking lot depends on what the world external to S is like, namely, on whether there are three cars in the parking lot. Facts about a person's status as a knower hence supervene[28] on (i.e., are dependent on) facts about the world external to the knower.[29]

According to a common view, however, the same is not true of facts

---

26. John McDowell, "Knowledge and the Internal," in *Meaning, Knowledge, and Reality* (Cambridge, MA: Harvard University Press, 1998), p. 395.

27. John McDowell, "Knowledge and the Internal Revisited," *Philosophy and Phenomenological Research* 64, no. 1 (2002): 97-105.

28. Supervenience is an asymmetric relationship of dependence or determination holding between facts or properties. "A set of properties *A* supervenes upon another set *B* just in case no two things can differ with respect to *A*-properties without also differing with respect to their *B*-properties" (B. McLaughlin and K. Bennett, "Supervenience," in *Stanford Encyclopedia of Philosophy* (Winter 2011 ed.), ed. Edward N. Zalta: http://plato.stanford.edu/entries/supervenience/ (accessed May 7, 2013). For example, the shape of a surface supervenes on the microphysical properties of the surface.

29. We can understand "external" in a straightforward physical sense here. Everything outside the subject's skin is external to him.

about a person's justification for his knowledge — the reasons that underpin or support it. Whether a person has a rational entitlement (justification) to believe something about the external world is, on the common view, a question that can be settled independently of considering what the external world is like. What matters for the person's rational entitlement is not how he is related to the external world, but only how he reasons on the basis of "inner," subjective entities such as his beliefs and perceptual appearances. A person who is, in fact, a brain in a vat can hence — if things subjectively appear to him the right way — have exactly the same rational entitlement to believe that there is a tree in front of him as a subject who actually sees a tree. Facts about a subject's rational entitlement do not, according to this view, supervene on facts about the subject's objective environment.

McDowell criticizes this common view of rational entitlement. He refers to it as "the interiorization of the space of reasons" and argues that it is responsible for creating the Cartesian gulf between the mind and the world that much modern philosophy has struggled, in vain, to bridge. The interiorization is not only responsible for generating the standard skeptical problems that have plagued modern philosophy (How can I know that I am not a brain in a vat?); but it also tends to make it unintelligible how our thoughts can have world-directed contents, how they can be *about* an objective world in the first place.[30]

McDowell argues that we must resist the temptation to "interiorize" the space of reasons. We should not think of our reasons or justifications for believing things about the objective world as consisting exclusively of "inner" items and conditions. Instead, our rational entitlement to such beliefs should be thought of as depending on cognitive relationships to worldly objects and states of affairs. This view of rational entitlement is congruent with common sense. Common sense allows that my justification for believing that there is a tree before me could be captured by saying, "I *see* that there is a tree before me." The verb "see" is factive, which means that it is only correct to say that I see that there is a tree before me if there really is a tree before me. A genuine "seeing" is a state that objectively relates me to something in the external world.

Why, then, have epistemologists generally been unwilling to allow

---

30. McDowell, "Knowledge and the Internal." Most of my presentation of McDowell's general view of knowledge is based on this essay. Hereafter, page references to it appear in parentheses within the text.

that a subject's justification for believing things about the objective world can be captured by factive expressions such as that *S sees that there is a tree before her?* Why do only "inner," subjective items, such as perceptual *appearances,* figure in the typical epistemologist's reconstruction of how our beliefs about the world are justified? The reason is the possibility of mistaking a mere appearance for a genuine seeing. It can happen that when I take myself to see a tree, I am in fact the victim of a hallucination. Even though it visually appears to me exactly as if there is a tree before me, in fact there is no tree present. The possibility of misleading perceptual appearances is usually taken to entail that reason must take subjective appearances and other "inner" items as its only starting points when it deliberates about what to believe about the objective world. To presume that one actually sees a tree — without having arrived at this conclusion by a chain of (tacit or explicit) reasoning from how things subjectively appear — would be to take an irresponsible risk.

This traditional line of thought is, according to McDowell, motivated by a desire to make reason "self-sufficient within its proper province" (p. 405). Everybody agrees that I am not capable of guaranteeing, by my own autonomous powers, that I *know* that there is a tree before me. No matter how cautious I have been when I concluded that there is a tree before me, it is still possible that I am wrong (consider, for instance, the possibility of a Cartesian demon). Therefore, I cannot guarantee, by my own autonomous powers, that I have knowledge. However, if we conceive of the justifications for our beliefs about the objective world as consisting of arguments from "inner" entities such as perceptual appearances, then we can claim that we are capable of guaranteeing that our beliefs are *justified.* While knowledge, in this view, is a status that requires "cooperation" from the objective world (the world must actually be as we take it to be if we are to have knowledge), justification is a world-independent status, achievable by our own autonomous powers, without dependence on "favors" from the world. This traditional line of thought results in a conception of the "space of reasons" as interiorized, as removed from the objective world; this is, according to McDowell, the root cause of a host of philosophical problems.

McDowell's suggested cure is that we give up the "fantasy of a sphere within which reason is in full autonomous control" (p. 408). We need to accept that our reasons — our rational standings with respect to empirical claims — can be dependent on circumstances in the external world that are beyond our immediate control. We need to conceive of the "space of reasons" as "coalescing" with the objective world instead of as "interiorized" (pp. 406-7). To picture the world and the space of reasons as coalescing means to acknowledge that the world *itself* — and not just "inner" representations of the world — can figure in the justifications/reasons that underpin our empirical knowledge. According to this "exteriorized" conception of the space of reasons, our rational entitlements to believe things about the world can be construed as factive perceptual states such as *seeing that there is a tree before us*. The latter perceptual state is not a purely "inner" item, but a state that one can only be in if the mind-independent world is a certain way. For McDowell, this does not disqualify *seeing that there is a tree before one* from being a paradigmatic *mental* state, since the mind, in his view, is not in the head. That the mind is not in the head does not mean that the mind is an immaterial soul. Rather, it means that the mind is a *relational* phenomenon that essentially involves the "external" world.[31] Knowledge and specific ways of knowing (such as *seeing that p)* are mental states that are relational in precisely the relevant sense. They relate the person to the objective environment and are constitutively dependent on the environment. Nevertheless, they are *mental* states — states of the mind.

McDowell's externalist conception of the mind and mental phenomena implies that the mind cannot be conceived of as a domain of reality that is totally transparent to the subject. Since mental states are world-involving, we can sometimes be wrong about the contents of our own minds, in the same way as we can be wrong about the contents of the world. The mind does not, in McDowell's conception of it, constitute a "cognitive home" in which everything that occurs is infallibly accessible to the subject.[32]

An important feature of McDowell's anti-Cartesian concept of mind and knowledge is, as we have seen, that it denies that epistemic justifica-

---

31. This view is called "externalism" and represents, in different versions, the majority view within the philosophy of mind today. Åsa Wikforss writes: "Externalism is widely perceived to have overthrown traditional theories . . . of the nature of psychological states. Indeed, externalism has been so successful that the primary focus of today's debate is not so much on whether externalism is right or wrong, but rather on what its implications are" (Åsa Wikforss, "Semantic Externalism and Psychological Externalism," *Philosophy Compass* 3, no. 1 (2008): 158-81; 158). However, McDowell goes further in the externalist direction than many are comfortable with.

32. John McDowell, "Singular Thought and the Extent of Inner Space," in *Meaning, Knowledge, and Reality* (Cambridge, MA: Harvard University Press, 1998). I have borrowed the term "cognitive home" from Timothy Williamson, *Knowledge and Its Limits* (Oxford: Oxford University Press, 2000), p. 93. The idea that the mind is *totally* transparent is defended by very few, if any, today.

tion (rational entitlement to take the world to be a certain way) is a status that we can achieve without dependence on "favors from the world." For McDowell, the world about which we form beliefs plays itself an important part in the justification of those beliefs. If I really see a tree before me, then I have a satisfactory rational entitlement to take it that there is a tree before me. I then have a "factive standing in the space of reasons" — a reason/justification that puts me in direct cognitive contact with an objective fact. However, if the world is "unkind" and does not present me with a real tree, but merely with a hallucination, then the relevant rational entitlement is lacking. I might not be aware that it is lacking, but it is lacking nonetheless. This means that I am dependent on "favors" from the world at the very level of epistemic rationality. Whether my epistemic postures with respect to how the objective world is are justified or not depends on how I am in fact related to the objective world. According to McDowell, we should face up to the epistemic vulnerability that this entails instead of trying to picture ourselves as rationally autonomous:

> The very idea that reason has a sphere of operation within which it is capable of ensuring, without being beholden to the world, that one's postures are all right . . . has the look of a fantasy, something we spin to console ourselves for the palpable limits on our powers.[33]

McDowell's view of the world-involving and world-dependent character of rational entitlement is especially plausible when we consider the entitlement that pertains to testimonial knowledge. Most philosophers agree, as we have seen, that it is possible to acquire knowledge by believing what other people tell us. It seems, however, to be extremely difficult to account for the justification of this kind of knowledge merely in terms of the individual's own perceptions, memories, and reasoning. An individual usually does not have access to a cogent argument that starts from what he knows on the basis of firsthand experience to the conclusion that what another person tells him is true. Anti-reductionists usually respond to this problem by positing a presumptive right to trust, but it is unclear what the basis of such a right is. However, if we abandon the fantasy that reason is self-sufficient — that it can do without "favors" from the world

---

33. McDowell, "Knowledge and the Internal," p. 405. An exposition and defense of McDowell's view of knowledge and rational entitlement, as well as of his view of the mind-world relationship, can be found in Mats Wahlberg, *Reshaping Natural Theology: Seeing Nature as Creation* (Houndmills, UK: Palgrave Macmillan, 2012), chaps. 2-4.

REVELATION AS TESTIMONY

— then we need not see the difficulty of accounting for the justification of testimonial knowledge in *individualistic* terms as a problem. We need no longer presume that a rational entitlement to believe what another person tells us must be something that an individual can achieve by her own autonomous powers, with or without appealing to an individualistic "right to trust." We can, instead, allow that whether I am rationally entitled to believe that p depends on whether my informant who has told me that p really knows that p.

The underlying idea here is that, even though testimonial knowledge obviously is mediated by the subject's hearing and understanding of the utterances he encounters, such knowledge need not be construed as inferential, that is, as based on an *argument* from the mediating circumstances (the latter being that he has heard and understood the relevant utterances). Instead, we can construe testimony as a cognitive process that, like perception and memory, can constitute a noninferential, cognitive "connection" between the subject and an objective fact. If I encounter truthful testimony about the fact that p, then I have access to a perfectly good reason/justification to believe that p. The reason/justification is the testimony, which makes knowledge that p noninferentially available in a similar way as *seeing that* p or *remembering that* p make knowledge that p noninferentially available. In other words, testimony can provide a subject with factive standings in the space of reasons. The rational entitlement that pertains to testimonial knowledge is not, according to this conception, due to a general and arbitrary "presumptive right to trust."

This means that in the same way as the justification/reason for my knowledge that p can be that I *see* that p, it can also be that *I have learned from S* that p. "See" is a factive expression (I can only see that p if it is the case that p), and we should also understand the expression "having learned" as factive in the present context. This means that if I have *learned* from S that p (in the technical sense of "learned" that I will henceforth work with), then p must be the case, and S must know that p. If S did not know that p, but happened to be right about p by chance, then I did not *learn* that p from S's utterance. There was, in the latter case, nothing to *learn* from S's utterance, since it did not express *knowledge.* This view, of course, does not entail that I cannot (falsely) *believe* that I have learned from S that p. In such a "bad" case, when I trust unreliable testimony, I have (maybe due to no fault of my own) a much weaker justification for my belief that p than when I trust reliable testimony.

From my subjective point of view, those two situations may be indistinguishable, so there may be nothing I can do to avoid ending up in the unfavorable situation. Nevertheless, the justification I have for believing that *p* differs between the two cases. This is because unreliable testimony does not connect me cognitively to the facts in the way reliable testimony does. And my rational entitlement is, on the McDowellian model, dependent on how I am related to the world. This is a consequence of the rejection of the "interiorized" conception of the space of reasons.

McDowell explains his account this way:

> One cannot count as [having learned] from someone that things are thus and so, in the relevant sense, unless, by virtue of understanding what the person says, one is in a position to know that things are indeed thus and so. If it turns out that things are not thus and so, or that although things are thus and so, the person from whom one took oneself to have [learned] it did not know it, one cannot persist in the claim that one [learned] from him that things are thus and so. One must retreat to the claim that one heard him say that things are thus and so. Just as one captures a knower's justification for believing what he does by saying that he sees that things are thus and so, or that he remembers that things are thus and so, so one can capture a knower's justification — his knowledge-constituting standing in the space of reasons — by saying that he has [learned] from so-and-so that things are thus and so.[34]

However, a person who mindlessly accepts whatever he is told cannot, according to McDowell, count as acquiring testimonial knowledge, even if what he is told is true. Knowledge is a standing in the space of *reasons*. This means that acquiring it has to do with an exercise of rationality. To exercise rationality importantly involves deliberating about what to believe and what not to believe in the light of one's background knowledge and current evidence. Therefore, acquiring knowledge from testimony requires that one *has* a certain amount of relevant background knowledge, for instance, about the risks inherent in accepting testimony. It also requires that one allows the awareness of those risks to affect one's epistemic behavior, for example, by causing one to be on the lookout for signs of deception or ignorance in one's informant. Only when a subject has this

---

34. John McDowell, "Knowledge by Hearsay," in *Meaning, Knowledge, and Reality*, p. 434. I have substituted "learned" for "heard" in this quote in order to harmonize the terminology. But the meanings are the same.

kind of rational sensitivity to the implications of background knowledge and current evidence is he capable of acquiring a standing in the space of reasons by believing testimony.

A condition for acquiring testimonial knowledge is, in other words, that one exercises a certain amount of *doxastic responsibility:*

> A person sufficiently responsible to count as having achieved epistemic standing from someone else's words needs to be aware of how knowledge can be had from others, and rationally responsive to considerations whose relevance that awareness embodies. That requires his forming beliefs on the say-so of others to be rationally shaped by an understanding of, among other things, the risks one subjects oneself to in accepting what people say.

However,

> although it is obviously doxastically irresponsible to believe someone about whom one has positive reason to believe he is not trustworthy, or not likely to be informed about the subject matter of the conversation, doxastic responsibility need not require positive reasons to believe that an apparent informant is informed and speaking his mind.[35]

In order to count as doxastically responsible, one has to be rationally sensitive to evidence that indicates that one's informant is unreliable as a source of the relevant information. If one becomes aware of such evidence, one should consider withholding belief in his testimony. This is quite different from saying that one must have evidence *for* the reliability of one's informant in order to be entitled to accept his testimony. The basic insight of anti-reductionism is, as we remember, that the latter requirement is too demanding.

In sum, doxastic responsibility, which is a necessary condition for acquiring knowledge from testimony, entails only a *negative* rational sensitivity. In the absence of reasons to believe that one's informant is untrustworthy, it is fully responsible to trust his words.

Even if we act responsibly when believing what somebody tells us, this does not mean that our belief is *justified*. Doxastic responsibility and justification (rational entitlement) are, according to McDowell's conception, two different things. Whether one's testimonial belief that p is justi-

---

35. McDowell, "Knowledge by Hearsay," pp. 434-35.

fied depends on whether the testimony that the belief is based on actually makes knowledge that *p* available, that is, on whether one's informant knows that *p* and expresses this knowledge in words. One's reason/justification for believing that *p* is, in the beneficial case when one's informant is reliable, that one has *learned* from so-and-so that *p*. This testimonial reason is excellent, since it constitutes a factive standing in the space of reasons, like *seeing that p* or *remembering that p*. Having this kind of justification entails that *p* is true. However, one cannot have a standing in the space of reasons of this kind without displaying a rational sensitivity to the implications of background knowledge and independent evidence. *Having learned from S that* p is thus (again, like seeing that *p* or remembering that *p*) a mediated epistemic position in the sense that whether one occupies it or not depends on whether certain other conditions are satisfied. One important condition is that one must not act in a doxastically irresponsible way when one takes oneself to learn from S that *p*. If one has good reason to believe that S is insincere when she asserts that *p,* then even though she in fact speaks her mind and knows what she is talking about, one still does not acquire a satisfactory position in the space of reasons by believing what she says. One's standing in the space of reasons — one's testimonial justification for believing that *p* — is undermined by one's lack of doxastic responsibility.

Doxastic responsibility is, therefore, a necessary but insufficient condition for having a satisfactorily justified testimonial belief, and hence for having testimonial knowledge. Testimonial beliefs are satisfactorily justified when based on factive standings in the space of reasons, such as *having learned from S that* p. If a piece of testimony that one relies on does not provide one with such a factive standing — maybe because one's informant did not know what he was talking about — then the belief that it purports to support will fail to be properly justified. This is true even if it was fully compatible with the requirements of doxastic responsibility to believe the testimony.

This means that two people who believe that *p* on the basis of other people's say-so can both satisfy the requirements of doxastic responsibility to the same degree, while only one of them has a satisfactory *justification* for believing that *p*. This can happen if the world has granted one of the persons the favor of consuming trustworthy testimony, while the other person (due to no fault of his own) has had the bad luck of running into a clever liar. The crucial point to appreciate here is that the latter circumstance affects the *rational standing* of the deceived subject. His rational entitlement to believe what he believes depends, in other words, on circumstances he cannot directly control — or control for.

Those who find such a dependence on luck or misfortune at the level of epistemic rationality unacceptable are, if McDowell is right, in the grip of an untenable fantasy: the fantasy of reason's autonomy with respect to the world and other people. That fantasy may express itself in questions such as: How can *my* rational entitlement to believe that *p* depend on whether some *other* person knows that *p,* and whether that person speaks truthfully? Doesn't *my* rational entitlement to believe that *p* merely depend on what *I* have done with the input that my environment (including other people) has provided me with?

When we consider these seemingly reasonable questions, we should remember that the project of reducing testimony as a source of epistemic justification to individualistic sources, such as the individual's own perceptions, memories, and inferences, seems to be very problematic. This suggests that we might either have to deny that testimony can provide knowledge or accept that testimony is an irreducible, sui generis source of justification. Accepting the truth of anti-reductionism means accepting that I as an individual cannot, by my own cognitive resources, establish that trusting the words of other people is, in general (or in most particular cases), conducive to knowledge.

In light of the problems that plague reductionism, we should be much less inclined to reject McDowell's analysis of testimonial knowledge on the grounds that it portrays the individual's rational powers as fundamentally dependent on "favors" from the world and other people. Perhaps we must accept that we cannot conceive of our own epistemic rationality, not even in principle, as fully within our control as isolated individuals. Perhaps reason cannot be thought of as operating within an interior zone, removed from the external world, in which it is immune to the effects of luck. The phenomenon of testimonial knowledge is especially suited to reveal our cognitive dependence on factors that we as individuals cannot directly control, such as the trustworthiness and epistemic competence of others.

Coady has suggested that traditional epistemology's focus on the individual's own autonomous resources is the result of an individualistic bias:

> When one thinks of investigating knowledge in a systematic philosophical way it can seem somehow inevitable to start from the epistemically isolated self; beginning with the idea of an individual who initially lacks knowledge altogether, we ask what it would be for him

to acquire it. . . . Nonetheless, it is surely clear that this starting-point is a product of cultural and philosophical predilection rather than a priori inevitability. . . . Indications that the egocentric premise owes much of its obviousness to cultural and ideological factors come from the fact that it has also been prominent within a specific political tradition in the derivation of moral and especially political duties, rights, and obligations. A good deal of social-contract theory begins with the isolated individual who is bereft of political, and often social, ties, obligations, or responsibilities and who must construct them on a basis of enlightened self-interest.[36]

As we have seen, an adequate understanding of the phenomenon of testimonial knowledge seems to require that we abandon the idea of the "epistemically isolated self" and the related fantasy of reason's autonomy with respect to the world and other people.

36. Coady, *Testimony: A Philosophical Study,* pp. 149-50.

CHAPTER 6

Entrance into God's Own Knowledge

It is possible, as we saw in chapter 4, for God to speak by authorizing or appropriating human speech. This possibility, however, raises a difficult epistemological question. A person who hears a human being speak can identify the speaker perceptually. But a person who hears God speak through a divinely authorized spokesperson (such as a prophet) cannot perceive God. How, then, could speech that is in fact divine be *identified* as divine by a human hearer?

An answer to this question must, in effect, explain how humans can acquire knowledge of God. To identify divine speech as divine (i.e., as God's speech) means to acquire knowledge that God speaks, knowledge entailing, of course, that God exists. How this kind of knowledge is possible is a main topic of this book. In the preceding chapter I argued that testimony is best conceived as a sui generis source of justification. A person's justification for believing that p (a justification good enough for knowledge that p) can be — according to the view defended — that she has learned that p from somebody's testimony. In this chapter I will argue that God, by testifying to humans through human spokespersons, could transmit some of his knowledge to us, including — crucially — knowledge of his own divine identity. The account of revelation as divine testimony that follows builds on John McDowell's explication of testimonial knowledge. This does not mean that my argument stands and falls with McDowell's theory. The same basic account could, with some adjustments, be defended on the basis of other anti-reductionist theories of testimony as well.[1]

1. The element that is crucial for my argument is anti-reductionism itself, i.e., the claim that testimony is a sui generis source of epistemic justification.

6.1 The Prophet P

Suppose that the prophet P speaks in the name of God. This means that (some of) P's utterances constitute divine speech-acts. When P speaks, God speaks. Suppose, furthermore, that P — speaking in the name of God — *says* that she speaks in the name of God. Since God knows what he is talking about, and since P's utterance constitutes ("counts as") a divine assertion, it follows that P's utterance makes knowledge of the proposition *that P speaks in the name of God* publicly available.[2]

However, it is one thing for knowledge to be made available by an act of testimony; it is another thing for knowledge actually to be transmitted to a hearer by such an act. In order to acquire testimonial knowledge to the effect that P speaks in the name of God, the hearer must, of course, believe the relevant testimony. As we saw in the last chapter, however, acquiring knowledge by believing testimony also requires one to exercise doxastic responsibility. If it would be doxastically irresponsible for a person to believe what God says through the prophet P, then that person cannot acquire testimonial knowledge from the prophet's utterance.

It is quite obvious that it would, in normal cases, be utterly irresponsible to believe somebody who claims to speak in the name of God. But I will argue that there are possible circumstances in which it would not. Before we address the issue of responsibility at length, we need to clarify some logical issues. In order to do so we need to assume, for now, that there *are* possible circumstances in which it would not be irresponsible for a subject to believe what the prophet P says — and that such circumstances actually obtain.

In this imagined scenario, it would be possible for a hearer of P's utterance to "pick up" the knowledge that the utterance makes available. In other words, a hearer could, under the special circumstances we imagine, acquire testimonial knowledge of the proposition *that P speaks in the name of God,* which obviously entails that God exists. Accordingly, knowledge of the former proposition amounts to knowledge that God exists. How to understand the word "God" in this context depends on the word's meaning in the linguistic milieu in which P makes that utterance. If P speaks in a linguistic context where "God" is understood to mean an infinite, personal

---

2. If P says "I speak in the name of God," we can, by changing the "rhetoric-conceptual structure" of the utterance, interpret it as *God's* saying, "P speaks in the name of God" (see sec. 4.4).

being on whom everything finite is dependent, and if this meaning is what God intends to communicate through P, then P's utterance makes available knowledge that an infinite, personal being on whom everything finite is dependent exists.

My story about P does not presuppose that P *herself* knows (before she makes the relevant utterance) that God exists. If this were to be taken for granted in the story, then I would tacitly and illegitimately have assumed that the kind of knowledge I am trying to account for already exists. The only thing that the scenario presupposes, however, is that P has had some kind of experience that has convinced her that God wants her to say certain things in his name. This means that P *believes* that God exists. Let us assume, however, that P's beliefs that God exists and wants her to say things in his name do not have the status of knowledge or even the status of being justified.

The unjustified status of P's belief in God does not prevent her from being God's spokesperson. What matters is only that God has *in fact* deputized P to speak in his name. This requires merely that God has done something that counts as an act of deputization, such as inducing some kind of religious experience in P that convinces her that God wants her to speak in his name. (Inducing this kind of religious experience in P is not the same as *telling* P about her divine commission. The experience need not involve any words or assertions.) If P, after being deputized, publicly proclaims that she speaks in the name of God, then knowledge of P's divine commission becomes available to humans through her utterance. In this scenario it becomes available not only to other humans but also (for the first time) to P herself.[3]

A hearer who, without doxastic irresponsibility, believes P's utterance thereby acquires a testimonial reason that justifies knowledge of God. The testimonial reason is that he (the hearer) has *learned from P's utterance* that P speaks in the name of God. If McDowell is right, genuine testimonial reasons such as *"having learned from so-and-so that . . ."* are factive standings in the space of reasons, like *seeing that p* or *remembering that p*. Having such a reason entails that the fact testified to really obtains. It is irrelevant,

---

3. However, if God deputizes P by *telling* it to her in a religious experience, then knowledge of her divine commission becomes available to P as soon as she receives the divine testimony. The question remains, however, whether the dictates of doxastic responsibility would allow P to believe what she is told in an experience of this kind. Probably only if the experience occurs in the context of some remarkable circumstances could P responsibly do so.

in this context, that having a piece of false testimony as one's reason for believing a proposition can be indistinguishable, from the hearer's point of view, from having a factive testimonial reason for believing that proposition. A subject in the latter situation has a knowledge-constituting reason for his belief, while the subject in the former situation does not.

P's utterance is, *ex hypothesi,* a speech-act by God. But it is probably the case that the utterance is also a speech-act by P, the same kind of speech-act as the one God performs, namely, an assertion that P speaks in the name of God.[4] P's own assertion, however, does not *as such* make knowledge of God available, since P does not, as we have stipulated, have any knowledge of God. She just believes, without a satisfactory justification, that she speaks in the name of God. But since P's assertion also constitutes a divine assertion, it nevertheless puts the relevant knowledge into the public domain, where it might (as we here suppose) be picked up. The subject from whom the hearer *learns* that P is speaking in the name of God is, accordingly, God himself.

Elisabeth Anscombe identifies testimonial belief with belief that takes a *person* as its object.[5] For instance, I believe you when you say that *p,* or I believe my mother when she claims that *p.* This view seems to imply that a person who acquires testimonial knowledge must be able to *identify* the person who testifies prior to accepting her testimony. In order to believe my mother, I must already know (or at least believe) that it is my mother who speaks to me. Analogously, in order to believe God, I must already know (or believe) that it is God who speaks to me. Does this view contradict the account of how knowledge of God could be acquired that I have sketched in the scenario involving the prophet P?

It does not. Even if the hearer of P's utterance does not, initially, believe that it is God who speaks, the hearer is nevertheless capable of identifying the utterance as *somebody's* speech, and hence capable of believing that person (whoever he/she is). If we were to deny that I can believe a person about whom I know nothing (except that he is a person), we would have to deny that most high-school students have acquired knowledge from reading textbooks. High-school students, as I pointed out earlier, usually do not know anything about the authors of their textbooks.

---

4. It is not necessary, however, that P's act is a speech-act. It is also consistent with the scenario that P merely performs a *locutionary* act — that she utters certain words.

5. G. E. M. Anscombe, "Faith," in *The Collected Philosophical Papers of G. E. M. Anscombe,* vol. 3: *Ethics, Religion and Politics* (Oxford: Basil Blackwell, 1981).

Often they have not bothered to run through the list of authors, so they do not even know their names. Still, what students acquire from reading textbooks is, we should presume, testimonial *knowledge.* They believe the unknown persons who have written the books. Consider also beliefs acquired from Wikipedia. Wikipedia is surely a possible source of knowledge (about some topics) even though the person who testifies is anonymous. The crucial issue is not whether the person who acquires knowledge from Wikipedia knows who the author of the article she reads is, but whether it is compatible with the requirements of doxastic responsibility for the reader to believe the testimony contained in the article. In the case of Wikipedia, it arguably is (with respect to some topics).

In cases where the testifier is unknown, it may be more appropriate to characterize testimonial beliefs as beliefs that take a piece of *testimony* as its primary object rather than a person. We can, for instance, say that I believe the stranger's claim that *p,* or the assertions contained in a certain book. Claims and assertions are, of course, acts that essentially involve a person.

McDowell's account of testimonial knowledge does not require that testimonial reasons make explicit reference to a certain person — or even a certain source. It is possible, according to McDowell, to characterize the epistemic standing one acquires from testimony (i.e., one's testimonial reason) without mentioning the source of the testimony. He asks us to "consider . . . the expression 'I gather that . . .' which claims knowledge from testimony without identifying the source. (Compare 'I heard it through the grapevine.'")[6]

The above considerations should not in any way be taken as a denial that the properties of the person who testifies are relevant for the epistemic standing that a hearer acquires by believing her testimony. A testimonial belief is justified (when it is justified) because it is based on the assertion of somebody who is trustworthy. However, as we saw in the previous chapter, one need not have prior knowledge of the trustworthiness of one's informant in order to be able to acquire testimonial knowledge from her words. If one's informant is in fact trustworthy, and if one's act of believing her testimony is not doxastically irresponsible, then the testimony transmits knowledge.

It is true, as both John Lamont and Anscombe point out, that Christian faith is best characterized as *believing God* when he speaks. A logical

---

6. John McDowell, "Knowledge by Hearsay," in *Meaning, Knowledge, and Reality* (Cambridge, MA: Harvard University Press, 1998), p. 433, n. 29.

Entrance into God's Own Knowledge

presupposition for being able to believe God is that one first believes that God exists and that what one is confronted with is God's speech. In my story, the prophet P's hearers do not (initially) believe that what they are confronted with is God's speech. They naturally assume that it is merely P's speech. So when they believe the testimony expressed by P's utterance, which is in fact God's testimony, they can nevertheless not be said to believe God. So it seems that believing the assertion made by God through P could not constitute an act of Christian faith.[7]

This is not a problem for my account. The belief that P speaks in God's name, even though it is in my story a testimonial belief, may be viewed as a "preamble" of faith. After the hearer has acquired testimonial knowledge that P speaks in God's name (and thereby knowledge that God exists), the hearer is in a position to know that the rest of what P says comes from God. The hearer can then believe *God* when he believes what P says.

The reader may have a feeling that it is logically problematic to claim that knowledge of God's existence can be acquired on the basis of God's own testimony. But this is a misconception. There may be all sorts of problems pertaining to the question of whether testimony about God can be responsibly accepted (problems to be addressed below), but there are no *logical* problems with the idea that divine testimony can provide knowledge of God's existence. By believing what is in fact God's testimony, but what one is not initially capable of *identifying* as God's testimony, one can acquire knowledge that the agent whose testimony one consumes is God. This is no more *logically* problematic than that one can acquire knowledge that the agent whose testimony one consumes is Barack Obama. If one has never heard of Barack Obama and bumps into a person who truthfully presents himself as Barack Obama, one gets to know that the agent whose

---

7. However, it is possible that P's hearers already believe (for whatever reason) that P speaks in the name of God, prior to encountering P's speech. If so, the hearers would indeed believe God when they believe what P says. Of course, since they already believe that P speaks in the name of God prior to hearing P's assertion to this effect, the hearers cannot be said to *acquire* the relevant belief from P's assertion. However, they might nevertheless acquire *knowledge* that P speaks in the name of God from P's assertion. This would happen if the hearer's prior belief that P speaks in the name of God is unjustified. By hearing P say that she speaks in the name of God, they would acquire a new reason to believe that P speaks in the name of God, a reason that is sufficient to give this belief the status of knowledge. Compare: If I have a true but unjustified belief that alcohol is lighter than water, I can acquire knowledge that alcohol is lighter than water by acquiring a new reason for believing the relevant proposition, for example, the testimony of a physics professor.

testimony one consumes is Barack Obama. In other words, one gets to know that Barack Obama exists by testimony from Barack Obama.

6.2 Doxastic Responsibility

Now to the crucial question: Can it ever be doxastically responsible to believe an assertion of the kind that we imagined God making through the prophet P? In order to answer this question, we need first to remind ourselves about what doxastic responsibility involves, and to clarify what work this notion is supposed to do in McDowell's account of testimonial knowledge.

If I know that p on the basis of S's testimony, then my justification for believing that p is not, according to McDowell, to be construed as an argument starting from the premise that *S said that* p, together with additional premises such as *S is usually trustworthy about these things,* or *people in general are usually trustworthy about these things.* Rather, the testimonial transaction itself (one's *having learned from S that* p) constitutes one's standing in the space of reasons with respect to p (i.e., one's reason or justification for believing p). The standing in the space of reasons constituted by *having learned from S that* p is factive, which means that having that standing entails that p is true.

However, acquiring knowledge from testimony is not a mindless reception of information. *Having learned from S that* p is a standing in the space of reasons and can, as such, only be correctly ascribed to a subject who is sensitive to the requirements of doxastic responsibility. Believing that p on the basis of S's testimony can only yield knowledge that p if one's acceptance of S's testimony is not doxastically irresponsible.

We need to clarify what this means. A hearer H who acquires testimonial knowledge that p from a speaker S is usually in a number of informational states that can be credited to him without presupposing that what he acquires from S is knowledge. For instance, H is in the state of hearing S say that p, which is a state that can be ascribed to H without presupposing that what he acquires from S is knowledge. Likewise, H may believe and know — independently of what he learns from S — a lot of things that are relevant for assessing the likelihood of p's being true, or the likelihood of S's knowing that p, or the likelihood of S's testifying sincerely. For instance, if p is the proposition *Bert is at home,* H may possess information that makes it unlikely that p is true, such as his having seen Bert drive away just a moment ago. Or H may possess information that suggests that S is a liar. Accordingly, the proposition that S testifies to stands in rational relations, such as probabilification or improbabilification, to the contents of other informational states that H is in. These inferential relations "constitute a rational structure to which one must be sufficiently responsive, largely in the negative way that one must not fly in the face of its revelations about belief-worthiness, if one is to be capable of being credited with [the knowledge that testimony makes available]."[8] Flying in the face of what the rational structure (consisting of one's other beliefs and knowledge) reveals about belief-worthiness is to act in a doxastically irresponsible way.

The crucial thing to remember about the notion of doxastic responsibility is that it is not — in McDowell's account — supposed to do the job of the notion of *justification*. Being doxastically responsible when forming a belief on the basis of a piece of testimony does not, by itself, make the belief satisfactorily justified. Responsibility, instead, is a precondition for acquiring a satisfactory justification in the form of a factive testimonial reason.

I might be capable of ensuring, by my own autonomous powers, that I form beliefs in a doxastically responsible way, but I cannot ensure that my testimonial beliefs are satisfactorily justified. For my testimonial beliefs to be satisfactorily justified, I am dependent on "favors" from other people (such as that they testify sincerely and know what they are talking about). Doxastic responsibility cannot guarantee that one receives the necessary favors, and hence not guarantee that one's testimonial beliefs are justified. To think that the notion of justification can be explicated wholly in terms of the notion of doxastic responsibility is to indulge in the "fantasy of a sphere in which reason is in full autonomous control."[9]

It is obvious that being doxastically responsible is compatible with having a lot of false beliefs. In the Middle Ages one could, without doxastic irresponsibility, believe that the earth does not move, that everything consists of four elements, that bodily fluids determine one's temper, and so forth. There seemed to be good arguments in favor of those views. From our perspective, these arguments do not hold water. This is because

8. McDowell, "Knowledge by Hearsay," p. 435.
9. So we have to reject deontological conceptions of epistemic justification, conceptions according to which "*being justified* is being within our rights, flouting no epistemic duties, doing no more than what is permitted" (Alvin Plantinga, *Warrant: The Current Debate* [New York: Oxford University Press, 1993], p. 13). Such accounts, one might say, try to explicate the concept of justification in terms of doxastic responsibility.

we have access to information and methods that medieval people did not know about. However, when it comes to assessing the doxastic responsibility of medieval people, we surely need to view things from *their* perspective. Furthermore, as we saw in the preceding chapter, people are inescapably dependent on testimony for most of their beliefs. If a culture is soaked with false beliefs (about, say, cosmology, medicine, chemistry) then nobody in that culture can avoid having her worldview shaped by them. Nobody, not even the most responsible subject, can depend only on her own reasoning and observation. Even if one could, one's very perception of the world would still be mediated by the concepts of one's culture. Even Elisabeth Fricker admits, as we saw in the preceding chapter, that in the "developmental phase" a subject has no choice but to rely uncritically on testimony, and Fricker also admits that there is no way of retrospectively justifying, in a noncircular way, all the beliefs thus acquired. We have an "irredeemable debt" to past testimony.

This means that "the rational structure to which a subject must be sufficiently responsive" in order to count as doxastically responsible is to a substantial degree constituted by inferential relationships among beliefs that the subject has absorbed from the surrounding culture through testimony. So whether a subject's acceptance of a new piece of testimony counts as responsible depends on what beliefs the subject already has, and what beliefs he has will depend, to a great extent, on what propositions are generally accepted as true within the culture in which he lives. This does not mean that a subject, without deserving blame for lack of doxastic responsibility, can accept *any* proposition that most other people within his culture accept. There are surely cases in which it is doxastically irresponsible to believe what most people believe. We cannot, however, expect that a subject, in order to count as doxastically responsible, must be able to extricate himself from the general worldview of the culture he inhabits.

6.3 Jesus

In addressing the issue of doxastic responsibility, I will — for reasons that will soon become apparent — change the example from being about the generic prophet P to being about the historical figure Jesus of Nazareth, as portrayed by the Gospel narratives. As before, the scenario is hypothetical: it is a scenario involving the historical Jesus that could (I claim) *possibly* be

Entrance into God's Own Knowledge

true.[10] Already at this stage, I must preface this by saying that the doctrine of the incarnation will be bracketed in my account. I will not assume, in this hypothetical scenario, that Jesus is God. Instead, I will picture him as being related to God in the same way that any prophet is — as a person who is deputized to speak in the name of God.[11]

If the Christian tradition is right, Jesus knows things about God "in advance" (i.e., prior to performing divine speech-acts). His utterances are thus expressive not only of God's knowledge but also of Jesus' knowledge. However, this circumstance will not figure in my argument. I will not appeal to Jesus' own knowledge in order to explain how knowledge can be transmitted from God to humans by means of Jesus' utterances. Therefore, we may equally well disregard the circumstance that Jesus (according to the Christian tradition) has prior knowledge of God, and we may view him as being in the same epistemic situation as the prophet P, whose belief that God has deputized her to speak for him is initially unjustified — a mere conviction.

Suppose, then, that Jesus sometimes spoke in the name of God, and that his utterances therefore constituted divine speech-acts. Suppose, furthermore, that Jesus, speaking in the name of God, asserted that he spoke in the name of God. (One can, of course, assert something to this effect without using these exact words, or their Aramaic equivalents.) Since God knows what he is talking about, and since the relevant assertion by Jesus also constitutes a divine assertion, it expresses *knowledge* of the fact that Jesus speaks in the name of God. The God Jesus claims to speak in the name of is the God of Israel, and hence a personal reality on whom everything finite depends — the kind of reality that Kant and Kaufman deny that people can have knowledge of.[12]

---

10. By "the historical Jesus" I do not mean the portrait(s) of Jesus that biblical scholars produce by using historical-critical methods. I simply mean the flesh-and-blood man who lived about two thousand years ago and to whom the name "Jesus of Nazareth" (as used in the Gospel narratives) refers. Most scholars believe that there was such a man (sometimes called "the real Jesus"). See, e.g., Francis Watson, "The Quest for the Real Jesus," in Markus Bockmuehl, ed., *The Cambridge Companion to Jesus* (Cambridge: Cambridge University Press, 2001), p. 156. My hypothetical account is supposed to be consistent with what the Gospels and our best historical knowledge tell us about Jesus and his environment.

11. I bracket the doctrine of the incarnation because it is not necessary for explaining how Jesus' words could transmit knowledge of God. However, the doctrine is unproblematically compatible with my account.

12. Marianne Meye Thompson says that "the traditions regarding Jesus' convictions about God remain relatively stable throughout various forms and sources, in all likelihood

153

It would, however, be doxastically irresponsible in any culture to believe a random guy off the street who says that he speaks in the name of God. There are good reasons to suspect that his assertion indicates, for example, some delusion. So how could the knowledge that Jesus' utterance makes available in our hypothetical scenario possibly be picked up by a hearer?

Well, suppose that for some reason you start following behind the guy off the street. You learn that he is an excellent person in moral respects, and you are swept away by his teaching. You find that what he teaches is anchored in Scripture and congruent with what you previously believed about God and Israel, and yet it casts a new light on Scripture and tradition. Moreover, Jesus' behavior resonates deeply with what he says. The man does not *seem* to be delusional or fraudulent, which he must be if his claim about being commissioned by God is false. On the contrary, he seems to be the most clear-sighted and honest person you have ever met.

It is not *obvious* that it would be doxastically irresponsible for a first-century Jew in this scenario to believe Jesus. For a first-century Jew, it was simply self-evident that there is a God. (Hasn't Richard Dawkins himself said that it was *Darwin* who made it possible to be an intellectually fulfilled atheist?[13]) We should assume, furthermore, that a first-century Palestinian Jew could, without doxastic irresponsibility, share his social environment's general beliefs about God, the law, Scripture, and so on.

---

because so much of the picture of God in the Gospels reflects core convictions found in the Old Testament and in early Judaism" (Marianne Meye Thompson, "Jesus and His God," in Markus Bockmuehl, ed., *The Cambridge Companion to Jesus* [Cambridge: Cambridge University Press, 2001], p. 43). It could be argued that it is unclear whether the Judaism Jesus knew taught that God created the world "out of nothing," and hence whether the God Jesus talks about is the "all-sufficient primordial being" that Kant and Kaufman claim we cannot know. The majority of scholars at least deny that Genesis 1 teaches creation ex nihilo. In 2 Maccabees 7:28, on the other hand, we read: "I beg you, my child, to look at the heaven and the earth and see everything that is in them, and recognize that God did not make them out of things that existed." This seems to indicate that Judaism, well before Jesus' time, taught creation ex nihilo. However, the passage may not have this implication (see John Goldingay, *Israel's Gospel* [Downers Grove, IL: InterVarsity, 2003], p. 78). Even if it is true that a creation-ex-nihilo doctrine was explicitly formulated only in the second century CE, it is certainly plausible that something like that doctrine was implicit in Jewish monotheism at the time of Jesus.

13. Richard Dawkins, *The Blind Watchmaker: Why the Evidence of Evolution Reveals a Universe without Design* (New York: Norton, 1986), p. 6.

Otherwise, we must expect a doxastically responsible subject to be able to extricate himself rather drastically from the general worldview of his fellows. Setting the bar for doxastic responsibility that high should be avoided. We should therefore assume that a first-century Jew can responsibly believe that Scripture records God's dealings with his people, and that it contains passages spoken by God through prophets commissioned by him. A first-century Jew may also responsibly believe that Scripture predicts the coming of a Davidic or priestly messiah sometime in the future. He would believe these things because they are generally accepted in his society, confirmed by the say-so of religious experts, and maybe appear to be confirmed by his own religious experience.

Note that I do not claim that a first-century Jew has a satisfactory *justification* for believing these things. Doxastic responsibility is, as we saw, a weaker notion than justification. A whole culture can have beliefs that are quite unjustified — or at least not justified to a satisfactory degree — but that does not mean that most of the inhabitants of that culture can be accused of doxastic irresponsibility. If the basic beliefs of first-century Judaism about God, Scripture, the law, and so on are false, then it is probably the case that quite a number of people further back — those who founded and spread the religion — did form beliefs about God and so on in a doxastically irresponsible way. But this does not imply that a person who enters the scene at a point when the religion is well entrenched and provides the conceptual framework by means of which people in general apprehend the world could be accused of doxastic irresponsibility just by virtue of sharing this religious framework and its foundational beliefs.

However, though a first-century Palestinian Jew may have background beliefs that give rise to a rational expectation of the coming of a Messiah or some other agent of God, I am still unsure whether it *would* be doxastically responsible for a first-century Jew simply to accept the assertion of a man who claims to speak in the name of God — even if this man turns out to be excellent in moral respects, a brilliant teacher, and so forth. A doxastically responsible subject should be aware of the possibility that Jesus is something like a delusional genius. Jesus cannot be *just* a madman, since his teaching is not that of a lunatic. But Jesus could be a lunatic *genius.* Great genius can coexist with delusion, a fact that ancient cultures also knew.

Let us set the bar for doxastic responsibility very high (possibly too high) in this case. Let us assume that in order for it to be possible for Jesus' hearers to believe him without doxastic irresponsibility, they must be aware of some circumstance or circumstances that rule out, or make highly unlikely, the mad-genius hypothesis.[14] What kind of circumstances could do that? Suppose you see Jesus perform some extraordinary acts of healing. Suppose, furthermore, that nobody in Jerusalem — not even those who have an interest in doing so — questions that the grave where Jesus was put after his crucifixion was empty a couple of days later. Finally, suppose that you encounter Jesus (or a person you are completely convinced is Jesus) some days after his death by crucifixion.

The mad-genius hypothesis, which provides an excellent explanation of why Jesus is such a brilliant teacher and yet makes the outrageous claim that he speaks for God, does not provide any explanation for these unusual events. But the hypothesis that Jesus really is commissioned by God does. This means that the total evidence to which Jesus' closest disciples have access, in this imagined scenario, supports rather than undermines the credibility of Jesus' claim. Therefore, his claim can be responsibly believed by the disciples.

The fact that the total amount of (nontestimonial) evidence to which Jesus' closest followers have access supports Jesus' credibility does not, of course, mean that this evidence proves that Jesus' claim is true. It does not, and it need not. The reader will remember that my basic thesis is that knowledge that Jesus speaks in the name of God can be had on the basis of testimony. If a subject H knows that Jesus speaks in the name of God on the basis of testimony, then H's *reason* for believing this is not an argument from premises such as *that Jesus did this and that act of healing, Jesus returned from the dead,* and so on.[15] H's reason for believing that Jesus speaks in the name of God is *that he learned it from Jesus' assertion.* The healings and the resurrection are relevant, in the present context, only as

---

14. That doxastic responsibility may require that Jesus' hearers are able to rule out the mad-genius hypothesis before they can believe Jesus's claim does not mean that doxastic responsibility requires them to rule out *all possible* alternative explanations of the evidence. To require this would be to require that they have a watertight argument to the truth of Jesus' claim before they can responsibly believe it. This is obviously setting the bar for doxastic responsibility too high. However, the suspicion that Jesus could be a delusional genius is, arguably, rather natural. It should be a cause of concern for a doxastically responsible subject.

15. A person who has witnessed the healings and some of Jesus' postresurrection appearances is, of course, in a position to construct an argument of this type, which would (to a certain degree) justify the belief that Jesus is commissioned by God. But would such an argument provide a justification that is good enough for knowledge? I do not think so.

Entrance into God's Own Knowledge

factors that ensure that H can believe Jesus' assertion without violating the dictates of doxastic responsibility. Doxastic responsibility clearly requires that one's initial attitude toward claims about divine commission is a highly skeptical one. In order for it to be responsible to believe somebody who claims to speak in the name of God, there must be some evidence that undermines the obvious reasons for skepticism. Observed "miracles" of the kind we have considered can do this. Even Terence Penelhum admits that "if the gospel records are true, the events they record are indeed (I would submit) both probative and revelatory."[16]

If it is possible, as I have argued, for Jesus' followers in the above scenario to believe his assertion without doxastic irresponsibility, then they are in a position to pick up the knowledge that it makes available. Because Jesus' assertion (according to our scenario) constitutes a divine speech-act, the latter knowledge is God's own. This means that Jesus' hearers can *know* that Jesus speaks in the name of God, and hence that God exists. Of course, they already believed that God exists, but it is questionable whether their belief was satisfactorily justified.

At this point I have already established what I set out to establish. I take it that I have shown that it is possible for humans to acquire testimonial knowledge of God's existence. I have done this by imagining a scenario in which God speaks through the first-century Palestinian Jew Jesus, who performs some extraordinary acts and undergoes an extraordinary event. These extraordinary occurrences (or even the *seeming* occurrence of them[17]) are sufficient to clear Jesus' followers of the charge of doxastic irresponsibility. So the followers are, in the imagined scenario, in a position to pick up God's own knowledge, expressed by the utterance of Jesus.[18]

---

16. Terence Penelhum, *Problems of Religious Knowledge* (London: Macmillan, 1971), p. 110.

17. Jesus's followers could, arguably, be acquitted of the charge of being doxastically irresponsible if they were completely convinced that Jesus healed some people and returned from the dead, and if these convictions themselves were not arrived at in a doxastically irresponsible way.

18. I have presumed that a first-century Palestinian Jew can, without doxastic irresponsibility, share his culture's general beliefs about God, the reliability of Scripture, etc. However, even if this presumption is rejected (a rejection that seems to commit one to believe that most individuals in human history have acquired most of their important beliefs in a doxastically irresponsible way), the conclusion still stands. A first-century Palestinian who followed Jesus around, but who did not initially believe that Scripture relates God's dealings with his people, and that prophets had been commissioned by God in the past, would nevertheless be able to believe Jesus's claim about his own divine commission without

However, it would be bad news for Christians if Jesus' utterances could be responsibly believed only by those who had seen him perform some miraculous healing or had witnessed some of his postresurrection appearances. Need one witness a miracle in order to be able, without doxastic irresponsibility, to trust testimony that purports to express knowledge of God? Below I will argue that one does not. First, however, we must situate my account of the epistemic function of miracles in the context of the Christian tradition. I will work here with an intuitive concept of "miracle" and will postpone the discussion about what a miracle is until later.

6.4 The Epistemic Function of Miracles

There is "a deeply rooted scriptural principle that miracles (performed within the framework of divine revelation) legitimate divinely authorized agents." This principle applies to the prophetic figures of the Old Testament, to Jesus, and to the apostles of the New Testament. In the case of Jesus, the miracles "support and promote the identity of Jesus as God's eschatological agent, the Messiah."[19] When the disciples of John the Baptist ask Jesus if he is the "one who is to come," Jesus tells them to tell John what they had *heard* and *seen,* namely, that "the blind receive their sight, the lame walk, the lepers are cleansed, the deaf hear, the dead are raised" (Matt. 11:4).

This is not to say that the miracles and the resurrection are *primarily* intended as — and seen by Jesus' contemporaries as — evidence for Jesus' divine status or commission. The miracles are closely connected to the message about the coming kingdom of God. Raymond Brown says:

> The miracle was not primarily an external proof of the coming of the kingdom . . . but *one of the means by which the kingdom came.* The acts of power were weapons Jesus used to reclaim people and the world from the domination of evil.

---

doxastic responsibility. Even in the eyes of an (initially) *unbelieving* first-century Palestinian Jew, the hypothesis that Jesus speaks truly about himself would appear to be (and in fact be) a very good explanation of Jesus' powerful deeds and his resurrection, especially in light of the scriptural passages that predict the coming of a messiah.

19. B. L. Blackburn, "Miracles, Miracle Stories I: Gospels," in D. G. Reid, ed., *The IVP Dictionary of the New Testament* (Downers Grove, IL: InterVarsity, 2004), p. 811.

However, by his miracle-working Jesus "clearly presents himself as changing the governance of the world and of human lives, introducing God's dominion in place of the oppressive Satanic rule."[20] The miracles, in other words, say something about *Jesus'* role in the inbreaking of the kingdom. They identify him as the one through whom the kingdom comes — as God's agent.[21] E. P. Sanders writes that "it is reasonable to think that [Jesus], as well as his followers, saw his miracles as testifying to his being a true messenger from or agent of God."[22]

In the apologetics of the church through the centuries, miracles have been given an important epistemic role. Origen says that "without miracles and wonders" the apostles "would not have persuaded those who heard new doctrines and new teaching."[23] According to Justin Martyr, Jesus "raised the dead and gave them life and by his actions challenged the men of this time to recognize him."[24] For Gregory of Nyssa, "His very miracles have convinced us of his deity."[25] Augustine claims that "miracles were necessary before the world believed, in order that it might believe."[26] Aquinas says that miracles "are rightly appealed to in proof of the Faith.... For a pronouncement issued by a man with a claim to divine authority is never more fittingly attested than by works which God alone can perform."[27] For Calvin, Moses' doctrine was "sanctioned for all time" by the wonders he wrought, and Jesus' divinity is "plainly

---

20. Raymond Brown, *An Introduction to New Testament Christology* (New York: Paulist Press, 1994), pp. 64, 65.

21. An all-too-common line of argument says that "if Jesus had offered his miracles as proofs either of his messiahship or of the coming reign of God, he would have completely contradicted his own conception of faith as free decision rather than coerced opinion" (Reginald Fuller, *Interpreting the Miracles* [London: SCM Press, 1963], p. 44; quoted in Joe Houston, *Reported Miracles: A Critique of Hume* [Cambridge: Cambridge University Press, 1994], p. 85). Houston demolishes this argument (and some other theological arguments against the epistemic role of miracles) in chap. 6 of his book. (The account of the role of miracles that I am defending does not, of course, portray miracles as "proofs.")

22. E. P. Sanders, *Jesus and Judaism* (London: SCM Press, 1985), p. 173.

23. Origen, *Against Celsus* 1.46; quoted in Colin Brown, *Miracles and the Critical Mind* (Grand Rapids: Eerdmans, 1984), p. 4.

24. Justin Martyr, *Dialogue with Trypho* 69; quoted in Brown, *Miracles and the Critical Mind,* p. 4.

25. Gregory of Nyssa, *An Address on Religious Instruction* (also known as *Catechetical Oration*) 34; quoted in Brown, *Miracles and the Critical Mind,* p. 4.

26. Augustine, *The City of God* (New York: Modern Library, 1978), p. 819.

27. Thomas Aquinas, *Aquinas's Shorter Summa* (Manchester, UK: Sophia Institute Press, 2002), p. 153.

and clearly" shown in miracles.[28] The First Vatican Council expresses similar views:

> In order that the obedience of our faith be nevertheless in harmony with reason . . . God willed that exterior proofs of his revelation, viz., divine facts, especially miracles and prophecies, should be joined to the interior helps of the Holy Spirit; as they manifestly display the omnipotence and infinite knowledge of God, they are the most certain signs of the divine revelation.[29]

Vatican II de-emphasizes the evidential role of miracles and prophecies, and presents them, according to Avery Dulles, "not as extrinsic signs of credibility but rather . . . as integral parts of revelation itself."[30] Nevertheless, the traditional function of miracles (to identify Christ as God's agent) is also present in the council's writings:

> For this reason Jesus perfected revelation by fulfilling it through his whole work of making Himself present and manifesting himself: through his words and deeds, his signs and wonders, but especially through his death and glorious Resurrection from the dead and final sending of the Spirit of truth.[31]

Traditionally, then, miracles have been assigned — among other things — an *epistemic* function with respect to Christian faith. Miracles have been viewed as occurrences that make possible — or facilitate, or play a part in — the recognition of divine revelation for human subjects. (*Recognition* is an epistemic concept: to recognize x is to *know* that the object of one's attention is x.) However, there are important differences between how different thinkers within the Christian tradition have understood the epistemic function of miracles. Hard-line evidentialists have claimed that miracles have a "logically coercive force," which means that a miracle, by itself, is sufficient to establish that God has spoken. Samuel Clarke and Hugh Farmer are examples of this position. Farmer writes: "The proof

---

28. Brown, *Miracles and the Critical Mind*, pp. 16-17.
29. Heinrich Denzinger, *Compendium of Creeds, Definitions, and Declarations on Matters of Faith and Morals*, ed. Peter Hünermann, 43rd ed. (San Francisco: Ignatius Press, 2012), §3009.
30. Avery Dulles, *The Assurance of Things Hoped For: A Theology of Christian Faith* (New York: Oxford University Press, 1994), p. 140.
31. Denzinger, *Compendium of Creeds*, §4204.

from miracles of the divine commission and doctrine of a prophet is, in itself, decisive and *absolute*. . . . The proof arises out of the nature of the miracles, independent of everything else."[32] John Locke represents a softer form of evidentialism, in which miracles have their evidential force in the context of other considerations. Colin Brown says: "Locke's approach to miracles involved what might be called a gestalt judgment. It not only took account of the paranormal particulars of a report [of a miracle], but also considered its moral and spiritual aspects in their immediate and wider contexts." Miracles, for Locke, "function within the wider context of what is already known and believed about God." The same is true of most premodern Christian thinkers. As Brown points out, "in the early Church, the appeal to miracles hardly ever stood on its own as a single, knockdown argument."[33] The church fathers did not view the miraculous as an unambiguous mark of the divine. Only in the context of Jesus' or the prophet's life and teaching was a miracle taken as an indication of divine attestation, as opposed to, say, demonic influence. Origen, well aware that Jesus' deeds could be interpreted as magic, says that "no sorcerer uses his tricks to call spectators to moral reformation; nor does he educate by the fear of God people who were astounded by what they saw, nor does he attempt to persuade the onlookers to live as men who will be judged by God."[34]

There are hence differences within the tradition as to what degree of probative or evidential force miracles are seen as having, and as to whether this evidential force belongs to the miracles taken in isolation, or only against a background of other knowledge and belief about God.

A completely separate question is whether miracles (or knowledge/beliefs about miracles) are appropriately conceived as *grounding* belief in divine revelation. Do Christians believe what God has said/revealed, and that he has said/revealed it, *because of* (i.e., on the basis of) knowledge of the occurrence of certain miracles? John Lamont summarizes the views of important patristic figures, such as Clement, Origen, Chrysostom, and Augustine, on this matter:

> All of them react to pagan criticism of the irrationality of Christian belief by flatly contradicting it. They claim that it is rational; and the

---

32. Hugh Farmer, *A Dissertation on Miracles: Designed to Shew, That They Are Arguments of a Divine Interposition, and Absolute Proofs of the Mission and Doctrine of a Prophet* (London: Printed for T. Cadell and J. Buckland, 1771), pp. 522-23.

33. Brown, *Miracles and the Critical Mind*, pp. 55, 44, 5.

34. Origen, *Against Celsus* 1.68; quoted in Brown, *Miracles and the Critical Mind*, p. 5.

reason they give for its rationality is the fact that it is believing God, who has the highest possible degree of authority. This authority gives faith [i.e., *what* is believed] a certainty that is equal to, or greater than, that of any other kind of knowledge. This certainty is *not* conferred by the signs or evidence [such as miracles] for God's having spoken, although these signs suffice to make the fact of his having spoken *beyond reasonable doubt*.[35]

For major church fathers, then, Christian belief in divine revelation is not based on "signs or evidence for God's having spoken." Even though there *is* good evidence for God's having spoken, Christians do not believe the Christian message as a result of inferring from that evidence that God has spoken. Christian belief arises in some other way.

In the Catholic tradition, the debate about the grounding of belief in divine revelation is often framed in terms of the role of the so-called motives of credibility. The latter are "the publicly available evidence, accessible to believer and unbeliever alike, that can be used to support the contention that the Christian message is communicated by God" (p. 47). Miracles, of course, figure importantly in this category. William of Auxerre seems to have been the first to raise the question of whether faith is based on the motives of credibility or not. Lamont discerns three different answers to this question within the Christian tradition: that Christian belief in divine speaking is *not* rationally grounded on the motives of credibility; that it is *partly* grounded in these motives; and that it is *entirely* so grounded (p. 52). He claims that the last position only emerges in early modernity as a result of the skeptical crises of the sixteenth and seventeenth centuries. It is represented by thinkers such as William Chillingworth, John Tilotson, and John Locke.

Lamont regards Thomas Aquinas — as most commentators seem to today — as representing the first view (pp. 53-73). For Aquinas, faith is an instance of belief in testimony, and testimonial beliefs are not justified by arguments from evidence for trustworthiness. This means that Christians do not believe the contents of the Christian faith on the basis of some argument that, starting from premises about miracles and so forth, demonstrates or makes likely that God has spoken those contents, from which it would follow that they are true. Instead, for Aquinas, "God's having said

---

35. John Lamont, *Divine Faith* (Aldershot, UK: Ashgate, 2004), p. 46 (italics added). Hereafter, page references to this work appear in parentheses within the text.

certain things is the reason why we believe them in faith" (p. 63). "Faith assents to something only because it is said by God" (p. 62). The basis of Christian faith is a testimonial reason *(that we have learned that* p *from God),* not an argument. On the other hand, Aquinas also says that "the miracles which Christ worked were a sufficient proof of His Godhead."[36] So there is some "hard" evidence in favor of the Christian revelation, and Aquinas is eager to emphasize this.

In sum, if we look at the Christian tradition, we find a strong insistence that miracles have an epistemic function to perform. Miracles and other motives of credibility are, the tradition insists, important for the rational standing of Christian belief. On the other hand, the view that Christian belief is *based* on arguments from miracles and so forth is relatively new, and constitutes a minority view within the tradition. Today this view is less popular than ever.

My account of how knowledge of God can be had through testimony reconciles these two elements of the Christian tradition. In the scenario we imagined, the hearers of Jesus believe that Jesus is commissioned by God on the basis of a testimonial reason. Accordingly, their belief is not justified by inference from Jesus' miracles. But the miracles have an important epistemic function in the account. They provide a context in which believing Jesus is not doxastically irresponsible. The extraordinary events that accompany the mission of Jesus make it possible for Jesus' hearers to "pick up" the knowledge made available by Jesus' words. Because of the miracles, the "surrounding considerations," which a rational subject must be sufficiently sensitive to if she is to be able to acquire knowledge by testimony, are such that they support rather than undermine the credibility of Jesus. The miracles do not *demonstrate* that Jesus' assertion is true; but this is not required. It is sufficient if the miracles neutralize considerations that a first-century Palestinian Jew must face up to — on pain of being doxastically irresponsible ("really, what are the chances that *this* messianic pretender is the genuine article?")

I do not claim that the miracles by themselves could perform the epistemic function of making belief in Jesus' assertion doxastically responsible for a first-century Palestinian Jew. If Jesus had been a morally despicable person who performed miracles in order to make money, believing Jesus' assertion about his own divine commission would probably not have been doxastically responsible. My claim is that, when the miracles are seen in

---

36. *ST* III, q. 43, a. 4.

the context of Jesus' life and teaching, and when Jesus' mission is seen (as Jesus clearly wanted it to be seen) in the context of the scriptural narrative of God's dealings with Israel, then the miracles seem to ask for a theistic interpretation, and they can therefore serve to defeat certain natural and inevitable suspicions about the credibility of Jesus' claim about himself. The disciples followed Jesus around, took part in his life and teaching, and got to know his character. They were also familiar with the scriptural narratives and were in a position to see that Jesus' life, teaching, and miracles resonated in a creative way with those stories.

Could something else fill the same epistemic function that I have assigned to physical miracles? It is quite possible. Maybe the sheer beauty of the Christian story as it is presented by the Christian church and in its central texts can do the job by itself.[37] Maybe the gestalt of Jesus and his message have some other intrinsic quality that makes it compatible with doxastic responsibility to believe Jesus' claim about himself. Or maybe what Jesus says has such beneficial moral effects on people's lives that believing that he speaks for God is not doxastically irresponsible.[38] Again, maybe the history of the church's growth and development is enough to defeat the natural skepticism toward Jesus' claim.[39] In what follows, however, I will not assume that reasons such as the ones suggested, either individually or collectively, suffice to make it compatible with doxastic responsibility to believe Jesus' claim to speak in the name of God. This is because it is unclear whether the suggested reasons really can do the job.

---

37. Hans Urs von Balthasar argues that the credibility of the Christian revelation derives from the splendor of the divine love that is manifested on the cross. We perceive that love as overwhelming beauty ("glory"), and this beauty possess its own intrinsic "credibility" in the same way as a great work of art does. "Divine Love can appear in such an overwhelming way that its glorious majesty throws one to the ground" (Hans Urs von Balthasar, *Love Alone Is Credible* [San Francisco: Ignatius Press, 2004], pp. 56-57). See also Hans Urs von Balthasar, *The Glory of the Lord: A Theological Aesthetics,* vol. 1: *Seeing the Form* (San Francisco: Ignatius Press, 1982).

38. Lamont, *Divine Faith,* p. 199. John Owen exemplifies this logic: "The work which is effected by [the divine word], in the regeneration, conversion, and sanctification of the souls of believers, doth evidence infallibly unto their consciences that it is not the word of man, but of God" (John Owen, "The Reason of Faith," in William Goold, ed., *The Works of John Owen,* vol. 4 (Edinburgh: Johnstone and Hunter, 1852), pp. 94-95; quoted in Lamont, *Divine Faith,* p. 201). Owen's claim is, however, far too strong.

39. Newman argues along these lines. See John Henry Newman, *An Essay in Aid of a Grammar of Assent* (Oxford: Oxford University Press, 1985). This kind of argument, of course, is only available for later generations of Christians.

It is unclear, for instance, whether the beauty of the Christian story really supports a claim about the existence of God. The theory of relativity is an extremely brilliant construct; but if its author were to claim that the theory was revealed to him by God, it is doubtful whether the brilliance of the theory would provide any significant support for that claim. Perhaps the brilliance of the theory would support the claim about divine origin to a significant extent if Einstein had been known to be a stupid and ignorant man who could not possibly have come up with the theory himself. But then we would really be talking about a kind of miracle. Analogously, even if the narrative about Jesus's life, death, and resurrection is beautiful, it does not seem to follow that it could not be a purely human construct. So even if reasons such as the ones suggested certainly could contribute to making belief in Jesus' claim compatible with doxastic responsibility, it is at least uncertain whether they could do the job all by themselves. I will therefore follow the tradition in assigning an important epistemic function to miraculous events.

6.5 The Task Ahead

I have noted above that it would be bad news for Christianity if one must witness a miracle in order to be able to pick up the knowledge expressed by Jesus' utterance. However, it might seem that this is the conclusion that I am approaching. Have I not suggested, albeit tentatively, that knowledge of miracles might be a necessary condition for doxastic responsibility in the context of believing claims about divine commission?

Knowledge of the occurrence of miracles might, however, be had even by people who have not *witnessed* any miracle. Below I will argue, following a number of philosophers, that knowledge of miraculous events can be had on the basis of testimony. Before I address this and related topics at length in the next chapter, I will end this chapter with a brief overview of the account I am going to defend. The account is an extension of the hypothetical scenario we have worked with above. Its purpose is to illustrate how people who have not witnessed any miracle performed by Jesus could, possibly, acquire knowledge of God from Jesus' testimony that is recorded in the Gospels. The details of the account will be elaborated in the next chapter.

Above we assumed, in accordance with Wolterstorff's theory of divine speech, that Jesus' utterances constitute divine speech-acts. This means that Jesus' utterances can make God's own knowledge of himself available, provided that Jesus speaks about God. We assumed, further, that Jesus does speak about God: Jesus asserts that he speaks in the name of God. This scenario is presupposed in the following.

I will argue below (7.1) that it is possible that people living today can know things about what Jesus said, did, and underwent on the basis of the church's testimony. The church's testimony about what Jesus said, did, and underwent consists primarily of the canonical Gospels.[40] Within the community of biblical scholars there is disagreement about how much knowledge of the historical Jesus can be gained from the Gospels. Some say "quite a lot," others "almost nothing." These debates are usually pursued against the background of a false assumption, namely, that the Gospels and other documents can only provide evidence of the *nontestimonial* type about the life of Jesus, evidence such as that the author of Mark wrote that Jesus said this and that. The task of the biblical scholar, as it is commonly understood, is to construct arguments from this kind of evidence and background knowledge to conclusions about what Jesus actually said, did, and underwent. As I have argued, however, testimony need not — and usually should not — be approached in this way. Testimony can provide sui generis testimonial reasons for belief. There are few biblical scholars who show an awareness of this. Richard Bauckham, however, is an exception. I will argue, following Bauckham, that a correct attitude toward testimony is essential for the acquisition of *historical* knowledge of Jesus.

There is, however, a special problem about those Gospel reports that concern miraculous events. A tradition from Hume argues that such reports can never be responsibly believed. If this is true, then knowledge of the occurrence of miraculous events cannot be had on the basis of the Gospel testimony. (It must be possible for one to believe a report without violating the dictates of doxastic responsibility, if one is to acquire *knowledge* from that report.) However, the Humean arguments are bad, and they are perceived as bad even by philosophers who are unsympathetic to religious miracles. I will argue, contra Hume, that there are no

---

40. So I do not need to address the question of how to identify the church in the contemporary world. In the first century CE there were communities who identified themselves as bearers of knowledge about Jesus, based on eyewitness testimony and preserved first in oral traditions, then in the canonical New Testament writings. These communities are the "church" in the sense relevant in the present context. The question concerning which ecclesiastical bodies in the contemporary world are in continuity with this early church can, for my present purposes, be left aside.

general obstacles for believing in well-attested miracles (7.2). I will also specifically argue (7.3) that a person who lives today can believe, without doxastic irresponsibility, the Gospel reports about Jesus' resurrection. If this is correct, knowledge of Jesus' resurrection could possibly be had on the basis of testimony.

If the arguments I have mentioned succeed, it is possible that people in our time can know certain facts about what Jesus said, did, and underwent, including that he was unexplainably alive after being dead for a considerable time.[41] Contemporary people can know this on the basis of the church's testimony, recorded in the canonical Gospels.

Here is a suggestion about how the mentioned knowledge could have been transmitted to people living today: There exists in the early Jesus movement some knowledge, based on eyewitness testimony, about Jesus. In accordance with our hypothetical scenario, we assume that the relevant knowledge includes knowledge that Jesus claimed to speak in the name of the one God of Israel, and that he died on the cross but was alive some days after. This knowledge is committed to writing in the canonical Gospels, which constitute the community's testimony. By reading this testimony, a subject H, who is a normal, well-educated person living today, comes to believe that Jesus claimed to speak in the name of God and that he was miraculously alive some days after his death by crucifixion. If H, in believing these things, does not thereby violate the requirements of dox-

---

41. The resurrection of Jesus is, in Christian theology, usually conceived of as an "eschatological event" and thus as fundamentally different from a mere resuscitation of Jesus' dead body. I agree completely with this common characterization. The fact that the resurrection is an eschatological event does not, however, mean that my admittedly rather blunt description of this event (that Jesus was "alive after being dead for a considerable time") is inadequate. The resurrection certainly means *more* than that Jesus was alive after being dead, but it does not mean less. The blunt description leaves open the question of the nature of Jesus' postresurrection existence, and of the relationship between this existence and Jesus' "old" body. The only thing that I need to insist on, in the present context, is that we understand the resurrection as something that happens to *Jesus,* and that Jesus' identity can, under certain circumstances at least, be clearly recognized after the resurrection. The fact that there is, in the New Testament stories about Jesus' resurrection appearances, a certain dialectic between "recognizing and not recognizing" and between "complete identity between the crucified and the risen Christ and complete transformation" (Joseph Ratzinger, *Introduction to Christianity* [San Francisco: Ignatius Press, 2004], p. 308) does not contradict the latter claim. Clear recognition is, after all, a very important element in the stories. Jesus' resurrection appearances "convinced [the disciples] *despite* their doubts and made them certain that the Lord had truly risen" (Ratzinger, *Introduction to Christianity,* p. 310 [italics in original].

astic responsibility — which, I will argue at length, he does not necessarily have to do — then H knows those things about Jesus. The justification that underpins H's knowledge is a testimonial reason (having *learned* from the Gospels that Jesus said so-and-so and underwent this and that).

Through the Gospel testimony, then, H knows that Jesus claimed to speak in the name of God. This means that H is in a position to *believe* or *disbelieve* Jesus' claim. If H believes it, and if this claim (as we here suppose) is true and gives expression to God's own knowledge, then H's believing it will transfer God's own knowledge to H. But can H believe Jesus' claim without being doxastically irresponsible? Since H knows, on the basis of the Gospel testimony, that Jesus miraculously returned to life after having been crucified, he can do so. This means that H can come to *know* that Jesus was speaking in the name of God, and hence that God exists.

In this scenario, H does not hear Jesus speak directly. His knowledge of Jesus' assertion is mediated by the Gospels. However, this circumstance is of no significance. One can believe or disbelieve Stephen Hawking even though his assertion is mediated by his voice generator, and one can believe or disbelieve Barack Obama even though his assertion is mediated by a newspaper article.

Jesus' contemporaneous disciples knew, as we have assumed, that Jesus underwent a miraculous event on the basis of their own *perceptions*. H knows, in our extended scenario, the same fact by *testimony*. H can also know, by testimony, facts about Jesus' moral character, the shape of his life, and his teaching. If it is compatible with doxastic responsibility for Jesus' disciples to believe what Jesus asserted about himself (which we have already established, in 6.3), then it can also be compatible with doxastic responsibility for H to believe this.[42] H's *testimonial* knowledge about Jesus' resurrection, his character, life, and teaching, makes the hypothesis that Jesus was a delusional genius very improbable. This hypothesis does not explain the resurrection. H's knowledge about the resurrection, therefore, undermines the natural reasons for skepticism about Jesus' claim to speak in God's name, reasons that, if undefeated, would prevent H from believing that claim on pain of violating the dictates of doxastic responsibility.

---

42. This is true even if H, unlike Jesus' contemporary disciples, does not have a (doxastically responsible) belief in the existence of God prior to accepting Jesus' testimony. The fact that Jesus seems to be a morally flawless person (and hence not disposed to lying or deceiving), together with the fact (as we here suppose) that certain "miracles" have taken place, make it compatible with doxastic responsibility for H to believe Jesus' claim even if H's initial stance is agnosticism.

Entrance into God's Own Knowledge

Moreover, H may have knowledge of many additional circumstances that speak in favor of the veracity of Jesus' claim — knowledge that, to a large extent, was unavailable to Jesus' contemporary hearers. H can know, for instance, about the rapid expansion of Christianity and its enormous significance for Western civilization. He can be aware of the intellectual fruitfulness, existential depths, and transformative power of the Christian message, the capability of the story about Jesus to inspire great art, the significance of Christian beliefs for the rise of modern science, and so on.[43] This kind of knowledge (just to take a few examples) may contribute to making it doxastically responsible for H to believe Jesus' claim about his divine commission.[44] An important factor is also the religious experiences that H may have as a result of encountering the figure of Jesus. If H finds that a Christian perspective is capable of making sense of these kinds of experiences in a way that naturalism and other perspectives do not, then this will contribute to making belief in Jesus' claim compatible with doxastic responsibility. There are, of course, alternative, nontheistic explanations of all the mentioned circumstances, but the cumulative force of those circumstances may nevertheless make the Christian explanation appear very plausible.

William Abraham says that

> miracles will not have the same degree of evidential value for those who have not themselves witnessed them. This follows not from Humean arguments ... but merely from the fact that we find it much more difficult to doubt the testimony of our own sense than reports of others.[45]

This statement reveals a confusion between psychology and epistemology. It is true that we often seem to be able to choose whether to believe a piece of testimony or not, while we usually do not choose whether to believe what our senses tell us. We just firmly believe it. However, to have a testimonial reason for believing that *p* — such as *having learned from*

---

43. See Amos Funkenstein, *Theology and the Scientific Imagination from the Middle Ages to the Seventeenth Century* (Princeton, NJ: Princeton University Press, 1986).

44. By roughly the following logic: If Jesus' claim about divine commission is false, then Jesus is a fraud or suffers from a delusion. It is more probable that a message preached by a person who is commissioned by God has the above-mentioned consequences than that a message preached by a fraudulent or delusional person has such consequences.

45. William Abraham, *Divine Revelation and the Limits of Historical Criticism* (Oxford: Oxford University Press, 1982), p. 41.

S that p — is, as we remember, to have a factive standing in the space of reasons. And a factive standing in the space of reasons with respect to *p* is the best reason for believing *p* that one can possibly have. When it comes to *epistemic* value, testimonial reasons are no worse than perceptual reasons. It is of no epistemic significance that we, as a matter of *psychological* fact, often find it easier to doubt beliefs acquired through testimony than beliefs acquired through perception.[46]

In summary, the church's testimony could provide H, who lives today, with knowledge that Jesus asserted that he speaks in the name of God. The church's testimony could also, as I will argue, give H knowledge about the occurrence of a miraculous event, the resurrection.[47] The latter knowledge, in combination with knowledge about Jesus' character and so forth, would make it compatible with doxastic responsibility for H to believe Jesus' assertion about himself. This means that H could pick up the knowledge expressed by that assertion.

The account I have sketched portrays the acquisition of knowledge of God through the utterances of Jesus as a two-step process. First, we get to know some of the things Jesus said, did, and underwent, from the church's testimony. This knowledge puts us in a position where we are able to believe (or not believe) what Jesus says. If Jesus spoke in the name of God, then his assertions make knowledge of God available, by virtue of constituting divine assertions. If we — without violating the requirements of doxastic responsibility — believe Jesus' assertions about God, then what we acquire is God's knowledge of himself.

I take it as established that if H *knows* that Jesus returned to life some days after having died as a result of crucifixion, then it would not be irresponsible for H to believe Jesus' claim to speak in the name of God. Most people, I assume, would agree with this. The crucial issue is thus whether

---

46. It should also be noted that sometimes we revise beliefs acquired by perception because they conflict with beliefs acquired through testimony. If I take myself to see an elephant at close range, but five of my friends, standing beside me, tell me that they do not see an elephant, it might be wise of me to reject my perceptual belief and trust the testimony of my friends.

47. When the event of Jesus' coming back to life is described as "the resurrection," it is implied that Jesus was brought back to life by *somebody* (God). In the present context we should forget about this implication, since the involvement of God is not observable. What I mean by "the resurrection" (in the present context) is simply the event of Jesus' returning to life (some way or other) after being dead for a considerable time. Under this description, the event is observable.

it is possible for a person who lives today to know the occurrence of the resurrection. The only way a contemporary person could possibly know it is on the basis of the testimony of the Gospels. Before we address the difficult question of whether the Gospels' testimony can provide us with knowledge of a *miraculous* event such as the resurrection, we must address the prior question of whether the Gospels can provide us with any interesting knowledge of Jesus at all.

CHAPTER 7

Responsible Belief

7.1 Trusting the Gospels

Trust is an essential condition for the acquisition of testimonial knowledge. This is true even if we (like John McDowell) do not want to appeal to a "presumptive right to trust" in order to explain how testimonial beliefs are justified.

Since we are not always in a position to know whether what *seems* to be a testimonial reason (i.e., a factive standing in the space of reasons, such as *having learned from S that* p) really is such a reason or whether it is an impostor, a case of somebody misleading us, we can only acquire testimonial knowledge by taking a risk — by exposing ourselves to epistemic danger. Testimonial knowledge can only be had by trusting the words of other people. To refuse to trust the testimony of another person, and instead to use the fact that she asserted that p as a premise in an argument that aims to establish that p is true, is not to acquire *testimonial* knowledge of p. It is to acquire *inferential* (inductive) knowledge of p.

Testimony, rightly understood, invites trust by its very nature.[1] An appropriate degree of trust is thus an epistemic virtue, not a vice. It is salutary to remember that the necessity of trust is not limited to the area of testimonial knowledge but belongs to perception and memory as well. We have to have a basic trust in the reliability of our senses and memory. Only against the background of a fundamental trust in these faculties can we

---

1. Richard Bauckham, *Jesus and the Eyewitnesses: The Gospels as Eyewitness Testimony* (Grand Rapids: Eerdmans, 2006), p. 478.

critically evaluate their deliverances. The current state of the philosophical debate about testimonial knowledge (see chap. 5 above) indicates that the idea that we can get along without a similar basic trust in the testimony of others is probably an illusion.

Trust is not, as some may think, opposed to critical appraisal. Coady writes:

> When we believe testimony we believe what is said because we trust the witness. This attitude of trust is very fundamental, but it is not blind. As Reid noted, the child begins with an attitude of complete trust in what it is told, and develops more critical attitudes as it matures. None the less, even for adults, the critical attitude is itself founded upon a general stance of trust, just as the adult awareness of the way memory plays us false rests upon a broader confidence in recollective powers.[2]

What happens if we approach the church's testimony about Jesus — the canonical Gospels — with these insights about the importance of trust in mind? The first thing we realize is that too skeptical an attitude can prevent us from acquiring historical knowledge. It may be the case that the Gospels make available knowledge of Jesus that can only be had by trusting the Gospel records, treating them as testimony. Suppose, for example, that the author of one of the Gospels knew, and reported in the Gospel, that Jesus had said that p. Then a reader of that Gospel has a satisfactory justification for believing that Jesus said that p and is thereby in a position to *know* that Jesus said that p. It may very well be the case, however, that the author's report about what Jesus said does not receive any support from evidence other than the author's assertion. In such a case, a skeptical reader may refuse to believe that Jesus said that p. He may, for instance, require that an independent source confirm that Jesus said that p before he is willing to believe that he did. If the reader acts in this way, he misses a chance to acquire a piece of historical knowledge.

This illustrates what the consequence can be of refusing to treat anything in the Gospels as *testimony*. Or to put it more accurately: To insist that any assertion found in a Gospel must be confirmed by independent evidence before it is believed is to assume that the Gospels cannot provide

---

2. C. A. J. Coady, *Testimony: A Philosophical Study* (Oxford: Oxford University Press, 1994), p. 46.

one with *testimonial reasons* for belief, only with premises for inductive or abductive arguments.

John Dominic Crossan assumes precisely this. In his quest for the historical Jesus he uses a methodological principle he calls "bracketing of singularity."[3] By this he means "the complete avoidance of any unit found only in a single attestation." A "unit" is a text reporting something about Jesus. If no additional, independent tradition confirms a certain report, then that unit constitutes a singularity, and it is to be ignored as a source of information about the historical Jesus. Crossan articulates his motivation for this methodological decision thus: "Something found in at least two independent sources . . . cannot have been created by either of them. Something found there but only in a single attestation could have been created by that source itself" (pp. xxxii-xxxiii).

This methodology reflects a decision not to treat any synoptic Gospel material as *testimony* about Jesus. The reason Crossan insists that a unit must be attested by two independent sources before he is prepared to credit it with any historic value is that he thereby does not have to rely on testimony at all. If two texts from independent sources assert that Jesus said that *p,* then we can construct a decent argument to the conclusion that Jesus said that *p.* The argument, very roughly, is that the best explanation of the fact that independent sources A and B assert that Jesus said that *p* is that Jesus actually did say that *p.*

Believing that Jesus said that *p* on the basis of such an argument is not to believe it on the basis of testimony. Of course, if the reductionists are right, then all knowledge acquired by hearing or reading what others say is justified by arguments similar to the one above. There are, according to reductionism, no sui generis testimonial reasons. There are, however, strong reasons to be suspicious of reductionism, as I have argued, and in the present context I will assume that there are distinctly testimonial reasons capable of justifying beliefs.

Crossan's methodology is not inconsequential. He says that "two-thirds of the complexes in the Jesus tradition as inventoried in appendix 1 have only a single attestation" (p. xxxiii). These two-thirds are "bracketed" in the quest for the historical Jesus. Crossan himself shows some awareness that this methodology may sometimes be an obstacle for the

---

3. John Dominic Crossan, *The Historical Jesus: The Life of a Mediterranean Jewish Peasant* (Edinburgh: T&T Clark, 1991), p. xxxii. Hereafter, page references to this work appear in parentheses within the text.

acquisition of historical knowledge of Jesus: "I agree that, in theory, a unit found only in a single source from the third stratum might be just as original as one found in fivefold independent attestation from the first stratum" (p. xxxiii).

Modern historical scholarship has developed methods that make it possible to extract knowledge from sources without relying on those sources as testimony. For example, a common modern approach to historical sources is to compel them to answer questions they were not designed to answer.[4]

> At least three fourths of the lives of the saints of the High Middle Ages can teach us nothing concrete about those pious personages whose careers they pretend to describe. If, on the other hand, we consult them as to the way of life or thought peculiar to the epoch in which they were written . . . we shall find them invaluable.[5]

There is absolutely nothing wrong with treating historical sources this way. It is, as Bauckham says, "virtually second nature to any modern practitioner of history" (p. 483). There is a danger, however, that historians come to *identify* historical knowledge with knowledge extracted without reliance on testimony. This identification is explicitly defended by R. G. Collingwood, who denies that knowledge based on testimony can ever be "scientific," "historical" knowledge. Historical knowledge is based on evidence, and by "evidence" Collingwood means *nontestimonial* reasons. "When testimony is reinforced by evidence our acceptance of it is no longer the acceptance of testimony as such; it is the affirmation of something based upon evidence, that is, historical knowledge."[6]

Collingwood's contrast between believing some claim on the basis of evidence and believing it on the basis of testimony is based on a misconception. Testimony (i.e., testimonial reasons) *is* a kind of evidence, albeit a sui generis kind. Testimonial reasons can underpin "historical" knowledge as satisfactorily as other kinds of reasons, such as inductive or abductive arguments. A better way of putting the contrast Collingwood is after is to distinguish between *forensic evidence* (what Collingwood calls "evidence")

---

4. Bauckham, *Jesus and the Eyewitnesses,* p. 482. Hereafter, page references to this work appear in parentheses within the text.

5. Marc Bloch, *The Historian's Craft* (New York: Knopf, 1953), p. 61.

6. R. G. Collingwood, *The Idea of History* (Oxford: Oxford University Press, 1946), p. 257.

and *testimonial reasons or evidence*.[7] A judge may believe what a criminal says because he realizes that it is in the criminal's own interest to tell the truth. The best explanation of why the criminal says what he says, in such a case, is that it is true. Here the judge can use the fact that the criminal makes a certain assertion as a premise in an argument to the conclusion that the content of the criminal's assertion is true. Treating assertions as "forensic" evidence in this way is a common and perfectly appropriate element in historical research, but it is not the same as treating them as testimony.

Modern historical research emerged when historians gradually moved away from treating the sources as testimony and increasingly started to treat them as forensic evidence. This development, of course, was partly positive. The Middle Ages approached historical sources with too much credulity, and the use of historical-critical methods has produced invaluable knowledge. The mistake is to think that forensic evidence is the only kind of evidence we need to rely on in the acquisition of historical knowledge. This attitude is an expression of modernist arrogance. The "claim to the historian's complete independence of testimony" is, as Bauckham argues, unsustainable (p. 485).

> In the medieval period scholars could think of themselves as dwarves standing on the shoulders of giants, able to see further than the ancients only by virtue of depending on the ancients. The more characteristic modern attitude is to celebrate, as Bloch does, a kind of triumph over the past, liberated from dependence on it to the extent that we can know "far more of the past than the past had thought good to tell us." (p. 483)

The modern quest for "liberation from dependence on the past" comes to expression in an excessive skepticism toward historical sources. Collingwood epitomizes this attitude: "If anyone ... hands [the historian] a readymade answer to his question, all he can do is to reject it: not because he thinks his informant is trying to deceive him, or is himself deceived, but because if he accepts it he is giving up his autonomy as an historian."[8]

Excessive skepticism may, according to Bauckham, be more pronounced in Gospel research than in other areas. Many Gospel scholars seem

---

7. This distinction is adapted from Lamont, who distinguishes between "forensic believing" and "belief in testimony" (John Lamont, *Divine Faith* [Aldershot, UK: Ashgate, 2004], p. 187).

8. Collingwood, *The Idea of History*, p. 256.

to be "anxious above all to avoid dogmatically influenced credulity." "Particularly in Gospel scholarship there is an attitude abroad that approaches the sources with fundamental skepticism, rather than trust, and therefore requires that anything the sources claim be accepted only if historians can independently verify it" (p. 486). Most scholars in the field, according to Bauckham, "have little or no experience of working as historians in other areas of history." It is thus easy for Gospel scholarship "to develop its own conventions for gauging the reliability of sources. These do not necessarily correspond well to the way evidence is treated in other historical fields. . . . Young scholars, learning their historical methods from Gospel scholars, often treat it as self-evident that the more skeptical they are toward their sources, the more rigorous will be their historical method" (p. 486).

While recognizing the value of modern historical methods, we should be on guard against the tendency to restrict the label "historical knowledge" to knowledge acquired by treating the sources merely as forensic evidence. There is, as Bauckham points out, "nothing about modern historical method [that] prohibits us from reading the explicit testimonies of the past for the sake of what they were intended to recount and reveal" (p. 483). We can combine treating (in appropriate cases) historical sources as *testimony* with a critical awareness of the ways in which sources can mislead. This is how we approach testimony in ordinary life.

It might be argued, however, that we have good reason to mistrust the Gospels. Even if we restrict ourselves to the synoptic Gospels, a comparison among them seems to reveal several inconsistencies — or at least discrepancies. However, this does not entail that the Gospels cannot give an accurate *general* portrait of Jesus and reliably provide knowledge of important events in his life. Take this analogy: different eyewitnesses may agree that there was a car accident and that two cars were involved, but they disagree on a number of details. Their disagreements should make us hesitant to regard any of them as completely reliable in matters of detail, but disagreements in detail need not undermine the eyewitnesses' trustworthiness concerning major features of the event. James Dunn regards it as a "clearly observable fact" that the synoptic tradition "provides *a remarkably consistent and coherent portrayal of Jesus*. Even allowing for all the diversity of the individual compilations and emphases . . . the Jesus portrayed is recognizably the same."[9] He approvingly quotes C. H. Dodd:

---

9. James D. G. Dunn, "Eyewitnesses and the Oral Jesus Tradition," *Journal for the Study of the Historical Jesus* 6, no. 1 (2008): 85-105; 86.

> The first three gospels offer a body of sayings on the whole so consistent, so coherent, and withal so distinctive in manner, style and content, that no reasonable critic should doubt, whatever reservations he may have about individual sayings, that we find here reflected the thought of a single, unique teacher.[10]

A question that needs to be addressed in this context is whether it is likely, given the commonalities and differences that exist among the synoptic Gospels, that the oral traditions behind them have reliably transmitted information about the historical Jesus. There are different answers to this question within the exegetical community. Kenneth Bailey has produced a typology of different models that purport to describe how the oral traditions behind the written Gospels operated. The so-called form-critical school, prominently represented by Rudolf Bultmann, worked with a model of *informal uncontrolled* tradition that is basically a form of "rumor transmission" (Bauckham, p. 253). According to this model, the early Christian communities had no interest in preserving authentic historical materials about Jesus, and thus there were no social mechanisms designed to place limits on the variability of the tradition. The transmission of Jesus material was, as Martin Hengel characterizes this model, "anonymous, collective and at the same time uninhibitedly 'creative.'"[11] If the form-critical school is right, the Gospels are not very reliable sources of information about Jesus.

The form-critical school's model of oral transmission has, however, been criticized by scholars who work with two other models of tradition transmission. Birger Gerhardsson has argued that the oral traditions behind the Gospels are *formal* and *controlled.* They are formal in the sense that there is a clearly identified teacher who passes on a clearly identified block of material to a clearly identified student (Bauckham, p. 253); they are controlled in the sense that the material is memorized and identified as "tradition." James Dunn, N. T. Wright, and Kenneth Bailey, on the other hand, think that a model of *informal controlled* oral transmission best explains the stability and variability we find between the synoptic Gospel accounts of what Jesus said and did. There is, according to this model, no clearly identified teacher. Instead, it is the community that exercises control to ensure that the tradition is faithfully preserved. If a storyteller

---

10. C. H. Dodd, *The Founder of Christianity* (London: Collins, 1971), pp. 21-22; quoted in Dunn, "Eyewitnesses and the Oral Jesus Tradition," p. 86, n. 3.

11. Martin Hengel, foreword to Samuel Byrskog, *Story as History — History as Story* (Tübingen: Mohr Siebeck, 2000), p. vii.

diverges too much from what the community perceives as the appropriate recital, he will be corrected by the listeners. In the case of certain types of material, such as proverbs and poems, the listeners may require verbatim reproduction (p. 255). This model can be seen as a middle way between the folkloric "rumor transmission" model of form criticism and Gerhardsson's model.

One type of criticism against Gerhardsson's view of the oral transmission process as a formal, controlled tradition after the rabbinic pattern is that it cannot explain the flexibility and variability among renderings of the same Jesus material by different Gospel traditions. The process seems too rigid to allow for such variability (p. 251). Bauckham argues, however, that a formal, controlled model does not, as such, entail inflexibility. The parameter of flexibility/variability is a third parameter, which can vary independently of the parameters of formality and control (p. 258).

Bauckham argues, building on the work of Gerhardsson and the latter's student Samuel Byrskog, that the Jesus material reached the written Gospels through formal, controlled transmission processes in which eyewitnesses played a central role. The period between the historical Jesus and the Gospels was, according to Bauckham, "spanned, not by anonymous community transmission, but by the continuing presence and testimony of the eyewitnesses, who remained the authoritative sources of their traditions until their deaths" (p. 8). Bauckham contends that

> in the period up to the writing of the Gospels, gospel traditions were connected with named and known eyewitnesses, people who had heard the teaching of Jesus from his lips and committed it to memory, people who had witnessed the events of his ministry, death and resurrection and themselves had formulated the stories about these events that they told. (p. 93)

Bauckham's thesis has a certain a priori plausibility, considering the short time span between the events that the Gospels recount and the writing of them. It is uncontroversial that at least Mark was written well within the lifetime of many of the eyewitnesses. If the disciples of Jesus were not "translated to heaven immediately after the Resurrection, why would they not have been consulted as authoritative sources of information about Jesus by the young Palestinian Christian communities?"[12]

---

12. Vincent Taylor, *The Formation of the Gospel Tradition* (London: Macmillan, 1935), p. 41.

Bauckham's case is supported by the argument of Byrskog, who has established that Greco-Roman historians valued eyewitness testimony highly, especially the testimony of people who were themselves participants in the events they recounted. Against the background of the central role of eyewitnesses in ancient historiography, Byrskog argues that eyewitnesses probably played a central role in the formation of the Gospel traditions as well.[13]

James Dunn agrees with Bauckham that the early churches would have wanted to hear eyewitness accounts about Jesus. He argues, however, that "the first disciples could not provide an authoritative check on the use made of the Jesus tradition in more than a few churches."[14] Many of the early churches must have received their Jesus tradition in second or third hand (p. 99). While Dunn recognizes that the eyewitnesses played an important role in formulating the Jesus tradition, he claims that they could not "bridge the gap" between the initial formulation and the writing down of the Gospels (p. 102). The difference between Dunn and Bauckham, however, is not very important in the present context. Although the eyewitnesses did not control the transmission process all the way to the written Gospels, according to Dunn's account, there was still "a mechanism (the process of oral tradition) whereby the initial impact [of Jesus] has been permanently retained in and transmitted through the oral tradition which became the Synoptic tradition" (p. 102). Dunn says, with reference to Gerhardsson and Bauckham, that "we all want to affirm the 'reliability' of the Gospel tradition (to use Gerhardsson's term)" (p. 89). I. Howard Marshall refers to the agreement that Dunn points out as a "new consensus on how the Gospels are to be understood," emerging between scholars such as Kenneth Bailey, Samuel Byrskog, James Dunn, Birger Gerhardsson, Martin Hengel, and Harald Riesenfeld.[15]

---

13. Samual Byrskog, *Story as History — History as Story* (Tübingen: Mohr Siebeck, 2000). Byrskog finds "numerous points of agreement" between his own work and Bauckham's (Samual Byrskog, "The Eyewitnesses as Interpreters of the Past: Reflections on Richard Bauckham's *Jesus and the Eyewitnesses*," *Journal for the Study of the Historical Jesus* 6, no. 2 (2008): 157-68; 158). Bauckham, according to Byrskog, "showed that eyewitnesses existed, that they played an important role, and that their names occasionally surface in the texts.... It is no longer possible to speak of the anonymous and collective force of the early Christian communities" (p. 159).

14. Dunn, "Eyewitnesses and the Oral Jesus Tradition," p. 98. Hereafter, page references to this essay appear in parentheses within the text.

15. I. Howard Marshall, "A New Consensus on Oral Tradition? A Review of Richard

If the form-critical understanding of the oral transmission process is correct, the Gospels are not reliable sources of information about Jesus. To treat them as *testimony* would, in that case, probably cause us to form a lot of false beliefs about the historical Jesus. If the proponents of the "new consensus" are right, however, it would be very beneficial for us to treat the Gospels as testimony. Treating them as testimony (which entails a basic attitude of trust) would, in that case, increase our knowledge about the historical Jesus.[16]

Is it, against the background of the unresolved debate within the exegetical community, compatible with *doxastic responsibility* to treat the Gospels as testimony (within appropriate limits)? In order to answer this question, we must recall what doxastic responsibility involves. We may remember what McDowell says:

> [A]lthough it is obviously doxastically irresponsible to believe someone about whom one has positive reasons to believe he is not trustworthy, or not likely to be informed about the subject matter of the conversation, doxastic responsibility need not require positive reasons to believe that an apparent informant is informed and speaking his mind.[17]

This means that we do not have to wait until the debate between the form-critical school and the "new consensus" is resolved before we can responsibly trust the Gospels. As long as the debate is unresolved, nothing has been established about the basic reliability or unreliability of the Gospel tradition. This means that no positive reasons to mistrust the Gospels' *general* portrait of Jesus have emerged. In the absence of positive reasons for mistrust, it is compatible with doxastic responsibility to trust. (Below I will treat the possible objection that the Gospels contain reports about miracles.)

Do the Gospels, as I have assumed, consistently testify that Jesus claimed to speak in the name of God? There is little doubt that they do. In Mark 9:37, Luke 9:48, and Matthew 10:40, Jesus says that "whoever welcomes me welcomes the one who sent me." About this text, Dunn says that "the thought is the familiar one of the prophet as speaking for

---

Bauckham's *Jesus and the Eyewitnesses*," *Journal for the Study of the Historical Jesus* 6, no. 2 (2008): 182-93; 183-84.

16. Bauckham, *Jesus and the Eyewitnesses*, p. 5.

17. John McDowell, "Knowledge by Hearsay," in *Meaning, Knowledge, and Reality* (Cambridge, MA: Harvard University Press, 1998), p. 435.

God, God's *saliah*."[18] E. P. Sanders does not hesitate to say that "Jesus claimed to be spokesman for God."[19] "He regarded himself as having full authority to speak and act on behalf of God."[20] According to Marianne Meye Thompson, "the consistent witness of the gospels [is that] Jesus believed himself to be acting and speaking by God's commission and in God's name."[21]

7.2 Believing Reports about Miracles

It could be argued that the Gospels cannot be regarded as reliable testimony because they report many miraculous events. The content of those reports is such that it shows the source to be unreliable. If David Hume is right about the impossibility of rationally believing miracle reports, this might be a sound argument. Hume flatters himself that he has "discovered an argument of a like nature, which, if just, will, with the wise and learned, be an everlasting check to all kinds of superstitious delusion." It is unclear exactly what the argument is, and even what the conclusion is. Central to the argument, however, seems to be Hume's claim that

> no testimony is sufficient to establish a miracle, unless the testimony be of such a kind, that its falsehood would be more miraculous, than the fact, which it endeavors to establish: And even in that case there is a mutual destruction of arguments, and the superior only gives us an assurance suitable to that degree of force, which remains, after deducting the inferior.[22]

Hume goes on to conclude that "no testimony for any kind of miracle has ever amounted to a probability, much less a proof." This formulation leaves open the possibility that testimony *may*, possibly, establish the probable occurrence of a miracle.[23] However, at another place Hume

---

18. James D. G. Dunn, *Jesus Remembered* (Grand Rapids: Eerdmans, 2003), p. 663.
19. E. P. Sanders, *Jesus and Judaism* (London: SCM Press, 1985), p. 271.
20. E. P. Sanders, *The Historical Figure of Jesus* (New York: Penguin, 1995), p. 238.
21. Marianne Meye Thompson, "Jesus and His God," in *The Cambridge Companion to Jesus,* ed. Markus Bockmuehl (Cambridge: Cambridge University Press, 2001), p. 54.
22. David Hume, *An Enquiry Concerning Human Understanding and Other Writings,* ed. Stephen Buckle (Cambridge: Cambridge University Press, 2007), pp. 97, 101.
23. In an earlier edition of the *Enquiry,* however, the claim is stronger: "[N]o testimony for any kind of miracle *can ever possibly* amount to a probability" (quoted in Elliott

concludes that "no human testimony can have such a force as to prove a miracle, and make it a just foundation for any such system of religion."[24] Here, and at other places, it seems that the possibility to establish a miracle by testimony does not even exist in principle.[25]

In this section I will express my disagreement with Hume on the issue of miracle reports. I cannot, of course, address the question of the believability of miracle reports at the length that a proper treatment would require. What I aim to show in this section is that there are good reasons to reject Hume's strong claim about the necessary irrationality of believing miracle reports, and the line of argument on which it is based, and that there are many contemporary philosophers who think the same. Before we go on, however, we must be clear about how Hume's argument against miracles is relevant to my general argument.

Hume claims that it is (nearly?) impossible for testimony to establish the occurrence of a miracle. His argument, however, takes for granted a reductionist view of testimony, according to which the justification of testimonial beliefs is reducible to a species of inductive inference. "The reason why we place any credit in witnesses and historians, is not derived from any *connexion,* which we perceive *a priori,* between testimony and reality, but because we are accustomed to find a conformity between them."[26] This view is in conflict with the anti-reductionist view I have defended, according to which testimonial justification is noninferential. A testimonial reason — such as *having learned from S that* p — is not just a premise in an inferential argument to the truth of *p,* but a *factive* reason, which taken by itself provides knowledge that *p.* That Hume's view of how testimony justifies beliefs differs from the one I am working with does not, however, render his argument irrelevant in the present context. This is because McDowell's account of testimonial knowledge requires that one's believing

---

Sober, "A Modest Proposal," *Philosophy and Phenomenological Research* 68, no. 2 [2004]: 487-94; 492 [italics added]).

24. Elliott Sober thinks that this formulation also leaves it open that miracles "as violations of presumptive laws of nature" can be established by testimony, but not the occurrence of a miracle "in the sense of a violation of a presumptive law *that is due to the intervention of a deity*" (Sober, "A Modest Proposal," p. 492 [italics added]).

25. "And what have we to oppose to such a cloud of witnesses, but the absolute impossibility or miraculous nature of the events, which they relate? And this surely, in the eyes of all reasonable people, will alone be regarded as a sufficient refutation" (Hume, *An Enquiry Concerning Human Understanding,* p. 110).

26. Hume, *An Enquiry Concerning Human Understanding,* p. 99.

that *p* on the basis of testimony must not be doxastically irresponsible if the belief in question is to be even a candidate for the status of knowledge. How can we determine whether believing a certain report is compatible with doxastic responsibility? We can determine that by looking at what reasons/evidence for the truth of the report we have *independent* of the reason that the testimony itself (if it is indeed expressive of knowledge) provides us with. If it turns out that the totality of independent evidence strongly suggests that the testimony is false, then it is clearly not compatible with doxastic responsibility to believe it.

Hume's anti-miracle argument aims to show that a situation such as this always (or nearly always) obtains whenever a report is about a miraculous event. The very fact that a report concerns a miraculous event means that there is extremely weighty evidence against it, namely, all the evidence for the laws of nature that the miracle allegedly violated. Therefore, Hume argues that in cases where the content of a report is the occurrence of a miraculous event, the "independent evidence" always strongly points to the conclusion that the report is false.[27] If this is correct, it follows that miracle reports can never be believed without violating the dictates of doxastic responsibility. However, if Hume's argument fails, then the mere fact that the Gospels contain reports about miracles cannot be taken to show that the Gospels are unreliable. Instead, it might be possible to acquire knowledge of the occurrence of miracles by reading the accounts in the Gospels.

One of the sharpest critics of Hume is John Earman, who writes:

> Section X ("Of Miracles") of Hume's *Enquiry Concerning Human Understanding* is a failure. In philosophy, where almost all ambitious projects are failures, this may seem a mild criticism. So to be blunt. I contend that "Of Miracles" is an abject failure.[28]

---

27. Craig Keener has recently questioned Hume's assessment of the empirical evidence. Keener claims, on the basis of an extensive survey of modern eyewitness reports about miracles from the Majority World as well as from the West, that "massive numbers of people [today] are claiming healings and other dramatic miracles throughout the world" (Craig Keener, *Miracles: The Credibility of the New Testament Accounts* [Grand Rapids: Baker Academic, 2011], p. 506). Even though the miraculous nature of the events reported can be contested, the sheer number of miracle reports calls into question whether the possibility of miracles really can be dismissed with reference to our common experience of the uniformity of nature.

28. John Earman, *Hume's Abject Failure: The Argument against Miracles* (New York: Oxford University Press, 2000), p. 3. Hereafter, page references to this work appear in parentheses within the text.

Furthermore, says Earman, "the essay reveals the weakness and the poverty of Hume's own account of induction and probabilistic reasoning. And to cap it all off, the essay represents the kind of overreaching that gives philosophy a bad name" (p. 3).

Earman is not a religious apologist. On the contrary, he finds the motivation behind Hume's project understandable. Hume wanted to devise a "litmus test" that would make it possible to reject in advance, without detailed investigation of particular cases, claims about the occurrence of miraculous events. Detailed investigations of miracle claims are often, according to Earman, "unrewarding" and "downright tedious" and make the reader "[hanker] after a silver bullet that will spare us further details by putting a merciful end to all the nonsense." He goes on to say:

> Joe Nickell's *Looking for a Miracle* (1993) casts a skeptical eye on the Shroud of Turin, weeping icons, bleeding effigies, etc. A few chapters are enough to make the reader yearn for a quick knockout blow to spare us further tedium. Hume himself, at the beginning of his miracles essay, confesses the desire to deliver such a blow.

The difference between Earman and Hume is that Earman does not think that it is possible to deliver that blow. The answer to the question of whether miracle claims are to be believed "cannot be supplied by a simple litmus test, but can only be reached by detailed, case-by-case investigations" (p. 3).

Earman uses Bayesian probability calculus to represent and criticize Hume's argument against miracles. In doing so he follows one of Hume's contemporary antagonists, Richard Price, who drew on Bayes's work in his critique of Hume's anti-miracle argument. In a letter to Price, Hume is very appreciative of Price's criticism, and is — according to Earman — "implicitly accepting the probabilistic form into which Price cast Hume's argument" (p. 25). Unfortunately, however, Hume did not avail himself of the knowledge of probability calculus available at the time.

Hume claims that a miracle is a "violation of a law of nature."[29] According to Earman, we must understand Hume to mean by "law" a *presumptive* law, since it is conceptually impossible to "violate" a genuine law of nature

---

29. In a footnote he also offers a definition that mentions a "deity," but that does not seem to play any role in the argument (see Sober, "A Modest Proposal," p. 490). See also Joe Houston, *Reported Miracles: A Critique of Hume* (Cambridge: Cambridge University Press, 1994), p. 64.

which by definition allows no exceptions.[30] Hume's main mistake, according to Earman, is to use what Hans Reichenbach later called the "straight rule of induction" to determine the probabilities of presumptive laws of nature. This rule says, roughly, that if we observe 1208 swans, and 1207 of them are white, the probability that the next swan we observe is white is 1207/1208. If *all* of a sufficiently large number of swans have been observed to be white, the straight rule tells us to assign the probability 1 to the presumptive law "all swans are white." "From this it follows that no further evidence (whether it is testimonial or takes some other form) can lower the probability of the presumptive law."[31] In such a case, we have what Hume calls a "full proof" of the presumptive law. Miracles are counterexamples to presumptive laws of nature. To affirm that a miracle has happened is to deny that the presumptive law(s) which it violates hold(s). But since a presumptive law of nature has the probability 1, no amount of evidence can justify such a denial. So we can know in advance that no testimony can do the job. Case against belief in miracle reports closed.

Earman observes that the straight rule "is both descriptively inadequate to actual scientific practice, and . . . stultifying to scientific inquiry" (p. 51). Presumptive laws of nature *can* be overturned by new observations. Earman says:

> Among the zillions of protons observed by particle physicists, none has been verified to decay. But particle physicists do not assign a probability of 1 to the proposition that the next proton to be observed will not decay, and they certainly do not think that they have adequate inductive grounds for probabilistic certainty with respect to the general proposition that no proton ever decays — otherwise the expenditure of time and money on experiments to detect proton decay would be inexplicable. (p. 31)

If Hume's argument against miracles is correctly interpreted by Earman, then it is, indeed, an "abject failure." Most contemporary philosophers would, I presume, agree with this.

---

30. Earman, *Hume's Abject Failure*, p. 12. Earman does not recognize that if we posit a distinction between nature and supernature, we can allow for the possibility that a law of nature is violated by intrusion from supernature. See Richard Swinburne, *Revelation: From Metaphor to Analogy*, 2nd ed. (Oxford: Oxford University Press, 2007), p. 114.

31. Sober, "A Modest Proposal," p. 491. Hereafter, page references to this essay appear in parentheses within the text.

The way to defend Hume is to deny — as commentators such as Robert Fogelin[32] and Elliott Sober do — that Hume's argument relies on the straight rule of induction. According to Sober, Hume merely claims that if all of the many swans we have examined so far have been white, we should be maximally skeptical that the next swan we examine is not white (p. 491).[33] If this is all Hume says, then it is possible that testimony could justify belief in a miracle (which Sober admits). It is true that to render more probable than not a proposition that has a very low prior probability (as miracle reports, according to Sober, always have), "a single witness must be *enormously* reliable" (p. 493). However, Sober admits that if there are many independent witnesses who agree in their reports about a miracle, and if each of them is at least minimally reliable, then their combined testimony might do the job. This is shown by Charles Babbage's demonstration that "it is always possible to assign a number of independent witnesses, the improbability of the falsehood of whose concurring testimonies shall be greater than that of the improbability of the miracle itself."[34] Hence, as Sober says, "What one imperfect witness cannot do, a number of such witnesses can easily achieve" (p. 493). Babbage shows that even if we have observed 1,000,000,000,000 persons who died without being resurrected, the combined testimony of eleven independent witnesses to the effect that the 1,000,000,000,001th person was resurrected would suffice to make that resurrection probable, if these witnesses are such that they tell the truth on 99 out of 100 occasions.[35]

So Sober wants to clear Hume's argument of the charge of being an "abject failure," and he does so by presenting it as no more than a "modest point": "I agree with Earman that Hume's general insight does not extend much beyond the thought that very strong evidence (testimonial or otherwise) is needed to render a proposition probable that we antecedently think is incredible" (p. 495). So Sober also denies that Hume has discovered a "silver bullet" — an argument against the very idea of testimonial knowledge of miracles. Sober, of course, is about as far from a religious apologist as you can get.

32. Robert Fogelin, *A Defense of Hume on Miracles* (Princeton, NJ: Princeton University Press, 2003).

33. I have substituted "swan" for "dead people" and "white" for "failing to return to life" in Sober's example.

34. Richard Swinburne, "Review: Hume's Abject Failure: The Argument against Miracles," *Mind* 111, no. 441 (2002): 95-99; 95.

35. Swinburne, "Review: Hume's Abject Failure," p. 96.

Earman concludes his case against Hume:

> In sum, Hume's contrary miracles argument has some effect against those who take miracles to be proofs of religious doctrines. But against those who take miracles only as providing confirmation of religious doctrines, Hume's argument is not vouchsafed by any valid principles of confirmation — at least not of the Bayesian variety. Hume is thus forced to leave the high ground and descend into the trenches where, as he must have been aware, there were opponents who had considered the contrary miracles argument and were prepared to argue on the basis of contextual details for the superiority of the New Testament miracle stories over heathen miracle stories. These opponents may or may not have been right. But Hume had no good reason for avoiding an engagement with them. (p. 70)

Another Bayesian attack on the Humean line of argument comes from Richard Swinburne. Swinburne's definition of a miracle is similar to Hume's. A miracle is a violation or quasi-violation[36] of a fundamental law of nature by an act of God (p. 112). If nature is all there is, so that the laws of nature are the ultimate determinants of what happens, then there can be no such thing as violations of fundamental laws of nature. "There can only be violations if some power from outside the system of natural laws (i.e., something non-physical, not acting in virtue of the powers and liabilities of physical objects), God or some lesser deity, determines whether a law operates" (p. 114). If violations occur, "they cannot be explained scientifically, and so we must look for a personal explanation . . . either in the agency of God . . . or that of some lesser spirit" (p. 117). We would have good reason to believe that some event was a violation (and hence that there exists some determining factor outside the system of natural laws) if it constituted an exception to some law of nature such that any attempt to amend or replace the purported law of nature so that it would predict the exception "would give us a purported new law so complicated internally and so disconsonant with the rest of scientific knowledge . . . that we would have no grounds for trusting its future predictions" (p. 115).[37]

---

36. Swinburne introduces this term to account for probabilistic laws of nature, which are not, strictly speaking, incompatible with any occurrence. A quasi-violation is an event that is very, very improbable given some nondeterministic law (Swinburne, *Revelation: From Metaphor to Analogy*, p. 116). Hereafter, page references to this work appear in parentheses within the text.

37. Joe Houston takes a view similar to Swinburne's on this matter: "There can be a

Against the backdrop of this view of natural laws and miracles, Hume's critique points to a real problem: The very fact that an alleged event would have been a violation of a natural law is in itself evidence against its occurrence (p. 118). This insight is derived from the general insight that our background knowledge about what the laws of nature are is highly relevant for the assessment of claims about what happened on particular occasions. Hume's main mistake, however, "was to assume that in cases of a purported violation of laws of nature, our evidence about what are the laws of nature is our main relevant background evidence." But it is not:

> All background evidence about whether there is or is not a God is also crucially relevant. For if there is a God, there exists a being with the power to set aside the laws of nature which he normally sustains; whereas if there is no God, there is far less reason to suppose that violations might sometimes occur. (p. 120)

Evidence for the existence of God can be gained from natural theology, according to Swinburne, and it affects the prior probability of miracles. Hume has failed to take this kind of background evidence into account. A critique along these lines was delivered against Hume as early as William Paley:

> As Mr. Hume has represented the question, miracles are alike incredible to him who is previously assured of the constant agency of a divine being, and him who believes that no such being exists.[38]

Like Swinburne and Paley, Keith Ward argues that Hume is insensitive to how background evidence and worldview commitments affect the assessment of the prior probability of miracles. Hume and his modern advocate J. L. Mackie contend that miracles are "maximally improbable" (as does Sober, who assumes that a miracle is something that we "antecedently think is incredible"). But this contention begs the question against theism,

---

case for treating as a natural law a generalization which gives best guidance about nature's usual course, even though there have been violations of that generalization" (Houston, *Reported Miracles*, p. 117).

38. William Paley, "A View of the Evidences of Christianity," in *The Works of William Paley . . . Containing His Life, Moral and Political Philosophy, Evidences of Christianity, Natural Theology, Tracts, Horae Paulinae, Clergyman's Companion, and Sermons* (Edinburgh: T. Nelson and P. Brown, 1831), p. 229; quoted in Houston, *Reported Miracles*, p. 127.

and neither a theist nor a rational atheist should accept it, according to Ward. Miracles are only maximally improbable given the assumption that natural laws are the only factors that may determine the course of events. But the claim that natural laws are the only determining factors — "scientific objectivism," as Ward calls the view — is a metaphysical theory of the same scope as theism, and its plausibility is differently assessed by different philosophers. It is a theory that is "clearly not entailed by the available evidence for it," and hence it has the status of a postulate or explanatory scheme. Since it has this status,

> it logically cannot be used to rule out any events which seem to cast doubt on it. If the postulate is accepted, it will make highly improbable the occurrence of any falsifying instances [such as events not determined by natural laws].... But such falsifying instances may occur, and must in a sense be looked for, if the explanatory postulate is to be reasonably upheld. That is, for the explanatory postulate to have force, we must at least be on the lookout for falsifying instances.... It will not be enough to say that, since they are maximally and improbably on the theory, no testimony to their occurrence will be acceptable.[39]

To dismiss all miracle reports on the ground that they are maximally improbable would be to render the explanatory scheme of "scientific objectivism" unfalsifiable. This is unacceptable. Therefore, even proponents of scientific objectivism must, on pain of irrationality, regard miracles as no more than highly improbable, or contrary to all expectations. This entails that sufficiently strong evidence for the occurrence of a miracle might be capable of upsetting those expectations and might disconfirm the explanatory scheme of scientific objectivism.

However, from a theistic perspective, the antecedent probability of miracles must be differently assessed. "If there is a God ... it is plainly possible that God might bring about events that no created cause has the power of itself to bring about." Such events can be called "miracles," but it is somewhat tendentious to conceive of them as "violations" of natural laws, according to Ward. The latter description suggests that it is somehow "improper, untidy, or arbitrary" for God to act otherwise than in accordance with general laws, and hence unlikely that he would do so. But "why should a personal God confine divine action to a set of absolute laws?" It is

---

39. Keith Ward, "Miracles and Testimony," *Religious Studies* 21, no. 2 (1985): 131-45; 136.

Hume who introduces a "hyperinflated" sense of "law of nature," according to which such laws are unbreakable and "absolute principles that govern the occurrence of each and every possible event in the history of the universe." It is only when theism is connected to this hyperinflated sense of law that "it can come to seem that it would be an imperfection in God's work for God to interfere in the presumably perfect order of laws that God has ordained."[40] The latter type of argument has been propounded by thinkers such as G. W. Leibniz, Friedrich Schleieremacher, David Friedrich Strauss, and Rudolf Bultmann.[41] However, it is "an extremely odd argument for those who believe in a personal God to put forth." Earlier thinkers, such as Aquinas, did not think in terms of a closed system of all-determining laws of nature. They spoke instead of the "natural, normal, or regular operation of things."[42] The normal operations of nature can be called "natural laws," but without the connotation that they must be capable of explaining *everything* that happens.

Against the background of belief in a personal God, then, supernatural actions by God (actions that transcend the normal operations of nature) are not to be viewed as antecedently improbable. A miracle, according to Ward, is a kind of supernatural action "of such an unusual, amazing or unprecedented sort that it is very improbable that it came about naturally, and very probable that it came about by the action of God, or some other supernatural power" ("Miracles and Testimony," p. 137). "Miracles, for a theist, are not even maximally unusual; they are irregular, rare, and exceptional. But good reasons might be found for their occurrence, insofar as they fit into a general web of beliefs that leads one to expect physical-law-transcending actions, unusual or not, from a Creator" ("Believing in Miracles," p. 746). Given certain theistic beliefs, then, "it is fairly probable that some miracle will occur." "The best statement of the position ... seems to be that a miracle is a physically improbable event, which is a member of a class of events, the instantiation of some member of which is quite probable" ("Miracles and Testimony," pp. 144, 139).

Both Swinburne and Ward claim that we have some background knowledge (or justified belief) about God that affects the antecedent probability of miracles. Thanks to this background, it is possible for sufficiently reliable testimony to establish that a violation of (or a "transcending of")

40. Keith Ward, "Believing in Miracles," *Zygon* 37, no. 3 (2002): 741-50; 742-43.
41. Houston, *Reported Miracles,* pp. 105-6. Houston judges that this line of argument is weak (Houston, *Reported Miracles,* p. 3).
42. Ward, "Believing in Miracles," p. 742. Hereafter, references to this work appear in parentheses in the text.

a natural law has occurred. This means that neither of them can claim that miracles *by themselves* can constitute the basis for belief in the existence of God. Swinburne says: "Hume might be right in his view that if evidence about possible violations of laws of nature were the only evidence for or against the existence of God, this evidence would never be sufficient to make such a violation 'a just foundation for any . . . system of religion.'"[43] Likewise, Ward says:

> Assessment of the claim that a miracle has occurred will thus depend upon assessment of the plausibility of an explanatory scheme for God's purpose and action in the world. Miracles cannot be considered in isolation, as evidences for supernatural intervention. They are confirming parts of an explanatory theory covering the whole of human history and knowledge. Reliable testimony to their occurrence helps to make such a theory plausible. . . . If the theory is very implausible, on other grounds, one will be less inclined to accept the occurrence of a miracle. ("Miracles and Testimony," pp. 141-42)

The reader will remember that my aim in this book is to explain how knowledge of (or justified belief in) God's existence can be had from God's testimony — without presupposing that the existence of God can also be established by natural theology. This means that I cannot appeal to a "potent" natural theology when arguing for the rationality of belief in miracle reports. If I were to do so, I would be presupposing the kind of knowledge of God that my account in this book is supposed to explain. This means that I cannot follow Swinburne and Ward, who explicitly appeal to a natural knowledge of (or justified belief in) God's existence when they defend the rationality of accepting miracle reports.

However, a potent natural theology (i.e., a natural theology that aims to establish the existence of *the God of theism*) is not the only thing that could generate background knowledge capable of making belief in miracle reports reasonable. A *modest* natural theology, which merely aims to justify belief in the existence of, say, some kind of creator or creators (an "Author of the world" in Kant's terms), could also do the job. This is implicitly acknowledged by Mackie when he says that people who believe "that there is an omnipotent deity, *or at any rate one or more powerful supernatural beings,* cannot find it absurd to suppose that such a being will occasionally interfere with the course of nature." If we have reason to believe that a

---

43. Swinburne, *Revelation: From Metaphor to Analogy*, p. 120.

powerful supernatural being exists (never mind whether this being has all or only some of the attributes of the God of theism), then "supernatural intervention, though prima facie unlikely in any particular occasion, is, generally speaking, on the cards: it is not altogether outside the range of reasonable expectation."[44]

Reasons to believe that a powerful supernatural being exists could be provided not only by a modest natural theology, but also by manifestational (special) revelation, such as, for example, by "mystical perception" of the kind William Alston defends, or by other forms of religious experience. I believe that, while many contemporary theologians are inclined to deny the existence of a potent natural theology, many of them would still agree that we have good ("natural") reasons to believe in the existence of some kind of creator, or at least in some kind of powerful personal agent whom we encounter in religious experience (and whom theologians often refer to as "God," even though the experiences themselves cannot establish that this being has the attributes of the God of theism).[45]

I could, therefore, without begging the question, concur with Swinburne and Ward that rational belief in miracle reports requires background knowledge derived from natural theology, as long as this background knowledge is not portrayed as knowledge of the existence of *the God of theism*. But I do not need to make this concession. The account I have been sketching need not rely on *any* kind of natural theology, not even a modest one. In what follows, I will argue, following Joe Houston, that miracle reports can be reasonably believed even if background knowledge from natural theology is lacking altogether.

Houston has argued, in his excellent book about miracle reports, that the kind of response provided by Swinburne and Ward fails to engage with Hume's argument. According to Houston, "the target for Hume's attack is . . . the apologist who sets out to supply a rational basis for a system of religion by appealing to miracle reports. This apologist can presuppose no assumed or previously established beliefs in a god, or gods, or other spirits."[46] For Hume, the question is not whether it could be reasonable

---

44. J. L. Mackie, *The Miracle of Theism: Arguments for and against the Existence of God* (Oxford: Oxford University Press, 1982), p. 27.

45. For instance, Alister McGrath, *The Open Secret: A New Vision for Natural Theology* (Malden, MA: Blackwell, 2008); Alister McGrath, *A Fine-Tuned Universe: The Quest for God in Science and Theology* (Louisville: Westminster John Knox, 2009).

46. Houston, *Reported Miracles,* p. 127. Hereafter, page references to this work appear in parentheses within the text.

for a person who already believes in the existence of God (or some other powerful, supernatural being) to accept a miracle report and use it as support for his system of religion. The question is whether a person who is undecided as to the existence of a god can reasonably accept such a report and thereby acquire a reason to believe that a god exists. Houston thinks that he can. He defends the anti-Humean contention that "[a] report of a putative miracle . . . can give weight to a theistic hypothesis, can support a case for theism, even when no theistic presupposition whatever (resting on natural theology) is made" (p. 158).

According to Houston, Hume's basic idea is that we, in deciding whether to believe that a miracle has occurred, should weigh the evidence *for* the miracle's occurring, against the evidence that suggests that it has not occurred. Then we should believe according to the stronger evidence. The kind of evidence in favor of a miracle that Hume considers is testimony.[47] The evidence against a miracle consists, primarily, of the vast body of human experience that has established the law of nature which the miracle, if it occurred, violated. This means that "it will be reasonable to believe a claim that a miracle has happened only if the evidence in favor of the claim outweighs the huge weight of evidence for the law of nature which is, allegedly, violated" (p. 52). The evidence in favor of a well-established natural law amounts to what Hume calls "a full proof," since it consists of a massive amount of uniform experience. This means that Hume only has to show that the evidence in favor of a miracle (i.e., testimony) is, by nature, "*somewhat* less weighty than a direct and full proof." If he can do this, his purpose is served. Since testimony, simply *as* testimony, falls short of being wholly and universally reliable (experience teaches us this), it seems to follow that (testimonial) evidence in favor of miracles is always, by nature, "less forceful than that which supports a natural law, and so any report of a miracle must be disbelieved by the reasonable person" (p. 57).

Hume's basic mistake, according to Houston, is to assume, without argument, that the evidence in favor of the natural laws that a reported

---

47. One wonders why Hume did not address the possibility of *perceptual* evidence for miracles. Mackie says that this possibility "does not make very much difference" (Mackie, *The Miracle of Theism,* p. 28). He seems to think that Hume's argument still applies. This means that one should not believe that a miracle has occurred no matter how strong perceptual evidence in favor of it one might have.

miraculous event allegedly violated is always relevant to the question of whether the miracle happened.[48]

Suppose that there is a report that Jesus walked on water. According to Hume, evidence for the natural law called Archimedes' Principle, and evidence that a human body's density is close to 1, is relevant for the question of whether the event occurred. However,

> suppose that there is any reason to think, or even consider the possibility, that a god has, on the occasion reported, so acted that generally obtaining patterns in events do not, on that occasion, obtain. On this supposition, a body of evidence, however vast, in favor of Archimedes' Principle [etc.] . . . cannot without further argument be taken as relevant to deciding the question of whether on the reported occasion Jesus walked on water. Perhaps the usual run of events, for which evidence for natural laws would be good evidence, has been departed from. (p. 134)

By regarding the evidence for Archimedes' Principle (etc.) as unproblematically relevant for deciding the question of whether Jesus walked on water, Hume assumes something that is at issue, namely, that no god has acted miraculously. This is to beg the question. One cannot, without further argument, assume that the inductive evidence that establishes how nature *normally* behaves is relevant for deciding the question of whether nature, on the relevant occasion, behaves normally or not.

The dialectical context that Hume's argument addresses is, according to Houston, a debate between a religious apologist and his interlocutor, who is as yet undecided about the existence of a god (p. 133). The topic of the debate is whether a particular alleged violation of a law of nature has occurred, such as Jesus' walking on water. Neither party of the debate may introduce as premises matters that are in dispute between them. To do so would be to break out of the dialectical context (as Swinburne and Ward recommend that the religious apologist do). Houston's anti-Humean point, presented above, is that by (without further argument) treating the

---

48. Houston has another important criticism of Hume. Hume assumes, without argument, that if an event is highly improbable (as Hume thinks any miracle must be), then it follows, from that fact alone, that the truth of a *report* of the event must also be highly improbable. But this does not follow. For example, the improbable nature of an event can make an observer more attentive and careful, which reduces the probability that he will be mistaken about what happened (see Houston, *Reported Miracles,* chap. 10). Ward has a similar criticism (Ward, "Believing in Miracles," p. 133).

evidence in favor of the allegedly violated natural law as *unquestionably relevant* for deciding the issue of whether a miracle has, on a certain occasion, occurred, Hume has in fact ruled out the possibility that a god might have suspended the normal course of nature. But this possibility can only be ruled out if atheism is presupposed.

Martin Curd summarizes Houston's argument:

> When we examine Hume's reasoning, we see that Hume has illicitly moved from (A) not presupposing that theism is true, to (B) presupposing that theism is false. . . . This slide from (A) to (B) occurs, according to Houston, when Hume uses the inductive evidence for a generalization being a natural law as counting decisively against the likelihood that the reported event violated that law.[49]

Houston considers a possible reply to his accusation that Hume presupposes something that he cannot legitimately presuppose:

> If certain of the conclusions of inductive reasoning are, as the apologist now insists, to be suspended or set aside because there is "good reason" for thinking that God may have brought about a violation of nature's normal course, the defender of Hume now wishes to know what "good reason" there could be which would not beg the question on the apologist's side. (p. 144)

Do we not have to assume that a god (probably) exists, in order to have "good reason" to take into account the proposal that a god may have acted miraculously? The answer, according to Houston, is no. In order for one to have good reason to consider the hypothesis that a god may have caused the event, one need not already accept that there is a god, or even that there *probably* is a god.

> "[H]aving a reason for thinking that God may have acted anomalously" does not necessarily involve the apologist in affirming something, or assuming something, which the non-believer does not accept, and thereby in begging a question that is in dispute between apologist and non-believer. Rather, it may be a matter of having a reason for entertaining and investigating a suggestion, a hypothesis . . . [that] holds out promise of explanatory power. (p. 149)

---

49. Martin Curd, "Reported Miracles by J. Houston: Review," *Mind,* new series 106, no. 422 (1997): 349-53; 350-51.

"There need be no *assumption,* even of a probability, that a god has miraculously acted for the apologist to urge that the proposal is promising-looking that a god has acted against nature's usual course" (p. 148). The latter claim by Houston should be clarified: the probability that a god has acted cannot, of course, be judged to be zero. If it is, the proposal that a god may have acted is not "promising-looking." However, to have "good reason" to consider the proposal that a god may have acted does not necessarily involve "attaching any firm judgment of determinate [prior] probability to the account or to any controversial part of it" (p. 147).

> There is no assumption needed even of a probability that there is a god. The proposal that a god has acted miraculously may still be regarded as promising-looking if it would effectively account for a good deal, including a good deal which is not otherwise easy to account for. The existence of testimony to the putative miracle may be difficult to account for well in any other way, and so may give strength to the apologist's claim to have an at least promising-looking proposal. (p. 148)

Below we will encounter a situation very much like this. According to prominent biblical scholars, there is evidence in connection with Jesus' alleged resurrection that is very hard to account for given the nonoccurrence of a miraculous event. The proposal that God has acted miraculously seems, in this context, to be promising-looking.

Houston's main point seems to be this: The availability of an explanatory story that accounts for some reported but problematic event (such as the resurrection of Jesus) and also accounts for a good deal else that is otherwise very difficult to explain (such as many independent testimonies about postmortem encounters with Jesus, the empty tomb, the faith of the disciples, etc.) will raise the probability that the problematic event actually occurred. This is true even if the explanatory story is not antecedently probable, but derives its plausibility merely from the fact that it constitutes the best explanation of the circumstances surrounding the putative event.

Houston illustrates how the consideration of a "promising-looking" explanatory story can, legitimately, affect how one judges the probability that a problematic event, which the story can account for, actually took place. I will quote his example at length:

Suppose that a man is seen at 02.00 hours hurrying down the street and into a car in which he drives speedily away. He is seen by a couple who each independently are fairly confident that the man is one Gordon Allen; but they are puzzled as to why he should be in this industrial part of town, when he lives and works miles away. The fire brigade comes by shortly afterwards to fight a warehouse fire nearby. The couple read in next day's newspaper that the warehouse belongs to William Allen and Co., and they think "William" was the name of a brother of Gordon. One of the couple is a solicitor, and they are able to discover that Gordon, who has a reputation for less-than-straightforward practice, is a shareholder in William Allen and Co., a family business which is not prospering. These discoveries suggest an account of events which would confirm the nocturnal identification of Gordon Allen, namely, that when seen he had been setting the warehouse on fire, for the insurance money. (If it had further transpired that the warehouse was not insured, that the Allens all knew this and that they were on good terms with one another, the identification would again have become more problematic.) Here is a question, the identification of someone, where what is seen may come to be understood as part of an interpretation involving and making sense of a number of factors together. The couple who thought they saw Gordon Allen but were unsure and puzzled had minds open to explanatory interpretations, or further considerations, of the kind which emerged. That does not mean that they concluded or assumed or believed that Gordon Allen was the torchman who set the warehouse on fire; rather they are open to that possibility, as to others, in trying to establish whether it was Gordon Allen whom they saw. There turns out to be reason to think that he may have been an arsonist because there are some facts which fit that interpretation, and so that interpretation comes to be entertained and thought about, perhaps to be believed in due course, perhaps to be rejected. It is at any rate a promising-looking hypothesis. However, "having reason" in this way to consider an account of something which is problematic (1) does not involve accepting that account or even any controversial part of it, prior to considering the account. Also, while it does involve thinking that the account seems, in view of the factors which have so far come to light, to have some probability, it (2) does not involve attaching any firm judgment of determinate probability to the account or to any controversial part of it, prior to evaluating the account taken as a whole.

Having a reason to take such an account seriously enough to assess it involves no argumentative circularity. (pp. 146-47)

If Houston is right, even a person who does not have any prior reasons to believe that a supernatural being exists could, without irrationality, believe a miracle report. If the fact that the report has been made (perhaps by several independent and trustworthy witnesses) and the circumstances surrounding it are sufficiently difficult to explain without supposing that the miraculous event actually occurred, then a rational subject should not dismiss the report, but should instead conclude that the hypothesis that a supernatural being has acted miraculously is promising-looking. If Houston is right, we do not even have to appeal to a *modest* natural theology, or religious experience, in order to defend the rationality of believing sufficiently well-attested miracle reports.

In this section I have focused strongly on the Humean critique of miracles. There are, of course, other lines of critique, both theological and philosophical. I mentioned above Schleiermacher's line of argument. I have ignored it because I find it too weak to require treatment. Houston seems to me to be right that "the Enlightenment arguments specifically against the apologists' use of miracle reports are due mainly to Hume" (p. 3). This is why Houston's book, which is a rather comprehensive treatment of philosophical and theological considerations about the epistemic value of miracle reports, has "the Humean constellation of arguments" as its primary focus.[50]

The purpose of this section has been to remove the prejudice, not unusual among theologians, that Hume's attack on the rationality of believing miracle reports is successful. The Humean arguments are weak. According to Ward, they are found acceptable "only by those who are (rightly) impressed by [Hume's] general philosophical acuteness — an acuteness that does not carry over into his remarks on miracles" ("Believing in Miracles," p. 742). Earman expresses a similar sentiment when, after saying that Hume's anti-miracle argument is "almost wholly without merit where it is original," he goes on to say that "there has been much too much genuflecting at Hume's altar."[51] Fogelin provides evidence that defenders of Hume fight against the current by observing that there has been, in the last

---

50. Houston also criticizes the anti-miracle arguments of F. H. Bradley and Ernst Troeltsch (Houston, *Reported Miracles,* chap. 5).
51. Earman, *Hume's Abject Failure,* p. vii.

few years, "a spate of attacks — 'bashes' might be a better word — aimed at Hume's treatment of miracles."[52] In a positive review of Houston's book in the journal *Mind,* Martin Curd concludes by saying that he thinks the author "overrates the originality of his project. After all, the vast majority of philosophers have been severely critical of Hume's evidential argument in 'Of Miracles,' and it is Mill and Mackie who belong to the small minority who have tried to defend Hume."[53]

7.3 Believing in the Resurrection

It seems that Hume and his followers have failed (at least in the eyes of many prominent commentators) to give a compelling in-principle reason to exclude propositions about the occurrence of miracles from the class of propositions that can be known on the basis of testimony. And the default position is surely that the occurrence of *any* kind of event that can be perceived and reported in words can also be the object of testimonial knowledge. One has to provide strong reasons in order to exclude miraculous events from the class of events knowable on the basis of testimony. The current state of the debate indicates that no such reasons have been provided.

The absence of cogent *general* anti-miracle arguments does not, of course, entail that the church's testimony about (e.g.) Jesus' resurrection can be responsibly believed. The failure of the Humean and other arguments only suggests that it is possible that *some* miracle reports can be responsibly believed. Whether the church's testimony about the resurrection belongs to this class is a question that can only be settled by looking at the particular details of this case.

The latter task falls, strictly speaking, outside the scope of this book. The main purpose of the book is to argue for the plausibility of a general model for knowledge transmission through divine testimony — a model that purports to be an explication of the Christian tradition's views on the matter. But it could turn out, after a detailed examination of the evidence for the resurrection and other miraculous events, that the church's testimony about them cannot be responsibly believed. Such a conclusion would not falsify the general model I have presented. Even if, in the actual

52. Fogelin, *A Defense of Hume on Miracles,* p. 32.
53. Curd, "Reported Miracles by J. Houston," p. 353.

world, the testimony for the resurrection of Jesus has some contingent properties that make it obligatory for a responsible subject to reject it, there are — if Hume is wrong — possible worlds in which the testimony for a resurrection does not suffer from such shortcomings, and in which it *can* be responsibly believed. So the general model I am proposing does not stand and fall with the outcome of the debate about particular features of the testimonial and other evidence for the resurrection of Jesus.

Of course, if it were obvious that the church's testimony about the resurrection of Jesus could not be responsibly believed, the model I am suggesting would lose much of its interest. I would still have proved Gordon Kaufman wrong, since my account would still have demonstrated that knowledge of a being with the properties of the God of theism could possibly be had on the basis of testimony, and without reliance on a potent natural theology. This, however, would be small comfort. The model is supposed to contribute to the debate about the Christian tradition's actual knowledge claims, and not merely to a debate about abstract possibilities.

Fortunately, it is not at all clear that the church's testimony about the resurrection of Jesus must be rejected in the name of doxastic responsibility. I am aware that there are many people who — without possessing extensive knowledge of New Testament scholarship — think that it is just obvious that the biblical testimony about the resurrection cannot be responsibly believed. But those people think that simply because the biblical testimony about the resurrection concerns a miraculous event. However, if Hume is *wrong,* one cannot justifiably reject reports about miracles simply because they are reports about miracles. Whether any particular miracle report can be responsibly believed or not must be judged on the basis of knowledge of the details of the particular case. The critic of miracle claims must, as Earman says, "descend into the trenches" and argue against particular miracle-claims on the basis of contextual detail.[54] To descend into the trenches requires, in the case of reports about Jesus' alleged resurrection, that one has extensive knowledge of New Testament scholarship.

Exactly how, then, is New Testament scholarship relevant for deciding the question of whether the Gospels' reports of Jesus' resurrection can be responsibly believed? To believe testimony in a doxastically responsible way requires that one be "responsive to the rational force of independently available considerations."[55] Such independently available considerations

---

54. Earman, *Hume's Abject Failure,* p. 70.
55. McDowell, "Knowledge by Hearsay," p. 429.

are, for example, evidence that suggests the untrustworthiness of the witness, or which indicates the falsity of the propositions testified to. New Testament scholarship (and modern historical research in general) deals precisely with this type of evidence, which I earlier called "forensic" (as opposed to "testimonial") evidence. As we saw above, modern historical scholarship has moved away from treating its sources as testimony (with the implied necessity of trust), and tries instead to reconstruct historical events on the basis of forensic-type evidence.

This is why New Testament scholarship is highly relevant for deciding whether the reports about the resurrection can be responsibly believed. Suppose we suspend trust in the New Testament witness, and ask in what direction the forensic-type evidence points. Does the forensic evidence (i.e., the total evidence minus testimonial, trust-requiring reasons) tend to undermine or support the credibility of the resurrection reports? This question is best answered by the methods of historical, "excavative" scholarship. If the forensic-type evidence that New Testament research uncovers strongly suggests that the reports are unreliable, then it would be necessary to conclude that one should not believe them. On the other hand, if the forensic evidence is very, very difficult to account for without assuming that Jesus was alive after being dead, then it can be compatible with doxastic responsibility to believe the reports.

The problem is that there is no clear consensus among scholars about the direction the forensic evidence points in. Gary Habermas has made a survey of over two thousand scholarly publications on the death, burial, and resurrection of Jesus, published between 1975 and 2005.[56] A rough estimate of these publications indicates, according to Habermas, that there is approximately a 3 to 1 ratio of works that fall into a category that Habermas has dubbed "the moderate conservative position." This is the position of those who hold that "Jesus was actually raised from the dead in some way, either bodily (and thus extended in space and time), or as some sort of spiritual body (though often undefined)." The essence of this view is the claim that "what occurred can be described as having happened to Jesus rather than only to his followers."[57]

---

56. Gary Habermas, "Resurrection Research from 1975 to the Present: What Are Critical Scholars Saying?" *Journal for the Study of the Historical Jesus* 3, no. 2 (2005): 135-53.

57. Habermas, "Resurrection Research from 1975 to the Present," p. 136. The historical Jesus scholar Dale Allison, who is currently very influential, has said that "there is some justice in all of Habermas's generalizations" (Allison, "Explaining the Resurrection: Conflicting Convictions," *Journal for the Study of the Historical Jesus* 3, no. 2 [2005]: 117-33; 125).

Alan Segal, on the other hand, says that "it does no good to argue that the consensus of NT scholars who have dealt with the problem of the resurrection actually agree that it was a literal resurrection of transformed flesh. I am not sure that such a claim is even valid."[58] It is no wonder that he is not sure of this, since Habermas does not make that claim. Habermas does not speak of a "consensus" concerning "a literal resurrection of transformed flesh." He only says that "the almost three-quarters of remaining scholars [after agnostics and those propounding naturalistic explanations have been discounted] hold either of the two views that Jesus was raised from the dead in some sense."[59] Segal then dismisses Habermas's study on the grounds that "there exists a group of scholars who are hostile to any other conclusion than that of literal resurrection. Under the circumstances, it is difficult to demonstrate that scholarly disinterestedness has been maintained." Segal's accusations imply that the field of New Testament research is a field where one can easily get poorly argued articles published. If the publications of the "faith-driven" scholars are well argued, then should we not pay attention to their conclusions, even if their authors are Christians? Segal goes on to argue that "this small scholarly consensus — really a school of scholarship — is beside the point because the vast majority of modern historians looking at the very same story would say that *no evidence at all would ever demonstrate that a unique resurrection took place.*"[60]

If this is what the vast majority of modern historians would say, then they are, as I have argued, probably wrong. Looking at it from the current state of the debate about the Humean anti-miracle arguments, those arguments do not seem to hold water. If the Humean arguments do not hold water — and if there are no other arguments that can justify the Humean conclusion — it is irrational to claim that "no evidence at all would ever demonstrate that a unique resurrection took place." It is as irrational as claiming that no evidence at all would ever demonstrate that I wear a blue shirt. So it is not the case that the "small scholarly consensus" consisting of those who have actually studied the evidence for the resurrection is "be-

---

58. Alan Segal, "The Resurrection: Faith or History?" in Robert Stewart, ed., *The Resurrection of Jesus: John Dominic Crossan and N. T. Wright in Dialogue* (Minneapolis: Fortress, 2006), p. 135.

59. Gary Habermas, "Mapping the Recent Trend toward the Bodily Resurrection Appearances of Jesus in Light of Other Prominent Critical Positions," in Stewart, ed., *The Resurrection of Jesus,* p. 91.

60. Segal, "The Resurrection: Faith or History?" p. 135.

side the point." Rather, it is Segal's claim about what "modern historians" *would* think about the resurrection — if they behave irrationally — that is beside the point.

The debate about whether evidence could "demonstrate" that a resurrection took place is, at any rate, irrelevant in the present context. I do not need to claim that there is a cogent argument from the forensic evidence to the truth (or even to a determinate probability) of the proposition *Jesus was alive after dying as a result of crucifixion.* All that is needed for my account is that the total evidence, including the forensic evidence uncovered by New Testament scholarship, is such that it does not make belief in the New Testament testimony irresponsible. If there is evidence that is very, very hard to account for without assuming the truth of the resurrection reports, then this condition is well satisfied. The existence of such evidence does not, however, rationally force a subject to believe in the resurrection, since there exists the possibility of the agnostic stance (taken, for instance, by Antony Flew[61]).

Nevertheless, a majority of the critical scholars who have studied this subject since 1975 seem to believe that the evidence actually makes it very probable that some kind of literal resurrection took place. Some of the most prominent scholars believe that there is a rather solid inference-to-the-best-explanation argument from the available forensic evidence to the truth (or at least great likelihood) of the proposition *Jesus was resurrected from the dead.* N. T. Wright, for instance, compares the skeptical attempts to explain away the evidence pointing to Jesus' resurrection with the familiar "mad scientist" hypothesis about the causes of our experiences of the "external world." He contends that "the proposal that Jesus was bodily raised from the dead possesses unrivalled power to explain the historical data at the heart of early Christianity."[62] This is quite a strong claim made by one of the most respected scholars in the field of historical

---

61. G. Habermas, A. Flew, and T. Miethe, *Did Jesus Rise from the Dead? The Resurrection Debate* (San Francisco: Harper and Row, 1987), p. 33. In a situation where the evidence is hard to account for without acknowledging the resurrection, it seems that the best explanation of the evidence is that Jesus was resurrected. But the skeptic has possible ways of countering. She can, for instance, claim that the agnostic posture is the most reasonable in light of the ontologically extravagant nature of the hypothesis that Jesus was resurrected.

62. N. T. Wright, *The Resurrection of the Son of God* (Minneapolis: Fortress, 2003), pp. 716-18. See also Wolfhart Pannenberg, *Jesus — God and Man* (London: SCM Press, 1968), chap. 3, sec. 4.

New Testament research. (Of course, my account does not need anything that strong.)

The fact that a majority of scholars believe that the resurrection is probable given the historical evidence does not entail that a resurrection probably took place, but it certainly indicates that believing the resurrection reports is compatible with respecting the requirements of doxastic responsibility. But it is unsatisfactory just to support my claim about doxastic responsibility by appealing to a survey of scholarly opinion. Even though I have neither the space nor the competence to argue the case with sufficient thoroughness here, certain basic facts about the historical question of the resurrection can and should be pointed out.

The fundamental fact that raises the credibility of the resurrection reports is that, very shortly after Jesus' death by crucifixion, the Jesus movement took off, starting with the disciples who, until then, had been secretive and anxious. The transformation of the disciples into enthusiastic and zealous missionaries is a fact that requires explanation, especially since Jesus' mission must have looked like an objective failure. It is almost universally agreed that only a strong belief in the resurrection on part of the disciples could explain how Christianity could emerge under these circumstances. Accordingly, Hermann Samuel Reimarus's old idea that the disciples promulgated the message of Jesus' resurrection as a deliberate attempt at deception is "promoted by next to nobody" today.[63] So the disciples really believed that Jesus had risen from the dead. This is, as Reginald Fuller says, "one of the indisputable facts of history."[64] The question is how this belief is to be explained. The best explanation is — or at least includes — that the disciples had some kind of experiences of Jesus being alive. According to Habermas's survey, "few critical scholars reject the notion that, after Jesus' death, the early Christians had real experiences of some sort." Even skeptical scholars like Crossan agree with this.[65] James Dunn writes: "What we should recognize as beyond reasonable doubt is that the first believers experienced 'resurrection appearances' and that those experiences are enshrined . . . in the traditions which have come down to us."[66] There are theories that try to explain the early belief in the

---

63. Allison, "Explaining the Resurrection," p. 119.

64. Reginald Fuller, *The Foundations of New Testament Christology* (London: Lutterworth Press, 1965), p. 142.

65. Habermas, "Resurrection Research from 1975 to the Present," pp. 149, 146.

66. Dunn, *Jesus Remembered,* pp. 861-62 (italics removed).

resurrection without positing experiences of (visual) appearances of Jesus, but these are notoriously weak.[67]

So there were powerful experiences taken as encounters with the risen Jesus. There are also good reasons to think that the tomb in which Jesus was laid was empty on the third day. There is a stable core tradition that comes to expression, with the usual flexibility and variability, in all four canonical Gospels, according to which

> Mary Magdalene and others (?) went to the tomb early on the first day of the week; they found the stone rolled away; according to the Synoptic versions, they saw (an) angel(s), who informed them, "He is not here; he has been raised"; at some point they (in John's Gospel, initially Peter and the other disciple) entered the tomb and saw for themselves.[68]

---

67. The idea that a "cognitive dissonance" could explain belief in the resurrection — the disciples could not face the harsh reality — is shown by N. T. Wright to be poorly supported and implausible. Many of the messianic movements between 150 BCE and 170 CE ended with the violent death of their founder. But it was, as Wright argues, simply not an option within Second Temple and later Judaism(s) to cling to the belief that a recently executed person was after all the Messiah. Something quite extraordinary would be required for this (Wright, *The Resurrection of the Son of God,* p. 700). Rudolf Pesch's theory, according to which a pre-Easter faith, established before the death of Jesus, eventually gave rise to legends about resurrection appearances and empty tombs, is likewise untenable. 1 Cor. 15:6-8 says that Jesus appeared to more than five hundred brothers, to James, and then to all the apostles. Scholars generally agree that Paul here hands on a tradition that is very old. According to Dunn, "This tradition, we can be entirely confident, *was formulated as tradition within months of Jesus' death*" (Dunn, *Jesus Remembered,* p. 855). So there was simply not enough time for a pre-Easter faith to develop into fanciful legends. (Pesch later changed his mind, and recognized that appearances of Jesus could be established by careful research: see Rudolf Pesch, "Zur Entstehung Des Glaubens An Die Auferstehung Jesu: Ein Neuer Versuch," *Freiburger Zeitschrift für Philosophie und Theologie* 30, no. 1-2 [1983]: 73-98.) The same critique can be directed against Edward Schillebeeckx's theory, according to which an original experience of grace and forgiveness eventually came to expression in "naïve" stories about a literal resurrection (Edward Schillebeeckx, *Jesus: An Experiment in Christology* [New York: Seabury Press, 1979]). See also Wright's criticism of Schillebeeckx (Wright, *The Resurrection of the Son of God,* p. 701). A remark by Dale Allison is highly relevant in the context of "legendary" theories: "It is, one might argue with some conviction, easier to create traditions about legendary figures from days gone by than about somebody who has been dead for just a few days; and the proclamation of Jesus' resurrection, there is reason to believe, goes back to the very first week after the crucifixion" (Allison, "Explaining the Resurrection," p. 131).

68. Dunn, *Jesus Remembered,* pp. 829-30; 832.

Responsible Belief

Dunn contends that the stability of this tradition is best explained by the assumption that its core was given its "definitive and lasting shape" by those who were involved in the episode at the tomb. He also says that "at the *historical* level it is very hard to explain how the belief in Jesus' resurrection arose unless his tomb was empty."[69] Dunn is not alone in this sort of judgment. According to Habermas's survey of scholarly opinion, "those who embrace the empty tomb as a historical fact still comprise a fairly strong majority."[70]

Dale Allison has listed arguments, pro and con, concerning the historicity of the empty tomb.[71] Some of the pro arguments are fairly strong. Here are the best: (1) There is no evidence of early Christians venerating Jesus' tomb, which would be expected given the Jewish piety surrounding the graves of saints.[72] (2) The confession of 1 Corinthians 15:3 implies an empty tomb. (3) The early Christians could not have preached Jesus' resurrection in Jerusalem unless his tomb was known to be opened and vacant. (4) The absence of scriptural intertextuality in Mark 16:1-8 (the discovery of the empty tomb episode) is striking considering how heavily Mark's passion narrative depends on the Old Testament. If Mark 16:1-8 were a "free Christian fiction," would it not have been more theologically interesting or apologetically useful? (5) The fact that the tradition unanimously ascribes the discovery of the empty tomb to women clearly suggests that the empty tomb tradition is not fictional, since if it were, more convincing witnesses than women would have been put on the scene. (6) Visions of a postmortem Jesus might, by themselves, "have given rise to the claim that he had ascended to heaven or that God had vindicated him, but not to the claim that God had raised him from the dead. Talk about resurrection

---

69. James D. G. Dunn, *The Evidence for Jesus* (Philadelphia: Westminster, 1985), p. 76.
70. Habermas, "Resurrection Research from 1975 to the Present," p. 141.
71. Allison, "Explaining the Resurrection."
72. Could the location of the grave have been unknown (as Peter Carnley argues in *The Structure of Resurrection Belief* [Oxford: Clarendon Press, 1987], pp. 55-7), or could it be that Jesus' body was not buried at all, but maybe eaten by dogs and crows (as John Dominic Crossan suggests in *Who Killed Jesus?* [New York: HarperCollins, 1995])? If either of these suggestions were correct, it could be expected that early anti-Christian polemic would have used these circumstances to counter the Christian preaching of Jesus' resurrection. ("How could you know that he is resurrected? For all you know, his bones could be rotting in his unknown grave right now.") But there is, as Dunn points out, not the slightest hint of such polemic (Dunn, *Jesus Remembered*, p. 836, n. 46). The anti-Christian polemic alluded to in Matt. 28:11-15 suggests, on the contrary, that the fact that the grave was empty was admitted by both sides.

was, in first-century Jerusalem, talk about bodies and bones. Other than an empty tomb, then, what could have moved early Christians to conceive of Jesus' vindication precisely as resurrection?"[73]

This last line of argument has been powerfully pursued by N. T. Wright. On the basis of a thorough study of early Christian resurrection belief, he concludes that

> Neither the empty tomb by itself . . . nor the appearances [of the postmortem Jesus] by themselves, could have generated the early Christian belief. The empty tomb alone would be a puzzle and a tragedy. Sightings of an apparently alive Jesus, by themselves, would have been classified as visions or hallucinations, which were well enough known in the ancient world. . . . However, an empty tomb and appearances of a living Jesus, taken together, would have presented a powerful reason for the emergence of the belief.[74]

Allison considers the two strongest arguments *against* the empty tomb to be: (1) That Christians could have come to believe that the tomb was empty as the result of an inference from visionary encounters with a postmortem Jesus. If Jesus was alive, must not the tomb have been empty? (2) That there are a lot of obviously fictional stories about empty tombs or disappearing bodies in biblical and postbiblical literature. (So the story about Jesus' empty tomb is, the argument implies, probably fictional.) The first contra argument is of this type: "It is possible that it happened this way, therefore it did." This is, *pace* Allison, a bad argument.[75] William Alston lists it as one of several fallacious patterns of argument that figure in New Testament research.[76]

Concerning the second contra argument, one might ask this: Should we conclude, from the fact that there are a lot of fictional stories about missing bodies, that no story about missing bodies is to be believed? Of

---

73. Allison, "Explaining the Resurrection," p. 124.
74. Wright, *The Resurrection of the Son of God*, p. 686.
75. Besides being fallacious, the argument is also, if N. T. Wright is right, based on a false premise. Wright argues that a first-century Jew would not infer, from visionary postmortem encounters with Jesus, that Jesus must have been resurrected in a bodily sense, and hence that his body must be missing. Only if he or she believed that Jesus' grave was empty would a first-century Jew come to believe in a bodily resurrection.
76. William Alston, "Biblical Criticism and the Resurrection," in Stephen T. Davis, Daniel Kendall, SJ, and Gerald O'Collins, SJ, eds., *The Resurrection* (Oxford: Oxford University Press, 1997), p. 181.

course not. If this principle were commonly obeyed, most of us would not know that grave robbery existed.

It is no surprise, given the weakness of the contra arguments, that Allison himself judges that the historical evidence points toward an empty tomb.[77] So the forensic evidence that mainstream historical-critical scholarship deals with makes it very probable (and most specialists agree with this judgment, according to the Habermas survey) that the early Christians had powerful experiences of a living Jesus, and that the grave in which Jesus was placed was known to be empty on the third day. Wright regards the dual facts of the experiences and the empty tomb as "coming in the same sort of category, of historical probability so high as to be virtually certain, as the death of Augustus in CE 14 or the fall of Jerusalem in CE 70."[78]

Now the question is: How do we explain the experiences plus the empty tomb? Hallucination theories have difficulties accounting for the fact that several people are reliably reported to have had the relevant experiences — and sometimes collectively.[79] Collective sightings are particularly hard to dismiss as purely subjective.[80] Moreover, Paul and James were not followers of Jesus prior to their experiences, so it is not quite easy to understand why their brains would produce experiences of the kind they are reported to have had (though more or less strained explanations could be produced).

The empty tomb is easier to explain in naturalistic terms. There are a number of possibilities. Maybe the women went to the wrong tomb, or maybe someone — such as the Jewish authorities — had removed the body.[81] Allison says about these speculations that there is not a shred of evidence for them, and that "they must all be deemed unlikely."[82]

Although there has recently been a "limited surge" of naturalistic explanations for the resurrection appearances, it is still the case that "the

---

77. Dale Allison, *Resurrecting Jesus: The Earliest Christian Tradition and Its Interpreters* (New York: T&T Clark, 2005), pp. 333-34.
78. Wright, *The Resurrection of the Son of God*, p. 710.
79. See Habermas, "Mapping the Recent Trend," p. 83.
80. Allison, "Explaining the Resurrection," p. 122.
81. However, the rabbinic polemic against Christian claims did not suggest this (Dunn, *Jesus Remembered*, p. 836). If it could be argued that the women had forgotten where the tomb was, this would have constituted a strong argument. The best explanation of the absence of any hints of such polemic is that this was a line of argument that could not be pursued in Jerusalem at that time.
82. Allison, *Resurrecting Jesus*, p. 334.

path of natural alternative theories is definitely a minority approach."[83] Not even Antony Flew thinks that there are any good naturalistic hypotheses on offer. When asked whether he was an adherent of some naturalistic explanation of the data pertaining to the (alleged) resurrection, he answered that he was not. "We are simply not in a position to reconstruct an account."[84]

It is clearly *possible* that a number of people, individually and collectively, had powerful (naturally caused) hallucinations of seeing Jesus alive, and that Jesus' body was secretly removed from the grave in which it was put without anything about this ever leaking out. This hypothesis explains the emergence of early Christian resurrection belief by positing two unrelated (and individually very unlikely) explanations for the postmortem experiences of Jesus and the fact of the empty tomb. The only incentive to buy this explanatory story is that something like it *must* be true if we have excluded, a priori, the possibility that the explanation that the earliest Christians themselves gave could be true. But a rational subject cannot, as we have seen, exclude this possibility.

The hypothesis that a powerful supernatural being has acted against the usual course of nature in order to resurrect Jesus is certainly, in Houston's words, "promising-looking" in light of the "forensic" evidence for the resurrection. And there exists, as even Flew admits, no satisfactory alternative explanation of the evidence. It can be argued that these circumstances alone make it compatible with doxastic responsibility to believe the reports about Jesus' resurrection.

The case for doxastic responsibility is further strengthened if we consider the undeniable, intrinsic beauty, depth, and transformative power of Jesus' message and the story about his life, death, and resurrection, seen in the context of the history of Israel as recapitulated in the Hebrew Bible. What are the odds that a religion that got started in the serendipitous way that the hallucination/grave-robbery hypothesis suggests would resonate so creatively and profoundly with the Hebrew narrative about Israel and also have the capacity to transform innumerable ordinary men and women into saints prepared to lay down their lives for God and their neighbor? What are the odds that such a religion would rapidly and extremely unexpectedly (considering that it worshiped a crucified man, and considering that it spread without the backing of state power) grow into a world reli-

---

83. Habermas, "Mapping the Recent Trend," p. 86.
84. Habermas, Flew, and Miethe, *Did Jesus Rise from the Dead?* p. 33.

gion? And what are the odds that it would create an intellectual mindset that, arguably, was more or less necessary for the emergence of modern science?[85]

A very slick explanation of the early Christian resurrection experiences, the empty tomb, and the rapid growth and intellectual and spiritual fruitfulness of Christianity is that Jesus really was resurrected, and that the God about whom Jesus spoke had something to do with it all. Rejecting that explanation, we are forced to conclude that we are facing an enormous confluence of unlikely coincidences, and that some of the available evidence cannot be satisfactorily explained.

The shift in perspective or general outlook that often comes as a result of Christian religious experience can also contribute to making belief in the resurrection responsible for individuals. If my experience of a personal encounter with Christ makes me see my fellow human beings in a new light — as infinitely valuable creatures worthy of divine love rather than as extras in the show of my life — then it is very natural to ask: Why do I feel what I feel now? Why do I experience the world like this? An individual believer may think (quite reasonably) that the nature and extent of the transformation that he has undergone is hard to explain given the falsity of the Christian story. This is a consideration in favor of its truth.

I do not claim that we can *know,* on the basis of an argument along the lines sketched above, that Jesus was resurrected. I agree with the skeptics (and contra N. T. Wright) that the "forensic" case for Jesus' resurrection is not that strong. The argument, by itself, does not give us a *knowledge-constituting* justification of the claim that Jesus was resurrected.[86] All I claim is that the circumstances surrounding the reports about the resurrection (i.e., the circumstances that the forensic case builds on) are such that it is not *doxastically irresponsible* to believe those reports. This is all I need to establish. If the reports can be responsibly believed, then we can "pick up" the knowledge that they (possibly) make available. The justification for this knowledge is not, then, the "forensic" argument sketched above, but a sui generis testimonial reason. I know that Jesus was resurrected (if I do) because I have learned it from the Gospels.

If you are still inclined to deny that a doxastically responsible person

---

85. See, for example, Amos Funkenstein, *Theology and the Scientific Imagination from the Middle Ages to the Seventeenth Century* (Princeton, NJ: Princeton University Press, 1986); Thomas Torrance, *Divine and Contingent Order* (Oxford: Oxford University Press, 1981).

86. The argument, of course, justifies belief in the resurrection to a significant degree, but not to a degree sufficient for knowledge.

can believe the Gospels' reports about Jesus' resurrection, you should ask yourself this: Under what circumstances would it be doxastically responsible to believe reports of this kind? How many more witnesses would be required? Or is the problem that the existing witnesses are not sufficiently trustworthy or competent? The answer better not be that there *are* no possible circumstances under which reports of this kind can be responsibly believed. This answer would reveal an adherence to the Humean misconception.

A completely watertight argument in favor of the resurrection would be very nice to have. However, it would be unreasonable to demand such an argument as a condition for responsible belief in the resurrection reports. Having a watertight argument would completely protect one from epistemic risk. However, forming beliefs in a doxastically responsible way is completely compatible with exposing oneself to epistemic risk. We expose ourselves to epistemic risk every time we trust the testimony of a stranger about, say, the whereabouts of the bus station. In such a case, we do not (if anti-reductionism is correct) have access to a cogent argument from premises we know to the conclusion that the testimony is truthful. The stranger might be misinformed, or hostile to tourists, even though there are no signs that indicate this. We take the same kinds of risks when we trust the testimony of textbooks in school, or encyclopedias whose authors we do not know. If we deny that doxastic responsibility allows us to take epistemic risks, we must deny that there is such a thing as testimonial knowledge.

Some readers might feel that my emphasis on the resurrection of Jesus (and miracles in general) as a condition for responsible belief in Jesus' claim about himself is misguided. You might think that Jesus can be responsibly believed even by people who lack knowledge of the resurrection or any other miraculous events. If this is your view, note that it is compatible with the *general* account I am defending in this book. Just replace knowledge of the resurrection with whatever you think makes responsible belief in Jesus' claim possible.

CHAPTER 8

Faithful Knowledge

Let me summarize the account I have been elaborating on. If Jesus claims that he speaks in the name of the one God of Israel, and if this claim is in fact a speech-act by God, then it expresses *knowledge* of God. It expresses the knowledge that there is one God, and that Jesus speaks in his name. However, if that knowledge is to be "picked up" by a human hearer, then believing the relevant utterance must not require her to violate the dictates of doxastic responsibility. Doxastic responsibility clearly dictates that a hearer must be very suspicious about claims that someone speaks in the name of God. But if a person who makes this kind of claim returns to life in the way that Jesus did after his crucifixion (and if he has the moral and other properties that the Gospels portray Jesus as having), then a very promising-looking hypothesis — indeed, the most promising-looking one — is that the person in question really was speaking in the name of God, and that God has vindicated him by raising him from the dead.

If a person *knows* that Jesus miraculously returned from the dead, she has, accordingly, independent evidence that clearly speaks in favor of the truth of Jesus' claim. The hypothesis that Jesus' claim is true would, for such a subject, appear (and also be) very feasible. This means that the person could *believe* Jesus' claim about his own divine commission without violating the dictates of doxastic responsibility. Jesus' contemporaneous followers, who *(ex hypothesi)* saw with their own eyes his miraculous return to life, were in precisely this situation. They had perceptual knowledge of the fact that Jesus had returned to life. If this eyewitness knowledge of Jesus' resurrection is committed to writing, either directly or through the mediation of a reliable oral tradition, and if it is compatible with doxastic responsibility for a reader of that written testimony to believe its content (which the above investigation indicates it could be), then the reader can "pick up" the knowledge expressed by it. This means that a person, living today, could possibly have testimonial knowledge about Jesus' miraculous return to life.

Against the background of that knowledge, it would be possible for a present-day person to accept Jesus' claim about his own divine commission (also made available by the written testimony) without violating the dictates of doxastic responsibility. This means that a present-day person could, possibly, get to *know* that Jesus speaks in the name of God, and hence that God exists.

8.1 Objections and Clarifications

Some people may feel that one cannot really *know* that Jesus miraculously returned to life unless one has seen "the mark of the nails in his hands, and put [one's] finger in the mark of the nails" (John 20:25). This opinion is probably the result of a confusion (which I referred to earlier) between one's *subjective* feeling of certainty and one's *objective* rational standing. This is surely understandable, but it should be regarded precisely as a confusion, and not as a sign of high intellectual standards. Refusing to believe something unless one has a certain subjective feeling of certainty, as well as believing something just because one has a certain subjective feeling of certainty, is not to be identified with critical thinking. What matters is not primarily how one feels but whether one's justification is satisfactory. I have argued that people possibly have factive reasons of the sui generis testimonial kind for the relevant belief about Jesus. Whether they actually have such reasons depends on what the objective world is like in certain specific respects. It depends, crucially, on whether Jesus really came back to life after being dead, and on whether the testimony in the Gospels about this event is reliable. If you still find it shocking that *your* rational standing with respect to the resurrection can depend on circumstances such as the ones mentioned — circumstances that you have no immediate access to, or ability to control — you should recall that this kind of dependence seems to characterize much of our knowledge (as I argued in chap. 5).

It cannot be expected of me that I prove that the testimony of the Gospels makes knowledge of the resurrection available. To prove that it does would mean to construct a cogent argument that establishes that the Gospels' testimony is trustworthy. But if anti-reductionism is correct, it is usually not possible to establish the trustworthiness of a particular testimony by argument, at least not on the basis of nontestimonial reasons only. Testimonial knowledge is knowledge that goes beyond what perception, memory, and inference (i.e., *arguments* from perceptions and memories) can establish. This is why testimony is irreducible as a source of justification.

It could be asked what the point of the present exercise is if it cannot be established that those who trust the Gospels' testimony actually acquire knowledge. The point is, first, to show that it is *possible* for those who believe the reports to acquire knowledge about Jesus' resurrection. I have argued that they *could* know that the resurrection happened even though they are incapable of proving (at least by argument from forensic evidence) *that* they know it, in much the same way as I can know I had a certain experience, though I cannot prove, by argument, that I had that experience. Of course, the mere possibility of this kind of knowledge is controversial. Many people would claim to *know* that nobody in our world today knows that Jesus was resurrected or that Jesus spoke in the name of God. The project of establishing the mere possibility of knowledge of the Christian message (or at least the possibility of justified belief in the same) is, in fact, very important. Unless this possibility can be established, Christians would have to live with rather unhealthy combinations of beliefs, for instance, "Jesus is the Son of God" and "I do not know or justifiably believe that Jesus is the Son of God."

Second, one aim I had in the preceding chapter was to argue that it is *plausible* that people have the relevant kind of knowledge. The forensic argument in favor of the resurrection of Jesus was meant to establish that the reports about the resurrection are very likely to be true. This was necessary to establish in order to show that those reports could be believed without doxastic irresponsibility. If it is plausible that the reports are true, then it is also plausible that what people acquire from believing those reports is *knowledge* of the resurrection.[1] Knowledge of the resurrection, in

---

1. Does not a person who knows that Jesus was resurrected also — and by necessity — *know that he knows*? Why, then, is it necessary for me to argue for the plausibility of resurrection knowledge? First, it is not at all obvious that a person who knows must also know that he knows. The so-called KK-thesis is highly controversial. Fred Dretske claims that, "unlike thirty years ago, there aren't many people around today who accept KK" (Fred Dretske, "Externalism and Modest Contextualism," *Erkenntnis* 61, no. 2 [2004]:

turn, significantly increases the plausibility that Jesus' claim to speak for God is true.

In this context it is suitable to address another possible objection to the project of this book. The Bible is not the only religious document that is taken by people to constitute or record divine testimony. A relevant question against the background of this is whether all religious communities that believe in divine testimony can appeal to the model for knowledge transmission presented in this book. If so, does not the model — despite my emphasis on the importance of rational justification — in practice encourage a relativistic attitude with respect to the claims of different faith communities?

I do not think so. The requirements of doxastic responsibility that I have emphasized are very difficult to meet when it comes to claims about divine revelation, especially in the context of modernity. The Christian community has a great advantage here with respect to other faith communities because of the enormous amount of historical-critical scholarship that has been devoted to the Bible. A consequence of this massive attention

---

173-86; 176). John McDowell says that it is "quite dubious that someone who knows must know that he knows" (McDowell, "Knowledge by Hearsay," in *Meaning, Knowledge, and Reality* [Cambridge, MA: Harvard University Press, 1998], p. 419). Second, however, my McDowellian account of testimonial knowledge actually seems to entail that a person who believes the resurrection reports, and thereby (as we assume) acquires knowledge of the resurrection, is thereby also in a position to *know that he knows* about the resurrection, or at least in a position to know that his belief in it is satisfactorily justified. This is because he is in a position to know that the resurrection reports are reliable and that his resurrection belief, consequently, is justified. He can know this by reasoning from the following premises. Premise 1: I believe, on the basis of the Gospel testimony, that Jesus was resurrected. Premise 2: If my belief in the resurrection is true, it is very likely that the Gospel testimony is reliable. (If my resurrection belief is true despite being based on *un*reliable testimony, then I have been remarkably lucky.) Premise 3: Jesus was resurrected. From these premises (which I know, the first two on the basis of introspection and relatively uncontroversial reasoning, and the third — as we here assume — by testimony) it follows that my belief in the resurrection is true (conclusion 1, from premises 1 and 3) and consequently that the Gospels' testimony is very likely to be reliable (conclusion 2, from premise 2 and conclusion 1). However, this knowledge of (or at least strongly justified belief in) the reliability of the testimony of the Gospels is a kind of "by-product" of the knowledge that Jesus was resurrected — a knowledge that is acquired by trusting testimony. Since the acquisition of knowledge by trusting testimony presupposes doxastic responsibility, it is necessary also for Christians to investigate the reliability of the Gospel testimony and the credibility of its assertions *while suspending trust in it,* that is, by appealing only to forensic evidence. When I argue in favor of the plausibility of the claim that people have knowledge of the resurrection, I argue from a standpoint where I have suspended trust in the Gospels' testimony.

is that the central event of the Christian religion, the alleged resurrection of Jesus, has been scrutinized much more than any other alleged miraculous event in world history. The resurrection has, as I have argued, withstood this scrutiny very well, and the majority of specialists in the area argue in favor of its historicity. Furthermore, not all religions point to some kind of miraculous event on the public stage of history to legitimate their claims about divine revelation.[2] I have argued, however, that there must be some extraordinary and very hard to explain, publicly available circumstance or circumstances connected to claims about divine revelation. Otherwise, the natural reasons for skepticism about such claims stand undefeated, and doxastic responsibility will dictate that the claims are not to be believed. Of course, this is not the place to evaluate the claims of faith communities other than the Christian church, and I neither can nor want to exclude the possibility that some of them could be defended as compatible with doxastic responsibility. My point is simply that it is not easy.

What about Christians who read the Gospels and believe in Jesus' resurrection but who have little or no knowledge about what the historical-critical or "forensic" evidence implies about the likelihood of that event? Can people like this acquire knowledge about Jesus' resurrection — and about Jesus' divine commission — from the Gospels' witness? It could be argued that they cannot, because a person who has not studied the "forensic" case for the resurrection cannot believe the resurrection reports without doxastic irresponsibility.

Doxastic responsibility, however, should not be analyzed in purely individualistic terms — no more than knowledge should be. It is clearly the case that I can responsibly believe that the speed of light is approximately 300,000,000 m/s even if I am not a physicist, and even if I have never been told (either orally or in writing) what the speed of light is by a physicist. It is sufficient if I know that physicists believe that the speed of light is 300,000,000 m/s. If I know this, I, too, can responsibly believe that the speed of light is 300,000,000 m/s. This shows that the doxastic rights of a certain epistemic elite (in this case, physicists) can be extended (to some degree) to those who do not belong to that elite.

2. The case of Islam is ambiguous. The Prophet Muhammad did not perform any miracle in order to confirm the revealed status of the Qur'an, but the Qur'an itself is usually seen as Muhammad's "miracle of confirmation" in Islamic theology. Swinburne, however, argues that the Qur'an's alleged "inimitability" and other allegedly unique properties are not sufficient to exclude natural explanations of its origin (Richard Swinburne, *Revelation: From Metaphor to Analogy,* 2nd ed. [Oxford: Oxford University Press, 2007], p. 128).

The Gospels are not documents primarily addressed to individuals, but to a community, the church. Therefore, the question we should ask is not whether a certain individual can responsibly believe the Gospels' testimony, but whether the church can. The church can responsibly believe this testimony if there is an epistemic elite within it that has the time and competence to study and assess the relevant evidence. If there is such an elite, and if this elite has found that the evidence clearly speaks in favor of the credibility of the resurrection reports, then the church can responsibly believe those reports. The doxastic rights that belong, in the first instance, to the epistemic elite can be extended to the church as a whole — and thereby to individual members.

However, the fact that the scholarly community as a whole is divided on questions about the historical Jesus, the resurrection, and the reliability of the Gospel traditions could be seen as a problem in this context. Since the specialists make different and contradictory assessments of the ("forensic") evidence connected to the resurrection, one can wonder whether it really is compatible with doxastic responsibility for a member of the church who has not studied the evidence thoroughly to believe the testimony about the resurrection.

However, if we deny that a nonexpert can responsibly form beliefs about issues that divide scholarly and scientific communities, then we would have to say that a nonethicist cannot responsibly have beliefs about the rightness or wrongness of war, of the death penalty, of abortion, of killing and eating animals, of infanticide, of euthanasia, of legalizing drugs, or of affirmative action. We would also have to say that a nonphilosopher cannot responsibly believe that we have beliefs,[3] that most of what we say has a determinate meaning,[4] that moral questions can be rationally decided, that life has a purpose, and that God does not exist. Furthermore, all noneconomists or non-social-scientists who have ever cast a vote in favor of a Keynesian or non-Keynesian political program, criticized the World Bank, or taken a stand in the debate between communism and capitalism have — if the objection we are considering is correct — acted in a doxastically irresponsible way. But this conclusion is actually too weak. Not all ethicists are experts on all of the controversial ethical issues men-

---

3. The position that there may be no beliefs is argued by (e.g.) Paul Churchland, "Eliminative Materialism and the Propositional Attitudes," *The Journal of Philosophy* 78, no. 2 (1981): 67-90.

4. The denial of determinate meanings is represented by W. V. Quine, *Word and Object* (Cambridge, MA: The MIT Press, 1960), chap. 2.

tioned, and not all economists or social scientists are familiar with all or even most of the research that is relevant for assessing the viability of the different economical-political issues mentioned. So if nonexperts cannot responsibly form beliefs about issues that divide experts, then we must say that even most social scientists and philosophers often form beliefs about topics *within their own disciplines* in a doxastically irresponsible way. I am able to support the last claim empirically by referring to a sociological study conducted by David Bourget and David Chalmers.[5]

Bourget and Chalmers surveyed the philosophical opinions of (mainly analytical) philosophers around the world. The survey targeted 1,972 faculty members in 99 leading departments of philosophy in the United States, Canada, Europe, and Australasia. A total of 931 philosophers completed the questionnaire (47 percent). Besides questions about their philosophical views, the survey also contained questions about the participants' areas of specialization within philosophy. This made it possible to study correlations between philosophical views and areas of specialization. According to the authors, the results "suggest that there is such a thing as specialist opinion in philosophy."[6]

A "specialization effect" is clearly discernible in the answers to several of the questions. One of the questions is about the existence of God. Of the total number of participants, 61.9 percent answered that they accept atheism (and another 11 percent said that they "lean toward" atheism). The difference between the specialists and nonspecialists with respect to this answer, however, is considerable. Only 20.9 percent of the specialists in the relevant area (the philosophy of religion) accepted atheism. Of the nonspecialists, 86.8 percent accepted atheism.[7]

Nonspecialists are, by definition, people who do not have a comprehensive grasp of the relevant literature, debates, and arguments in a certain area. A large majority of the philosophers who lack specialist knowledge in the philosophy of religion were apparently completely comfortable with taking a position on a question that is controversial and divides those who have specialist competence. The position that the majority of the nonspecialists took was, furthermore, clearly a minority position among the specialists. The participants in the survey were not

---

5. David Bourget and David Chalmers, *What Do Philosophers Believe?* http://philpapers.org/archive/BOUWDP (accessed May 23, 2013).
6. Bourget and Chalmers, *What Do Philosophers Believe?* p. 18.
7. Bourget and Chalmers, *What Do Philosophers Believe?* p. 19.

forced to express an unambiguous belief. They had the option of answering "agnostic/undecided." They also had the option of answering "lean toward" rather than "accept" for either theism or atheism. Yet 61.9 percent chose to mark the box for "accept" on atheism.

The objection we are considering says that if there are contradictory assessments of the evidence concerning a certain issue within the relevant scholarly or scientific community, then a nonspecialist should suspend belief with respect to that issue, and adopt an agnostic stance. To do otherwise — for instance, to accept the position of one side of the scholarly or scientific debate and reject the other — is to act in a doxastically irresponsible way. If this is correct, it seems that most analytical philosophers (assuming that Chalmer and Bourget's study is representative) act in a doxastically irresponsible way when they form beliefs about (e.g.) God. If one were to argue that philosophers in general are very knowledgeable about the literature, debates, and arguments concerning God's existence, and that all philosophers — even those who do not work within the philosophy of religion — are "specialists" with respect to that issue, I would say, based on my experience, that this is simply not true. It is as false as the claim that all natural scientists are specialists in evolutionary biology.

My conclusion, however, is not that analytical philosophers are doxastically irresponsible. I conclude instead that doxastic responsibility, at least sometimes, is compatible with taking a stand on a question that divides specialists, even if one is not a specialist oneself. The reason a layman may justifiably have greater confidence in the conclusions of one group of scholars rather than another in a particular scholarly debate can be, for example, that one has reason to think that the other camp is biased in a certain direction. It is possible, for example, that philosophers of religion in general find atheism less credible than do their nonspecialist colleagues because some philosophers of religion have chosen their field of specialization as a result of their prior belief in God. Likewise, one may reasonably suspect that certain scholars who work within the field of resurrection research have excluded in advance the possibility of confirming a miracle, as a result of their adherence to a certain naturalistic worldview, or to a certain form of methodological atheism. This would explain why a minority of scholars in the field assess the evidence differently than the majority do. Conversely, one can argue that the conclusions of the majority are unduly influenced by Christian beliefs. If one belongs to a community such as the church, and if there is an epistemic elite within the church with specialist competence in a certain area, it is not irrational to have more confidence

Faithful Knowledge

in the conclusions of that group of specialists than in the conclusions of specialists who do not share one's own basic worldview or values.

It is appropriate, in this context, to address and preempt another criticism that my account is likely to draw. The account portrays (at least tentatively) knowledge about Jesus' resurrection as a condition for acquiring knowledge that Jesus spoke in the name of God. However, many Christians will say that they came to believe in Jesus' divine commission first, and only later did they come to accept the resurrection as a historical event.

The temporal order in which beliefs arise is irrelevant in the present context. What I have been talking about is the logic of knowledge-acquisition, not the psychology of belief-acquisition. A person H may come to believe Jesus' claim to speak in the name of God first, and only later start to believe the Gospels' reports of his resurrection. My account implies that the belief that Jesus speaks in the name of God initially would be *irresponsibly* held by H, since he believes Jesus' claim without having knowledge of his resurrection. So the belief in Jesus' claim would not, initially, constitute knowledge. When H starts to believe the Gospels' reports about Jesus' resurrection, however, he would thereby acquire testimonial knowledge of that miraculous event, knowledge that would ensure that the first belief does not violate the dictates of doxastic responsibility anymore. As a result, the first belief would also come to constitute knowledge.

It could be objected, however, that this does not solve the problem. What if the reason H starts to believe in the resurrection is that he, after having been Christian for a while, now is so firmly convinced that Jesus speaks in the name of God that he does not perceive the resurrection as unlikely anymore? This is not at all an implausible scenario. Many Christians today are more reluctant to believe in miracles than they are to believe that Jesus is commissioned by God.

This objection cannot be defused by reference to the distinction between the logic of knowledge-acquisition and the psychology of belief-acquisition. The problem seems to be logical. If H's *reason* for believing in the resurrection is that he already believes Jesus' claim about being commissioned by God, then knowledge about the resurrection cannot, in turn, function as the factor that makes it doxastically responsible for H to believe Jesus' claim about being commissioned by God. This would be a case of vicious circularity.

The objection, however, is misconceived. Every person who believes that Jesus was resurrected does so because the Gospels or other New Testament writings tell us that Jesus was resurrected. If the New Testament did not tell us that Jesus was resurrected, nobody would believe that Jesus was resurrected. This means that everybody who believes that Jesus was resurrected has a (putative) *testimonial* reason for that belief — having *learned* it from the New Testament. In the above scenario, H does not think that the New Testament testimony is sufficient to justify belief in Jesus' resurrection. So he thinks he needs an additional reason. The additional reason that he points to is his firm conviction that Jesus was commissioned by God. If my account is correct, however, the testimonial reason is *by itself* sufficient to justify H's belief in Jesus' resurrection (it is, *ex hypothesi*, a factive reason). H is thus wrong in believing that an additional reason is needed. Moreover, H is also wrong in thinking that his belief that Jesus is commissioned by God provides epistemic support for the subsequently acquired belief that Jesus was resurrected. Since the former belief initially is *irresponsibly* held and therefore unjustified, it does not provide any epistemic support. All the epistemic work is done by the testimonial reason; it is this reason that justifies H's belief in Jesus' resurrection. This means that H's knowledge of Jesus' resurrection is epistemically independent of his belief that Jesus is commissioned by God (even though H does not think so himself). This, in turn, means that H's knowledge of the resurrection can do the job that it is supposed to do in my account, namely, to ensure that it is doxastically responsible for H to believe Jesus' claim about divine commission.

Finally, we may ask why God, if his intention was to make knowledge of himself available, chose to do so by means of human testimony, with all the uncertainties that this transmission process entails. Surely there are more reliable means for an omnipotent being to communicate knowledge — means that do not require that we trust people we have never met. It could be argued that the fact that God did not choose any such means indicates that the purpose of God's revelation was not to communicate knowledge at all.

It seems to me, however, that the frail and trust-requiring process of human testimony is exactly the kind of means that would be fitting for the God of the Bible to choose for making himself *known*. It is not farfetched to assume, with Laura Garcia, that this God "might desire that most persons should come to know Him . . . by hearing [His] message from others — originally from eyewitnesses of His miracles and His 'glory,' but later from those who have not seen and yet have believed. This method preserves the relationality of human beings better than . . . more direct, individualistic methods . . . and is perhaps a better introduction into the realm of personal relationships that comprises our final destiny and that characterizes even the inner life of God himself (according to the Christian doctrine of the Trinity)."[8] An interpersonal God (the Trinity) who saves by making himself vulnerable (the incarnation) might very well want to make himself known through an interpersonal and vulnerable process.

8.2 What about *Faith?*

This book has exemplified how knowledge of God could be had on the basis of God's testimony. The focus has been on the utterances of Jesus as instances of divine speech. The tradition, however, conceives of not only the words of Jesus and the prophets, but also the Bible itself as divine testimony. In an earlier chapter, I have suggested that this may be a tenable view and that many common objections to it can be overcome by the resources provided by (e.g.) Wolterstorff's philosophical analysis of divine speech. But the main concern of this book is to establish the general possibility of knowledge of God through divine testimony. Therefore, I will not expand on the topic of the Bible's status as divine speech.

John Lamont, in his fine work *Divine Faith,* has argued that Christian faith is a matter of believing God when he speaks. He conceives of the knowledge that the believer acquires by believing God as *testimonial* knowledge, and he appeals, as I do, to John McDowell's analysis of testimony. But there is a crucial difference between Lamont's account of how knowledge of God comes about and mine. The main purpose of my account is to explain how humans can get to know that a reality with the properties of the Christian God exists. Gordon Kaufman and others who follow Kant claim that knowledge of such a reality cannot be had, and that the Christian tradition must abandon its traditional realist conception of God. My testimonial account aims to solve this problem and to allow us to retain a realist conception of God, even without reliance on a potent natural theology.

Lamont's account has a very different focus and addresses Kaufman's Kantian challenge only in passing. Lamont acknowledges that in order to be able to believe God when he speaks, the believer must recognize the

---

8. Laura Garcia, "St. John of the Cross and the Necessity of Divine Hiddenness," in Daniel Howard-Snyder and Paul Moser, eds., *Divine Hiddenness: New Essays* (West Nyack, NY: Cambridge University Press, 2002), pp. 86-87.

identity of the speaker. The believer must, prior to believing the spoken message, recognize that it is *God* who speaks (otherwise the believer cannot *believe God*). To recognize that it is God who speaks means coming to know that it is God who speaks.

The weakest point in Lamont's otherwise very valuable book is his account of how the recognition of God happens. He says that "it is the effect of an utterance upon a hearer that enables the hearer to recognize it as being spoken by God." "A divine utterance can be recognized as divine when it enlightens us in a way that only God can, or when it changes us in a way that only God can." An example of this kind of enlightenment or change is when a "seared" conscience miraculously recovers:

> It is common for people to undoubtingly believe that evil actions they do are good, and to not be able to grasp . . . that these actions are not good. A conscience that is seared in this way does not have the power to realize that the evil actions in question are not good, or to be brought to realize this by other people. If such a conscience is brought to realize, through hearing the gospel preached, that the actions it thought good were in fact evil, this cannot happen through the action of any natural power. It can only happen through an exercise of divine power.[9]

However, even if the enlightenment of a seared conscience is such that it "cannot happen through the action of any *natural* power," it does not follow that "it can only happen through an exercise of *divine* power." It is surely possible that a spiritual (preternatural) being who is extremely powerful, but who is not the Creator of everything that exists (and hence not God) could enlighten a seared conscience in the way Lamont describes.[10] So the fact that a seared conscience is enlightened when the gospel is preached does not enable us to conclude that the gospel is divine in origin.[11]

---

9. John Lamont, *Divine Faith* (Aldershot, UK: Ashgate, 2004), pp. 198-99.

10. It could be argued that a preternatural power is still a *natural* power, and that any power that is not natural is, by definition, divine (a traditional definition). However, if we define the concept "natural power" so that it includes every imaginable (material or spiritual) power except divine powers, then we have no grounds to believe that the healing of a seared conscience "cannot happen through the action of any natural power." We have, for example, absolutely no reason to believe that a mighty spiritual (but nondivine) being who has the power to "magically" affect the functioning of the human brain could not possibly heal a seared conscience in the way Lamont describes.

11. Lamont gives other examples of enlightenment and change that, according to him,

Lamont can, of course, appeal to natural theology for support here. If we already know, independently of divine revelation, that God exists, then we may be on firmer ground in concluding that God is behind the miraculous enlightenment of consciences. But the ground would still not be very firm. Even if we know from natural theology that God exists, it is possible that some other spiritual being is responsible for the miraculous enlightenment of consciences. In order to exclude this possibility, we would have to know that the only existing spiritual being who has powers sufficient for the relevant kind of enlightenment is God. But this is not something that natural theology can tell us. The Christian tradition itself assumes the existence of very powerful spiritual beings besides God, such as angels.

Lamont, therefore, does not give a satisfactory answer to the question of how divine speech can be recognized as divine — at any rate, not an answer that is convincing in the absence of a potent natural theology.[12] My model, on the other hand, provides such an answer, as I have argued. We can believe God's *testimony* even though we do not (initially) recognize it as *God's* testimony. If God testifies (through human spokespersons) that it is he who is speaking, and if we believe his testimony without being doxastically irresponsible, then we acquire knowledge about the divine identity of the speaker. Admittedly, we cannot say, in this case, that we are "believing *God* when he speaks"; but this is a minor problem (as we saw in 6.1). The crux, instead, is the issue of doxastic responsibility. Addressing this issue has required us to look at, among other things, the epistemic function of miracles and the believability of miracle reports. The purpose of this investigation was to solve a problem that Lamont more or less

---

allow us to recognize God as their cause, such as enlightenment about "the goodness and desirability of the Christian life" (*Divine Faith,* p. 200). Charity, moreover, "requires grace that is strictly supernatural" (p. 201), and the existence of charity can thus be recognized as an effect of God's agency. None of these examples are convincing. A demon could brainwash us to find the Christian life desirable. If charity *by definition* "requires grace that is strictly supernatural," then the existence of charity is certainly "a sign of divine power" (only God is "supernatural"). But this only relocates the problem: How can we distinguish charity (which by definition has God as its cause) from merely human love, or love caused by some very mighty preternatural being?

12. The same can be said of St. Thomas Aquinas, understood in accordance with the currently most popular interpretation. Aquinas claims, according to Paul Macdonald, that the human intellect, as a result of a "supernaturally infused habit or 'light of faith'" can "*recognize* or *discern,* immediately and non-inferentially, what propositions . . . have been revealed by God" (Macdonald, *Knowledge and the Transcendent: An Inquiry into the Mind's Relationship to God* [Washington, DC: Catholic University of America Press, 2009], p. 201).

sweeps under the carpet, namely, how to get to know the divine identity of the speaker.

In the remainder of this chapter, I will argue that my account of how knowledge of God comes about is congenial to the nature of Christian faith, as this has been classically conceived. Lamont writes: "Traditional Christian thought has taken it for granted that God has spoken to humanity, and that the Christian message originates in this speech."[13] Speech is something that has a propositional content, and it is obvious that the tradition up to modernity presumes that one important aspect of Christian faith is intellectual assent to divinely spoken propositions. Even though other aspects of faith, such as its connection with trust, or its relational character, might be as important, or even more important, than the assent-to-propositions dimension, the latter cannot be denied to exist. This intellectual dimension is explicit in a few places in the New Testament itself, where "faith" refers to "the body of Christian truth implied in faith," such as Galatians 1:23, 1 Timothy 4:1, 6, and Jude 3.[14] In the Gospel of John, the object of the verb *pisteuo* ("I believe") is, on twelve occasions, a propositional content, namely, Christological convictions (believing that Jesus is the Messiah, that he is the Son of God, that he has come from God, etc.).[15] Moreover, an important part of trusting a person is, one may presume, believing what he says. An intellectual-assent dimension is thus probably implicit even when words like *pistis* and *pisteuo* take a person, such as Jesus (or God), as their object.

The tradition is ambiguous when it comes to the question of whether Christian faith is a form of *knowledge*. This question is itself ambiguous, since there is no univocal concept of knowledge used by patristic, medieval, and modern thinkers in common. Most of the fathers insisted that faith is a form of knowledge in the sense of *scientia*, despite the fact that the Christian faith concerns contingent events of history (p. 35). Aquinas's view is that faith lies between *scientia* and *opinio*. *Scientia* is (paradigmatically) the knowledge acquired by demonstration from "immediate" (self-evident) propositions. The assent involved in *scientia* is compelled by the rational force of the demonstrations. *Opinio*, on the other hand, happens

---

13. Lamont, *Divine Faith*, p. 5. Hereafter, page references to this work appear in parentheses within the text.

14. Geoffrey Bromiley, "Faith," in Geoffrey Bromiley, ed., *The International Standard Bible Encyclopedia* (Grand Rapids: Eerdmans, 1982), vol. 2, p. 270.

15. R. T. France, "Faith," in Joel B. Green and Scot McKnight, eds., *Dictionary of Jesus and the Gospels* (Downers Grove, IL: InterVarsity, 1992), p. 225.

when the intellect assents to a proposition without being fully certain of its truth. Faith lies between *scientia* and *opinio* because the assent involved in faith is firm, as in *scientia,* but it is not rationally compelled by some demonstration. The assent of faith is, instead, as in *opinio,* produced by the choice of the will (pp. 55-56).

My above account portrays Christian faith as involving *knowledge* of God, but it also concurs with Aquinas that the Christian believer's assent to the propositions spoken by God is dependent on the will. The assent is not rationally compelled by "forensic" evidence.

The Christian tradition has, according to Lamont, made three important affirmations about Christian faith (pp. 29-30). Believing God when he speaks (i.e., faith) —

(1) is voluntary;
(2) is theoretically reasonable;
(3) requires grace.

Theologians have wrestled with reconciling these affirmations, which all have a firm grounding in the tradition. However, the first affirmation is controversial. Martin Luther famously denied the existence of free will after the Fall, at least with respect to salvation.[16] The later Lutheran tradition, however, seems to acknowledge a role for a "freed will," which is able to "assent to" and "accept" God's word, "although in great weakness."[17] The Council of Trent emphasizes more strongly that "the will in coming to faith is indeed moved by God, but God does not move it coercively, as irrational creatures are moved, but freely, in such a way that it makes its own contribution."[18] This view receives support from New Testament texts that suggest that belief is to be praised, and its absence blamed — for

---

16. See, e.g., *Luther's Works,* vol. 31, ed. Harold J. Grimm (Philadelphia: Fortress, 1957), p. 40. Much of what Luther says about free will points in this direction. However, for a different interpretation of Luther, see William Placher, *The Domestication of Transcendence: How Modern Thinking about God Went Wrong* (Louisville: Westminster John Knox, 1996), pp. 124-25.

17. Robert Kolb and Timothy Wengert, eds., *The Book of Concord: The Confessions of the Evangelical Lutheran Church* (Minneapolis: Fortress, 2000), p. 557.

18. This description of the Tridentine view is Avery Dulles's (*The Assurance of Things Hoped For* [New York: Oxford University Press, 1994], p. 227). For the original anathema, see Heinrich Denzinger, *Compendium of Creeds, Definitions, and Declarations on Matters of Faith and Morals,* ed. Peter Hünermann, 43rd ed. (San Francisco: Ignatius Press, 2012), §1554.

example, Mark 16:9-14 and 1 John 5:10 (*Divine Faith,* p. 191). Praise and blame seem to presuppose that one has a choice whether to believe or not believe, that is, that one's will has something do with it. However, even theologians who, like Luther, deny the voluntary nature of Christian faith could admit that belief in the Christian message is voluntary in the sense of *not being rationally compelled* by the evidence for it.[19] This epistemic sense of "voluntary" is the most pertinent in the present context.

The theoretical reasonableness of Christian faith has been defended by the great majority of Christian thinkers through the ages. This is not that strange, since it would be odd if God, who has created humans with an ability for rational thinking, were to require them to believe something that could not reasonably be believed. Faith is not supposed to be, in the words of Vatican I, "a blind impulse of the mind."[20]

The claim that faith *requires grace* is embraced by all mainline churches, and it is implied in a host of biblical texts. Ephesians 2:8 states the matter clearly: "By grace you have been saved through faith, and this is not your own doing; it is the gift of God." Since faith justifies — and since justification is by grace — faith must be by grace.

The account that I have presented in this book is capable of reconciling the three affirmations above. Both the voluntary nature of believing God when he speaks, and its theoretical reasonableness, follow from the nature of testimonial knowledge, as the latter is conceived of above, together with my claim that believing Jesus' assertion to speak in the name of God can be compatible with doxastic responsibility. An important feature of testimonial knowledge is that its acquisition requires trust. Not blind trust, as we have seen, since a blind trust that violates the requirements of doxastic responsibility positively prevents one from acquiring knowledge from testimony. Nevertheless, to rely on testimony for one's belief that p is to believe p without possessing (or at least without basing one's belief on) a watertight argument from premises whose truth one can assure oneself of, to the truth of p. If one believes that p on the basis of such an argument, then one's belief is not testimonial but inferential.

This is why my account never says that Jesus' claim about himself, or the church's claims about Jesus' return to life, *must* be believed, on pain

---

19. Vatican I affirmed, contra Georges Hermes, that the assent to the Christian message is not "produced with necessity by arguments of human reason" (Denzinger, *Compendium of Creeds,* §3035).

20. Denzinger, *Compendium of Creeds,* §3010.

of irrationality. The account claims only that the testimonies of Jesus and the church make knowledge *available*. This knowledge is not forced on all rational subjects who are acquainted with the relevant (forensic) evidence. Believing Jesus' and the church's testimony can, I have contended, be compatible with doxastic responsibility, but so can *not* believing them. This means that believing the testimony is, in an epistemic sense, voluntary. We can say that choosing to trust the testimony gives us access to knowledge that would otherwise be unavailable.

The argument of this book hence portrays trust (exercised in a doxastically responsible way) as a precondition for knowledge of God. The origin of Christian faith was the disciples' trust in Jesus' claim to speak in the name of God. This trust was doxastically responsible (theoretically reasonable) because, among other things, the disciples had seen Jesus perform miraculous acts. The voluntary (not rationally compelled) choice they made to trust his assertion made knowledge of the fact that Jesus was speaking for God available to them, and through them, to us. Knowing that it was God who spoke through Jesus, the disciples could subsequently conceive of themselves as believing God when they believed what Jesus said.[21] Knowledge of God is, in this model, dependent on trust in Jesus. This means that it pictures faith in the sense of *cognitive assent* and faith in the sense of *trust* as inseparable. Moreover, the object of trust is Jesus. This resonates well with the Johannine saying: "I am the way, and the truth, and the life. No one comes to the Father except through me" (John 14:6).

So the account of this book entails that Christian faith — conceived as believing God when he speaks — is both voluntary and theoretically reasonable. What about the necessity of grace? The claim that grace is necessary for Christian belief (faith) is compatible with the account, given a reasonable interpretation of that claim. It is not only the case, according to the tradition, that grace is necessary for "living faith" — faith vivified by charity; Vatican I says that "faith itself, even when it is not working through love ... is a gift of God."[22] In other words, the mere intellectual assent to the Christian message requires grace.

We cannot, however, interpret this as meaning that no one can give an intellectual assent to the Christian message unless he is moved to do so

---

21. This does not presuppose that the disciples embraced the doctrine of the incarnation. Ordinary prophets also speak in the name of God, and believing what a prophet says is, accordingly, to believe what God says.

22. Denzinger, *Compendium of Creeds*, §§3010, 3035.

by grace. The Epistle of James says that even the demons believe — and they shudder. The purely intellectual assent of the demons to the Christian message is, everybody agrees, not caused by grace. According to Aquinas's reasonable interpretation, the assent of the demons is compelled by the evidence. It can be argued, following John Jenkins, that the case of the demons is irrelevant for whether *human* assent requires grace, since demons have greater cognitive powers than do humans.[23] So the demons may have access to evidence that humans do not have access to, which explains how they can assent to the Christian message without grace. However, even if the evidence available to us humans is not capable of rationally compelling our assent, it must be possible for us to assent *irrationally* to the Christian message.[24]

We can reconcile the possibility of a non-grace-produced assent to the Christian message with the traditional claim that grace is necessary for faith by pointing out that non-grace-produced assent would not be *Christian* faith. The intellectual assent involved in Christian faith is, by definition, produced by grace. The account of knowledge of God presented in this book leaves it open that, in the normal case, those who choose to trust Jesus and believe what he says are moved to do so by grace. The assent is not, as we have seen, compelled by the "forensic" evidence. However, it cannot be denied that a person may come to trust Jesus and believe what he says without being moved by grace, perhaps as a result of some idiosyncratic disposition. This possibility must be admitted by any reasonable account of Christian faith. The formulation of Vatican I seems to be compatible with this admission. The council says that "no one can accept the gospel preaching *in the way that is necessary for achieving salvation* without the inspiration and illumination of the Holy Spirit."[25] This seems to leave open that someone may come to accept the gospel preaching in a way that is *not* conducive to salvation without the inspiration and illumination of the Holy Spirit.

---

23. John Jenkins, *Knowledge and Faith in Thomas Aquinas* (Cambridge: Cambridge University Press, 1997), pp. 171-72.

24. It is true that there could be some psychological laws in virtue of which it is (naturally) impossible for human beings to accept the Christian message. However, even if this is the case, it is hard to deny that, e.g., physical damage to the brain could put these laws out of play.

25. Vatican Council I, *Dei Filius* [Dogmatic Constitution on the Catholic Faith], chap. 3, §6 (italics added): http://www.ewtn.com/library/councils/v1.htm (accessed May 7, 2013). This translation is clearer than the one provided by Denzinger, *Compendium of Creeds*, §3010.

Finally, I will argue that the perspective on revelation defended in this book promises to solve a problem that has figured importantly in modern theology. The problem is whether God's revelation is or is not in need of justification by reference to prior and independent criteria of rational justification. Karl Barth and Hans Urs von Balthasar represent one side of the debate. They are very critical of what Balthasar calls the "anthropological reduction" of revelation, the modern program that "set[s] the criterion for the truth of revelation in the center of the pious human subject," demanding that "every objective dogmatic proposition must be measured in terms of its suitability to the religious subject, in terms of its positive effects on and capacity to complete and fulfill that subject."[26] The central task that modern theology, in this spirit, has set for itself is "how to make religion, revelation and the relationship with God something which could also be understood as a necessary human predicate, or at any rate how to demonstrate that humanity had a potentiality, a capacity, for these things."[27] For Barth, the logical consequence of this attitude is the philosophy of Ludwig Feuerbach, whose openly declared aim is to "reduce theology to anthropology."[28]

Against the tendency to make the human being the "master, judge or protector" of revelation,[29] Barth and Balthasar emphasize that "man is no measure for God, and man's answer is no measure for the Word that is sent to him." The divine revelation cannot be grounded in, or justified by reference to, anything but itself. "There is no text that offers a 'foundation' for God's text, making it legible and intelligible.... It must interpret itself, and this is what it wishes to do."[30] In Barth's words:

> To say "God with us" is to say something which has no basis or possibility outside itself, which can in no sense be explained in terms of man and man's situation, but only as a knowledge of God from God, as free and unmerited grace. As the Bible bears witness to God's revelation and as Church proclamation takes up this witness in obedience, both

---

26. Hans Urs von Balthasar, *Love Alone Is Credible* (San Francisco: Ignatius Press, 2004), pp. 43, 40.
27. Karl Barth, *Protestant Theology in the Nineteenth Century: Its Background and History* (London: SCM Press, 1972), pp. 536-37.
28. Ludwig Feuerbach, *The Essence of Christianity* (New York: Cosimo, 2008), p. xxiii.
29. Karl Barth, *Church Dogmatics*, vol. I.1: *The Doctrine of the Word of God* (Edinburgh: T & T Clark, 1975), p. 31 (quoting Luther).
30. Balthasar, *Love Alone Is Credible,* pp. 147, 50.

renounce any foundation apart from that which God has given once and for all by speaking.

This means that "we must accept the fact that only the Logos of God Himself can provide the proof that we are really talking about Him when we are allegedly doing so."[31]

Barth and Balthasar are, as many theologians today feel, clear-sighted about the risk of God's revelation being domesticated and distorted when it is justified by reference to a set of prior, independently established criteria. However, there is also a legitimate concern among theologians that the opposite attitude — the refusal to justify Christian belief with reference to anything outside the "circle of faith" — is indistinguishable from fideism. Wolfhart Pannenberg has voiced this concern about Barth:

> When the foundation of theology is left to a venture [of faith] in this way, not only is its scientific status endangered, but also the priority of God and his revelation over human beings, on which, for Barth, everything rests. Barth's unmediated starting from God and his revealing word turns out to be no more than an unfounded postulate of theological consciousness. . . . Whereas other attempts to give theology a foundation in human terms sought support from common arguments, Barth's apparently so lofty objectivity about God and God's word turns out to rest on no more than the irrational subjectivity of a venture of faith with no justification outside itself.[32]

Pannenberg's criticism correctly points out the need for a *justification* of Christian belief. If Christian belief is unjustified — based on nothing but an "unfounded postulate" or a subjective "venture of faith" — then it is surely rationally unacceptable to be a Christian, and all lofty talk about "the priority of God and his revelation over human beings" is in fact empty.

To acknowledge the need for a justification is, however, completely compatible with heeding Barth's call to "renounce any foundation apart

---

31. Barth, *Church Dogmatics*, vol. I.1, pp. 119-20, 163.
32. Wolfhart Pannenberg, *Theology and the Philosophy of Science* (London: Darton, Longman and Todd, 1976), pp. 272-73. Wentzel van Huyssteen has a similar criticism: "Barth ultimately fell prey to precisely that psychological subjectivism from which he had sought to escape" (van Huyssteen, *Theology and the Justification of Faith: Constructing Theories in Systematic Theology* [Grand Rapids: Eerdmans, 1989], p. 19). Carl Henry has no doubt that Barth is a "fideist" (Henry, *God, Revelation and Authority*, vol. 3 [Wheaton: Crossway Books, 1999], p. 442).

from that which God has given once and for all by speaking." I have argued that testimonial knowledge is not justified by inferential arguments aimed at establishing the credibility of the testifier, or the plausibility of the proposition testified to. Testimonial knowledge is justified by sui generis testimonial reasons. The "ground," "basis," or "reason" on which a piece of testimonial knowledge rests is, in other words, *the testimony itself.*

This means that if God reveals by speaking, and if we acquire Christian beliefs by listening to what God says, then it is God's speech itself — his testimony, or our hearing it — that constitutes our justification for those beliefs. Therefore, Christian belief has no "foundation apart from that which God has given once and for all by speaking." There is, of course, a role for arguments and independent evidence in our appropriation of divine revelation (as we have seen), but it is not the role of *grounding* Christian belief.

The model of revelation that I defend in this book thus allows us to say, with Barth and Balthasar, that *belief in revelation is not grounded in anything but revelation itself.* It is God's speech that gives faith its only foundation. The insights about testimonial knowledge that this model builds on allow us, at the same time, to show why accusations of fideism are out of place. If Christian belief is based on reliable testimony (God's own), then it is fully and satisfactorily justified. We may not have a *proof* that Christian belief is indeed based on reliable testimony, but the same can be said of most other testimonial beliefs that people have. Testimonial beliefs are not, in general, justified by evidence or arguments for the reliability of the testimony. They are justified by reliable testimony.

Bibliography

Abraham, William. *Divine Revelation and the Limits of Historical Criticism.* Oxford: Oxford University Press, 1982.

Allison, Dale. "Explaining the Resurrection: Conflicting Convictions." *Journal for the Study of the Historical Jesus* 3, no. 2 (2005): 117-33.

———. *Resurrecting Jesus: The Earliest Christian Tradition and Its Interpreters.* New York: T & T Clark, 2005.

Alston, William. "Biblical Criticism and the Resurrection." In *The Resurrection,* edited by Stephen Davis, Daniel Kendall SJ, and Gerald O'Collins SJ, 148-83. Oxford: Oxford University Press, 1997.

———. "Internalism and Externalism in Epistemology." In *Epistemology: Internalism and Externalism,* edited by Hilary Kornblith, 68-110. Oxford: Blackwell, 2001.

———. *Perceiving God: The Epistemology of Religious Experience.* Ithaca, NY: Cornell University Press, 1991.

———. "Sellars and the 'Myth of the Given.'" *Philosophical and Phenomenological Research* 65, no. 1 (2002): 69-86.

Anscombe, G. E. M. "Faith." In *The Collected Philosophical Papers of G. E. M. Anscombe,* vol. 3: *Ethics, Religion and Politics,* pp. 113-22. Oxford: Basil Blackwell, 1981.

Aquinas, Saint Thomas. *The Summa Theologica.* Translated by L. Shapcote and D. J. Sullivan. 2nd ed. 2 volumes. Chicago: Encyclopedia Britannica, 1990.

———. *Aquinas's Shorter Summa.* Manchester, UK: Sophia Institute Press, 2002.

Augustine, Saint. *The City of God.* New York: Modern Library, 1978.

Baillie, John. *The Idea of Revelation in Recent Thought.* New York: Columbia University Press, 1956.

Balthasar, Hans Urs von. *Love Alone Is Credible.* San Francisco: Ignatius Press, 2004.

———. *The Glory of the Lord: A Theological Aesthetics,* vol. 1: *Seeing the Form.* San Francisco: Ignatius Press, 1982.

Barth, Karl. *Church Dogmatics.* Vol. I.1: *The Doctrine of the Word of God.* Edinburgh: T & T Clark, 1975.

———. *Church Dogmatics.* Vol. I.2: *The Doctrine of the Word of God.* Edinburgh: T & T Clark, 1956.
———. *Protestant Theology in the Nineteenth Century: Its Background and History.* London: SCM Press, 1972.
Bauckham, Richard. *Jesus and the Eyewitnesses: The Gospels as Eyewitness Testimony.* Grand Rapids: Eerdmans, 2006.
Baum, Gregory. *New Horizon: Theological Essays.* New York: Paulist Press, 1972.
———. Foreword to Andrew Greeley, *The New Agenda.* Garden City, NY: Doubleday, 1973.
Blaauw, Martijn. "The Nature of Divine Revelation." *The Heythrop Journal* 50, no. 1 (2009): 2-12.
Blackburn, B. L. "Miracles, Miracle Stories I: Gospels." In *The IVP Dictionary of the New Testament,* edited by D. G. Reid, 801-12. Downers Grove, IL: InterVarsity Press, 2004.
Bloch, Marc. *The Historian's Craft.* New York: Knopf, 1953.
BonJour, Laurence. *The Structure of Empirical Knowledge.* Cambridge, MA: Harvard University Press, 1985.
Bourget, David, and David Chalmers, *What Do Philosophers Believe?* http://philpapers.org/archive/BOUWDP (accessed May 23, 2013).
Brewer, Bill. *Perception and Reason.* New York: Oxford University Press, 1999.
Bromiley, Geoffrey. "Faith." In *The International Standard Bible Encyclopedia,* edited by Geoffrey Bromiley, vol. 2, 270-73. Grand Rapids: Eerdmans, 1982.
Brown, Colin. *Miracles and the Critical Mind.* Grand Rapids: Eerdmans, 1984.
Brown, Raymond. *An Introduction to New Testament Christology.* New York: Paulist Press, 1994.
Brunner, Emil. *The Christian Doctrine of God: Dogmatics.* Vol. 1. Philadelphia: Westminster Press, 1950.
Burnyeat, M. F., and Jonathan Barnes. "Socrates and the Jury: Paradoxes in Plato's Distinction between Knowledge and True Belief." *Proceedings of the Aristotelian Society, Supplementary Volumes* 54 (1980): 193-206.
Byrskog, Samuel. "The Eyewitnesses as Interpreters of the Past: Reflections on Richard Bauckham's, *Jesus and the Eyewitnesses.*" *Journal for the Study of the Historical Jesus* 6, no. 2 (2008): 157-68.
———. *Story as History — History as Story.* Tübingen: Mohr Siebeck, 2000.
Calvin, John. *Institutes of the Christian Religion.* Grand Rapids: Eerdmans, 1989.
Carnley, Peter. *The Structure of Resurrection Belief.* Oxford: Clarendon Press, 1987.
Churchland, Paul. "Eliminative Materialism and the Propositional Attitudes." *The Journal of Philosophy* 78, no. 2 (1981): 67-90.
Coady, C. A. J. "Testimony, Observation and 'Autonomous Knowledge.'" In *Knowing from Words,* edited by B. K. Matilal and A. Chakrabarti, 225-50. Dordrecht: Kluwer Academic, 1994.
———. *Testimony: A Philosophical Study.* Oxford: Oxford University Press, 1994.
Collingwood, R. G. *The Idea of History.* Oxford: Oxford University Press, 1946.
Crossan, John Dominic. *The Historical Jesus: The Life of a Mediterranean Jewish Peasant.* Edinburgh: T & T Clark, 1991.
———. *Who Killed Jesus?* New York: HarperCollins, 1995.

Curd, Martin. "Reported Miracles by J. Houston: Review." *Mind, New Series* 106, no. 422 (1997): 349-53.

Davidson, Donald. "A Coherence Theory of Truth and Knowledge." In *Truth and Interpretation: Perspectives on the Philosophy of Donald Davidson*, edited by E. LePore, 307-19. Oxford: Basil Blackwell, 1986.

Dawkins, Richard. *The Blind Watchmaker: Why the Evidence of Evolution Reveals a Universe without Design*. New York: Norton, 1986.

DeHart, Paul. *The Trial of the Witnesses: The Rise and Decline of Postliberal Theology*. Malden, MA: Blackwell, 2006.

Denzinger, Heinrich. *Compendium of Creeds, Definitions, and Declarations on Matters of Faith and Morals*. Edited by Peter Hünermann. 43rd ed. San Francisco: Ignatius Press, 2012.

Derrida, Jacques. *Positions*. Chicago: University of Chicago Press, 1981.

DeVries, Willem, Timm Triplett, and Wilfrid Sellars. *Knowledge, Mind, and the Given: Reading Wilfrid Sellars's "Empiricism and the Philosophy of Mind," Including the Complete Text of Sellars's Essay*. Indianapolis: Hackett, 2000.

Dodd, C. H. *The Founder of Christianity*. London: Collins, 1971.

Dretske, Fred. "Externalism and Modest Contextualism." *Erkenntnis* 61, no. 2 (2004): 173-86.

Dulles, Avery. *The Assurance of Things Hoped For: A Theology of Christian Faith*. New York: Oxford University Press, 1994.

———. *Models of Revelation*. Maryknoll, NY: Orbis, 1992.

Dummett, Michael. "Testimony and Memory." In *Knowing from Words*, edited by B. K. Matilal and A. Chakrabarti, 251-72. Dordrecht: Kluwer Academic, 1994.

Dunn, James D. G. *The Evidence for Jesus*. Philadelphia: Westminster Press, 1985.

———. "Eyewitnesses and the Oral Jesus Tradition." *Journal for the Study of the Historical Jesus* 6, no. 1 (2008): 85-105.

———. *Jesus Remembered*. Grand Rapids: Eerdmans, 2003.

Earman, John. *Hume's Abject Failure: The Argument against Miracles*. New York: Oxford University Press, 2000.

Farmer, Hugh. *A Dissertation on Miracles: Designed to Shew, That They Are Arguments of a Divine Interposition, and Absolute Proofs of the Mission and Doctrine of a Prophet*. London: Printed for T. Cadell and J. Buckland, 1771.

Farrer, Austin. "Revelation." In *Faith and Logic: Oxford Essays in Philosophical Theology*, edited by Basil Mitchell. London: George Allen and Unwin, 1957.

Feuerbach, Ludwig. *The Essence of Christianity*. New York: Cosimo, 2008.

Fogelin, Robert. *A Defense of Hume on Miracles*. Princeton, NJ: Princeton University Press, 2003.

Forgie, J. William. "Pike's Mystic Union and the Possibility of Theistic Experience." *Religious Studies* 30, no. 2 (2008): 231-42.

———. "The Possibility of Theistic Experience." *Religious Studies* 34, no. 3 (1998): 317-23.

———. "Theistic Experience and the Doctrine of Unanimity." *International Journal for Philosophy of Religion* 15, no. 1 (1984): 13-30.

Forster, Michael. "Friedrich Daniel Ernst Schleiermacher." In *Stanford Encyclopedia of Philosophy* (fall 2008 edition), edited by Edward N. Zalta, 2008: http://plato.stanford.edu/archives/fall2008/entries/schleiermacher/.

France, R. T. "Faith." In *Dictionary of Jesus and the Gospels,* edited by Joel Green and Scot McKnight, 223-26. Downers Grove, IL: InterVarsity Press, 1992.

Fricker, Elisabeth. "Against Gullibility." In *Knowing from Words,* edited by B. K. Matilal and A. Chakrabarti, 25-62. Dordrecht: Kluwer Academic, 1994.

———. "Telling and Trusting: Reductionism and Anti-Reductionism in the Epistemology of Testimony, a Critical Notice of Coady 1992." *Mind* 104, no. 414 (1995): 393-411.

Fuller, Reginald. *The Foundations of New Testament Christology.* London: Lutterworth Press, 1965.

Funkenstein, Amos. *Theology and the Scientific Imagination from the Middle Ages to the Seventeenth Century.* Princeton, NJ: Princeton University Press, 1986.

Garcia, Laura. "St. John of the Cross and the Necessity of Divine Hiddenness." In *Divine Hiddenness: New Essays,* edited by Daniel Howard-Snyder and Paul Moser, pp. 83-97. West Nyack: Cambridge University Press, 2002.

Geach, Peter. "Assertion." *The Philosophical Review* 74, no. 4 (1965): 449-65.

Goldberg, Sanford. *Anti-Individualism: Mind and Language, Knowledge and Justification.* Cambridge: Cambridge University Press, 2007.

Goldingay, John. *Israel's Gospel.* Downers Grove, IL: InterVarsity Press, 2003.

Grenz, Stanley, and Roger Olson. *20th Century Theology: God and the World in a Transitional Age.* Carlisle, UK: Paternoster Press, 1992.

Griffiths, Paul J. "Book Review of *Divine Discourse: Philosophical Reflections on the Claim That God Speaks,* by Nicholas Wolterstorff." *Anglican Theological Review* 78, no. 3 (1996).

Gunton, Colin. *A Brief Theology of Revelation.* Edinburgh: T & T Clark, 1995.

———. *Revelation and Reason: Prolegomena to Systematic Theology.* Edited by P. H. Brazier. Edinburgh: T & T Clark, 2008.

Habermas, Gary, Antony Flew, and Terry Miethe. *Did Jesus Rise from the Dead? The Resurrection Debate.* San Francisco: Harper and Row, 1987.

Habermas, Gary. "Mapping the Recent Trend toward the Bodily Resurrection Appearances of Jesus in Light of Other Prominent Critical Positions." In *The Resurrection of Jesus: John Dominic Crossan and N. T. Wright in Dialogue,* edited by Robert Stewart, 78-92. London: SPCK, 2006.

———. "Resurrection Research from 1975 to the Present: What Are Critical Scholars Saying?" *Journal for the Study of the Historical Jesus* 3, no. 2 (2005): 135-53.

Hammond, Guy. "Tillich on the Personal God." *The Journal of Religion* 44, no. 4 (1964): 289-93.

Hart, Ray. *Unfinished Man and the Imagination.* New York: Herder and Herder, 1968.

Hauerwas, Stanley. *A Community of Character: Toward a Constructive Christian Social Ethic.* Notre Dame, IN: University of Notre Dame Press, 1981.

———. *The Hauerwas Reader.* Durham: Duke University Press, 2001.

Heck, Richard. "Nonconceptual Content and the 'Space of Reasons.'" *The Philosophical Review* 109, no. 4 (2000): 483-523.

Helm, Paul. *The Divine Revelation: The Basic Issues.* Westchester, IL: Crossway Books, 1982.

BIBLIOGRAPHY

———. "Revealed Propositions and Timeless Truths." *Religious Studies* 8, no. 2 (1972): 127-36.
Hengel, Martin. Foreword to Samuel Byrskog, *Story as History — History as Story*, vii-viii. Tübingen: Mohr Siebeck, 2000.
Henry, Carl F. H. *God, Revelation and Authority.* Vol. 3. Wheaton, IL: Crossway Books, 1999.
Hordern, William. *The Case for a New Reformation Theology.* Philadelphia: Westminster Press, 1959.
Houston, Joe. *Reported Miracles: A Critique of Hume.* Cambridge: Cambridge University Press, 1994.
Hume, David. *An Enquiry Concerning Human Understanding and Other Writings.* Edited by Stephen Buckle. Cambridge: Cambridge University Press, 2007.
Insole, Christopher. "Seeing off the Local Threat to Irreducible Knowledge by Testimony." *Philosophical Quarterly* 50, no. 198 (2000): 44-56.
Jenkins, John. *Knowledge and Faith in Thomas Aquinas.* Cambridge: Cambridge University Press, 1997.
John Paul II. *Fides et Ratio* [Encyclical Letter on the Relationship between Faith and Reason]: http://www.vatican.va/holy_father/john_paul_ii/encyclicals/documents/hf_jp-ii_enc_15101998_fides-et-ratio_en.html (accessed May 7, 2013).
Kant, Immanuel. *Immanuel Kant's Critique of Pure Reason.* Translated by Norman Kemp Smith. New York: Palgrave, 1929.
———. *Prolegomena to Any Future Metaphysics That Will Be Able to Come Forward as Science, with Kant's Letter to Marcus Herz, February 27, 1772.* Translated by James Ellington. 2nd ed. Indianapolis: Hackett, 2001.
Kaufman, Gordon. *An Essay on Theological Method.* 3rd ed. Atlanta: Scholars Press, 1995.
———. *In Face of Mystery: A Constructive Theology.* Cambridge, MA: Harvard University Press, 1993.
Keener, Craig. *Miracles: The Credibility of the New Testament Accounts.* 2 vols. Grand Rapids: Baker Academic, 2011.
Kelsey, David. *The Uses of Scripture in Recent Theology.* Philadelphia: Fortress, 1975.
Kerr, Fergus. *Twentieth-Century Catholic Theologians: From Neoscholasticism to Nuptial Mysticism.* Malden, MA: Blackwell, 2007.
Kolb, Robert, and Timothy Wengert, eds. *The Book of Concord: The Confessions of the Evangelical Lutheran Church.* Minneapolis: Fortress, 2000.
Lamont, John. "Stump and Swinburne on Revelation." *Religious Studies* 32, no. 3 (1996): 395-411.
———. *Divine Faith.* Aldershot, UK: Ashgate, 2004.
Levine, Michael. "God Speak." *Religious Studies* 34, no. 1 (1998): 1-16.
Lindbeck, George. *The Nature of Doctrine: Religion and Theology in a Postliberal Age.* Philadelphia: Westminster Press, 1984.
Locke, John. *An Essay Concerning Human Understanding.* Edited by P. H. Nidditch. Oxford: Clarendon Press, 1975.
Lubac, Henri de. *The Discovery of God.* Grand Rapids: Eerdmans 1996.
Luther, Martin. *Luther's Works.* Vol. 31. Edited by Harold J. Grimm. Philadelphia: Fortress, 1957.

———. *Luther's Works.* Vol. 34. Edited by Lewis W. Spitz. Philadelphia: Fortress, 1960.
Macdonald, Paul. *Knowledge and the Transcendent: An Inquiry into the Mind's Relationship to God.* Washington, DC: Catholic University of America Press, 2009.
———. "A Realist Epistemology of Faith." *Religious Studies* 41, no. 4 (2005): 373-93.
MacDonald, Scott. "Theory of Knowledge." In *The Cambridge Companion to Aquinas,* edited by Norman Kretzman and Eleonore Stump, 160-95. Cambridge: Cambridge University Press, 1993.
Mackie, J. L. *The Miracle of Theism: Arguments for and against the Existence of God.* Oxford: Oxford University Press, 1982.
———. "The Possibility of Innate Knowledge." *Proceedings of the Aristotelian Society,* new series 70 (1969-1970): 245-57.
Marshall, Bruce. *Trinity and Truth.* Cambridge: Cambridge University Press, 2000.
Marshall, I. Howard. "A New Consensus on Oral Tradition? A Review of Richard Bauckham's *Jesus and the Eyewitnesses.*" *Journal for the Study of the Historical Jesus* 6, no. 2 (2008): 182-93.
Martin, M. G. F. "Perception, Concepts, and Memory." *The Philosophical Review* 101, no. 4 (1992): 745-63.
Matilal, B. K., and A. Chakrabarti. "Introduction." In *Knowing from Words,* edited by B. K. Matilal and A. Chakrabarti, 1-22. Dordrecht: Kluwer Academic, 1994.
Mavrodes, George. *Revelation in Religious Belief.* Philadelphia: Temple University Press, 1988.
McCormack, Bruce. *Orthodox and Modern: Studies in the Theology of Karl Barth.* Grand Rapids: Baker Academic, 2008.
McDowell, John. "Avoiding the Myth of the Given." In *The Engaged Intellect: Philosophical Essays,* 256-72. Cambridge, MA: Harvard University Press, 2009.
———. "Knowledge and the Internal." In *Meaning, Knowledge, and Reality,* 395-413. Cambridge, MA: Harvard University Press, 1998.
———. "Knowledge and the Internal Revisited." *Philosophy and Phenomenological Research* 64, no. 1 (2002): 97-105.
———. "Knowledge by Hearsay." In *Meaning, Knowledge, and Reality,* 414-44. Cambridge, MA: Harvard University Press, 1998.
———. *Mind and World.* Cambridge, MA: Harvard University Press, 1996.
———. "Singular Thought and the Extent of Inner Space." In *Meaning, Knowledge, and Reality,* 228-59. Cambridge, MA: Harvard University Press, 1998.
McGrath, Alister. *A Fine-Tuned Universe: The Quest for God in Science and Theology.* Louisville: Westminster John Knox, 2009.
———. *The Open Secret: A New Vision for Natural Theology.* Malden, MA: Blackwell, 2008.
McGrath, Matthew. "Propositions." In *Stanford Encyclopedia of Philosophy* (summer 2012 edition). Edited by Edward N. Zalta, 2012: http://plato.stanford.edu/archives/sum2012/entries/propositions/.
McLaughlin, B., and K. Bennett. "Supervenience." In *Stanford Encyclopedia of Philosophy* (winter 2011 edition). Edited by Edward N. Zalta, 2011: http://plato.stanford.edu/archives/win2011/entries/supervenience/.
Milbank, John. "Intensities." *Modern Theology* 15, no. 4 (1999): 445-97.

BIBLIOGRAPHY

———. *Theology and Social Theory: Beyond Secular Reason.* Cambridge: Basil Blackwell, 1990.
Milbank, John, Catherine Pickstock, and Graham Ward, eds. *Radical Orthodoxy: A New Theology.* London: Routledge, 1999.
Murphy, Nancey. *Beyond Liberalism and Fundamentalism: How Modern and Postmodern Philosophy Set the Theological Agenda.* Valley Forge, PA: Trinity Press International, 1996.
Newman, John Henry. *An Essay in Aid of a Grammar of Assent.* Oxford: Oxford University Press, 1985.
O'Collins, Gerald, and Mario Farrugia. *Catholicism: The Story of Catholic Christianity.* New York: Oxford University Press, 2003.
Owen, John. "The Reason of Faith." In *The Works of John Owen.* Vol. 4. Edited by William Goold. Edinburgh: Johnstone and Hunter, 1852.
Paley, William. "A View of the Evidences of Christianity." In *The Works of William Paley . . . Containing His Life, Moral and Political Philosophy, Evidences of Christianity, Natural Theology, Tracts, Horae Paulinae, Clergyman's Companion, and Sermons.* Edinburgh: T. Nelson and P. Brown, 1831.
Pannenberg, Wolfhart. "Dogmatic Theses on the Doctrine of Revelation." In *Revelation as History,* edited by Wolfhart Pannenberg, 123-58. New York: Macmillan, 1968.
———. *Faith and Reality.* Philadelphia: Westminster Press, 1977.
———. *An Introduction to Systematic Theology.* Grand Rapids: Eerdmans, 1991.
———. *Jesus: God and Man.* London: SCM Press, 1968.
———. "Response to the Discussion." In *New Frontiers in Theology,* edited by John Cobb Jr. and James Robinson. New York: Harper and Row, 1967.
———. *Systematic Theology.* Vol. 1. Grand Rapids: Eerdmans, 1991.
———. *Theology and the Philosophy of Science.* London: Darton, Longman and Todd, 1976.
Peacocke, Arthur. *Theology for a Scientific Age: Being and Becoming: Natural, Divine, and Human.* Minneapolis: Fortress, 1993.
Peacocke, Christopher. *A Study of Concepts.* Cambridge, MA: MIT Press, 1992.
———. "Phenomenology and Nonconceptual Content." *Philosophical and Phenomenological Research* 62, no. 3 (2001): 609-15.
Penelhum, Terence. *Problems of Religious Knowledge.* London: Macmillan, 1971.
Pesch, Rudolf. "Zur Entstehung Des Glaubens an Die Auferstehung Jesu. Ein Neuer Versuch." *Freiburger Zeitschrift für Philosophie und Theologie* 30, nos. 1-2 (1983): 73-98.
Pike, Nelson. *Mystic Union: An Essay in the Phenomenology of Mysticism.* Ithaca, NY: Cornell University Press, 1992.
Placher, William. *The Domestication of Transcendence: How Modern Thinking about God Went Wrong.* Louisville: Westminster John Knox, 1996.
———. *Unapologetic Theology: A Christian Voice in a Pluralistic Conversation.* Louisville: Westminster John Knox, 1989.
Plantinga, Alvin. *Warrant: The Current Debate.* New York: Oxford University Press, 1993.
———. *Warranted Christian Belief.* New York: Oxford University Press, 2000.
Polkinghorne, John. *Science and Religion in Quest of Truth.* London: SPCK, 2011.

Proudfoot, Wayne. *Religious Experience.* Berkeley: University of California Press, 1985.
Quine, W. V. *Word and Object.* Cambridge, MA: MIT Press, 1960.
Quinn, Philip. "Can God Speak? Does God Speak?" *Religious Studies* 37, no. 3 (2001): 259-69.
Rahner, Karl. *Foundations of Christian Faith: An Introduction to the Idea of Christianity.* New York: Crossroad, 1978.
Rahner, Karl, and Joseph Ratzinger. *Revelation and Tradition.* Freiburg: Herder, 1966.
Ratzinger, Joseph. *Introduction to Christianity.* San Francisco: Ignatius Press, 2004.
———. *On the Way to Jesus Christ.* San Francisco: Ignatius Press, 2005.
———. "Revelation Itself." In *Commentary on the Documents of Vatican II.* Vol. 3. Edited by Herbert Vorgrimler. New York: Herder and Herder, 1969.
———. "The Transmission of Divine Revelation." In *Commentary on the Documents of Vatican II.* Vol. 3. Edited by Herbert Vorgrimler. New York: Herder and Herder, 1969.
Reid, Thomas. *Essays on the Intellectual Powers of Man,* edited by James Walker. Cambridge: John Bartlett, 1852.
Rorty, Richard. *Philosophy and the Mirror of Nature.* Princeton, NJ: Princeton University Press, 1979.
Rosenberg, Jay. "Still Mythic After All These Years: On Alston's Latest Defense of the Given." *Philosophical and Phenomenological Research* 72, no. 1 (2006): 157-73.
Rowe, William. "The Meaning of 'God' in Tillich's Theology." *The Journal of Religion* 42, no. 4 (1962): 274-86.
Rowland, Tracey. *Ratzinger's Faith: The Theology of Pope Benedict XVI.* Oxford: Oxford University Press, 2008.
Russell, Robert. "Special Providence and Genetic Mutation: A New Defense of Theistic Evolution." In *Evolutionary and Molecular Biology: Scientific Perspectives on Divine Action,* edited by Robert Russel, William Stoeger, and Francisco Ayala, 191-223. Notre Dame, IN: University of Notre Dame Press, 1999.
Sanders, E. P. *The Historical Figure of Jesus.* New York: Penguin, 1995.
———. *Jesus and Judaism.* London: SCM Press, 1985.
Schantz, Richard. "The Given Regained: Reflections on the Sensuous Content of Experience." *Philosophical and Phenomenological Research* 62, no. 1 (2001): 167-80.
Schillebeeckx, Edward. *Jesus: An Experiment in Christology.* New York: Seabury Press, 1979.
Schleiermacher, Friedrich. *On Religion: Speeches to Its Cultured Despisers.* Cambridge: Cambridge University Press, 1996.
———. *The Christian Faith.* Edited by H. R. Mackintosh and J. S. Stewart. London: T & T Clark, 1999.
Schmitt, Frederick. "Socializing Epistemology: An Introduction through Two Sample Issues." In *Socializing Epistemology: The Social Dimensions of Knowledge,* edited by Frederick Schmitt, 1-28. Lanham: Rowman and Littlefield, 1994.
Searle, John. *Speech Acts: An Essay in the Philosophy of Language.* London: Cambridge University Press, 1969.
Segal, Alan. "The Resurrection: Faith or History?" In *The Resurrection of Jesus: John Dominic Crossan and N. T. Wright in Dialogue,* edited by Robert Stewart, 121-38. Minneapolis: Fortress, 2006.

BIBLIOGRAPHY

Smart, Ninian. "Interpretation and Mystical Experience." *Religious Studies* 1, no. 1 (1965): 75-87.

Smith, Wilfred Cantwell. *The Meaning and End of Religion: A New Approach to the Religious Traditions of Mankind.* New York: Macmillan, 1963.

Sober, Elliott. "A Modest Proposal." *Philosophy and Phenomenological Research* 68, no. 2 (2004): 487-94.

Soskice, Janet Martin. *Metaphor and Religious Language.* Oxford: Oxford University Press, 1985.

Stace, W. T. *Mysticism and Philosophy* Philadelphia: Lippincott, 1960.

Stenmark, Mikael. *Rationality in Science, Religion, and Everyday Life: A Critical Evaluation of Four Models of Rationality.* Notre Dame, IN: University of Notre Dame Press, 1995.

Stevenson, Leslie. "Why Believe What People Say?" *Synthese* 94, no. 3 (1993): 429-51.

Strawson, Peter. *The Bounds of Sense: An Essay on Kant's "Critique of Pure Reason."* London: Routledge, 1966.

Stump, Eleonore. "Review of *Revelation: From Metaphor to Analogy,* by Richard Swinburne." *The Philosophical Review* 103, no. 4 (1994): 739-43.

Swinburne, Richard. *The Existence of God.* 2nd ed. Oxford: Oxford University Press, 2004.

———. *Revelation: From Metaphor to Analogy.* 2nd ed. Oxford: Oxford University Press, 2007.

———. "Review: Hume's Abject Failure: The Argument against Miracles." *Mind* 111, no. 441 (2002): 95.

Taylor, Vincent. *The Formation of the Gospel Tradition.* London: Macmillan, 1935.

Thiemann, Ronald. *Revelation and Theology: The Gospel as Narrated Promise.* Notre Dame, IN: University of Notre Dame Press, 1985.

Thompson, Marianne Meye. "Jesus and His God." In *The Cambridge Companion to Jesus,* edited by Markus Bockmuehl, 41-55. Cambridge: Cambridge University Press, 2001.

Thompson, William. *Christ and Consciousness: Exploring Christ's Contribution to Human Consciousness: The Origins and Development of Christian Consciousness.* New York: Paulist Press, 1966.

Tillich, Paul. "The Religious Symbol." *Daedalus* 87, no. 3 (1958): 3-21.

———. *The Shaking of the Foundations.* New York: Charles Scribner's Sons, 1948.

———. *Systematic Theology.* Vol. 1. Chicago: University of Chicago Press, 1951.

Torrance, Thomas. *Divine and Contingent Order.* Oxford: Oxford University Press, 1981.

Towey, Anthony. "Dei Verbum: Fit for Purpose?" *New Blackfriars* 90, no. 1026 (2009): 206-18.

Tracy, Thomas. "Particular Providence and the God of the Gaps." In *Chaos and Complexity: Scientific Perspectives on Divine Action,* edited by Robert Russel, Nancey Murphy, and Arthur Peacocke, 289-324. Notre Dame, IN: University of Notre Dame Press, 1996.

Turner, Denys. *Faith, Reason and the Existence of God.* New York: Cambridge University Press, 2004.

Tye, Michael. *Ten Problems of Consciousness: A Representational Theory of the Phenomenal Mind.* Cambridge, MA: MIT Press, 1995.

Wahlberg, Mats. *Reshaping Natural Theology: Seeing Nature as Creation.* Houndmills, UK: Palgrave Macmillan, 2012.
Van Huyssteen, Wentzel. *Theology and the Justification of Faith: Constructing Theories in Systematic Theology.* Grand Rapids: Eerdmans, 1989.
Ward, Keith. "Believing in Miracles." *Zygon* 37, no. 3 (2002): 741-50.
———. *God, Chance and Necessity.* Oxford: Oneworld, 1996.
———. "Miracles and Testimony." *Religious Studies* 21, no. 2 (1985): 131-45.
———. *Religion and Revelation: A Theology of Revelation in the World's Religions.* Oxford: Oxford University Press, 1994.
Vatican Council I. *Dei Filius* [Dogmatic Constitution on the Catholic Faith]: http://www.ewtn.com/library/councils/v1.htm (accessed May 7, 2013).
Watson, Francis. "The Quest for the Real Jesus." In *The Cambridge Companion to Jesus,* edited by Markus Bockmuehl, 156-69. Cambridge: Cambridge University Press, 2001.
Webster, John. *Barth.* 2nd ed. London: Continuum, 2004.
Weiner, Matthew. "Accepting Testimony." *Philosophical Quarterly* 53, no. 211 (2003): 256-64.
Westphal, Merold. "The Importance of Overcoming Metaphysics for the Life of Faith." *Modern Theology* 23, no. 2 (2007): 253-78.
———. "On Reading God the Author." *Religious Studies* 37, no. 3 (2001): 271-91.
Wikforss, Åsa. "Semantic Externalism and Psychological Externalism." *Philosophy Compass* 3, no. 1 (2008): 158-81.
Willaschek, Marcus. Preface to *John McDowell: Reason and Nature.* Edited by Marcus Willaschek. Münster: LIT Verlag, 1999.
Williams, Rowan. *On Christian Theology.* Oxford: Blackwell, 2000.
Williamson, Timothy. *Knowledge and Its Limits.* Oxford: Oxford University Press, 2000.
Wisse, Maarten. "From Cover to Cover? A Critique of Wolterstorff's Theory of the Bible as Divine Discourse." *International Journal for Philosophy of Religion* 52, no. 3 (2002): 159-73.
Wolterstorff, Nicholas. *Divine Discourse: Philosophical Reflections on the Claim That God Speaks.* Cambridge: Cambridge University Press, 1995.
———. "Is It Possible and Desirable for Theologians to Recover from Kant?" *Modern Theology* 14, no. 1 (1998): 1-18.
———. "Response to Helm, Quinn, and Westphal." *Religious Studies* 37, no. 3 (2001): 293-306.
Wright, George Ernest. *God Who Acts: Biblical Theology as Recital.* London: SCM Press, 1952.
Wright, N. T. *The Resurrection of the Son of God.* London: SPCK, 2003.
Zangwill, Nick. "The Myth of Religious Experience." *Religious Studies* 40, no. 1 (2004): 1-22.

Index

Abraham, William, 169
Allison, Dale, 202n57, 206n67, 207-9
Alston, William, 62n26, 73-75, 78
Anscombe, Elisabeth, 147, 148
anti-reductionism (testimony), 6, 126-32, 214-15; John McDowell's version of, chap. 5.2
appropriation of discourse, 112, 113-14, 120-22
Aquinas, Thomas: on the beatific vision, 102-6; on faith, 1, 7, 9-11, 162-63, 225n12, 226-27, 230; on miracles, 159, 163; on *scientia*, 8-9, 11, 226-27
Augustine, 159
Austin, J. L., 109
authorization of discourse, 112, 120-22

Balthasar, Hans Urs von, 15, 164, 231-33
Barnes, Jonathan, 124
Barth, Karl: on the Bible, 4n12, 84; on revelation, 80, 84-89, 231-33
Bauckham, Richard, 175-80
Baum, Gregory, 89, 90n68
beatific vision, 102-6
Benedict XVI. *See* Ratzinger, Joseph
BonJour, Laurence, 94
Bourget, David, 219-20
Brown, Colin, 161
Brown, Raymond, 158

Brunner, Emil, 80, 81-83
Bultmann, Rudolf, 178
Byrskog, Samuel, 179-80

Calvin, John, 2, 22n7, 159-60
Chalmers, David, 219-20
Clement of Alexandria, 2
Coady, C. A. J., 127, 142-43, 173
coherentism, epistemological, 67n31, 93-96
Collingwood, R. G., 175-76
Crossan, John Dominic, 174-75, 205, 207n72
Curd, Martin, 200

deputization, 111-12, 113, 120-21, 146
divine action, 122-23. *See also* miracles
divine speech, 2, chap. 4; Barth on, 4n12; Ratzinger on, 17n42; Wolterstorff on, chap. 4
double-agency discourse, 96-97, 110-14
doxastic responsibility, 140-42, 150-52, 217-21, passim
Dulles, Avery: on models of revelation, 51, 52; on propositional revelation, 37-40
Dummett, Michael, 127-28
Dunn, James D. G., 177-78, 180, 181-82, 205-7

Index

Earman, John, 184-86, 188, 199
epistemic justification. *See* justification
externalism: epistemological, 22n7, 23n8; about the mind, 136, 136n31

faith, 7, 148-49, 226-30; Aquinas on, 1, 7-8, 9-11, 162-63, 225n12, 226-27, 230
Farmer, Hugh, 160-61
Farrer, Austin, 3
Flew, Antony, 210
Fogelin, Robert, 199-200
form-critical school, 178, 181
Fricker, Elisabeth, 128-32

Garcia, Laura, 222-23
Gerhardsson, Birger, 178-80
Gospels: as historical sources, 172-82; traditions behind, 178-81. *See also* historical knowledge of Jesus
Gregory of Nyssa, 159
Gunton, Colin, 7

Habermas, Gary, 202-3, 205, 207
Hauerwas, Stanley, 92n78
historical Jesus, 153n10. *See also* historical knowledge of Jesus
historical knowledge: in general, 175-77; of Jesus, 172-75, 177-82; of the resurrection, 201-12, 214-16
Houston, Joe, 159n21, 188n37, 193-200
Hume, David: on miracles, 166, 182-200; on testimony, 125-27, 129-30

illocutionary acts, 109-10, 121
Insole, Christopher, 131-32

Jenkins, John, 8n22, 105, 230
John Paul II, 7
justification, epistemic, 18n45, 23n8, 151; Aquinas on, 9-10; of Christian beliefs, 22-25, passim; coherence theories of, 67n31, 93-96; of testimonial beliefs, chap. 5
Justin Martyr, 159

Kant, Immanuel: on God, 46n55, 49n56; on natural theology, 43-44
Kaufman, Gordon, 44-46
Keener, Craig, 184n27
knowledge: Aquinas on, 8-11; of God, 25n11, chap. 2.2, chap. 3, chap. 6; *See also* historical knowledge; testimonial knowledge; propositional, 26-28.

Lamont, John, 27, 37-38, 115-16, 161-63, 223-26
Locke, John: on miracles, 161; on revelation, 21; on testimony, 124
locutionary acts, 109-10, 120-21. *See also* illocutionary acts
Lubac, Henri de, 68n33
Luther, Martin, 2, 227

Macdonald, Paul, 11, 44, 102-6, 225n12
MacDonald, Scott, 8-9
Mackie, J. L., 126, 189, 192-93, 194n47
manifestational revelation, 28-33, 41-42, 51, chap. 3
Marshall, Bruce, 96n84
McCormack, Bruce, 84-85, 87
McDowell, John: on knowledge and concepts, 23n8, 67n31, 68n32, 93, 215n1, 133-37; on testimony, chap. 5.2 (esp. 137-43), 148, 150-51
metaphorical language, 37-40, 119-20
Milbank, John, 3-4, 92n77, 97-101
miracles: epistemic function of, chap. 6.4; Hume on, 166, 182-200; reports about, chap. 7.2
motives of credibility, 162-63
mystical perception, 71-80
myth of the given, 66-68

natural theology, 21-22, 25n11, 43-44, 100-101, 192-93
nonconceptual content, 68n32

oral tradition, 178-81
Origen, 159, 161

245

INDEX

Pannenberg, Wolfhart: critique of Barth, 232; on revelation, 3, 53-59
Paley, William, 189
Penelhum, Terrence, 157
Pike, Nelson, 75-79
Plantinga, Alvin, 22n7, 23n8, 45-46
proposition: notion of, 26-28, 37-40
propositional revelation, 13-18, 20-21, 28-41
Proudfoot, Wayne, 61-62

Rahner, Karl, 64-71
Ratzinger, Joseph (Pope Benedict XVI), 14-15, 16-17, 167n41
reductionism (testimony), 124-32
Reid, Thomas, 129-30
religious experience, chaps. 3.2–3.3
resurrection of Jesus: as eschatological event, 167n41; evidence for, 201-12; knowledge of, 214-16
revelation: as conceptual experience (William Alston, Nelson Pike), chap. 3.3; as dialectical presence (Emil Brunner, Karl Barth), chap. 3.4; as history (Wolfhart Pannenberg), chap. 3.1; manifestational, 28-33, 41-42, 51, chap. 3; natural, 25n11; as new awareness (Paul Tillich), chap. 3.5; as nonconceptual experience (Friedrich Schleiermacher, Karl Rahner), chap. 3.2; "postliberal" views of (Ronald Thiemann, John Milbank), chap. 3.6; propositional, 13-18, 20-21, 28-41; Ratzinger on, 14-18; Second Vatican Council on, 13-14, 15; self-revelation, 15-17, 85-86

Sanders, E. P., 159, 182
Schleiermacher, Friedrich, 59-64
Schmitt, Frederick, 124-25, 127
scientia, 8-9, 11
Segal, Alan, 203-4
Sellars, Wilfrid, 66-67
sensus divinitatis, 22n7, 23n8, 108n1
Sober, Elliott, 187
space of reasons, 133, 134-36
speech-act theory, 108, 109-10
Swinburne, Richard: on biblical interpretation, 118-19; critique of Hume on miracles, 188-89, 192

Temple, William, 53, 98
testimonial knowledge: 1, 4-6, 12, chap. 5, 172-73; of God, 1-2, 10-11, 49-50, chap. 6; of miracles, chap. 7.2; of the resurrection, chap. 7.3, 214-15, 221-22
testimony. *See* testimonial knowledge
Thiemann, Ronald, 92-97
Thompson, Marianne Meye, 21, 153n12
Thompson, William, 89
Tillich, Paul, 90-91

Ward, Keith: on miracles, 189-92; on revelation, 40-41
Westphal, Merold, 21n5, 120-21
Wolterstorff, Nicholas: on biblical interpretation, 116-20; on divine discourse, chap. 4; on revelation, 28-33
Wright, N. T., 36n35, 204, 206n67, 208, 209

Zangwill, Nick, 72-73